ILLEGALITY IN THE HEARTLAND

The publisher and the University of California Press Foundation gratefully acknowledge the generous support of Michelle Ciccarelli Lerach and William Lerach in making this book possible.

ILLEGALITY IN THE HEARTLAND

Latinidad, Indigeneity, and Immigration
Policies during Times of Hate

ANDREA GÓMEZ CERVANTES

UNIVERSITY OF CALIFORNIA PRESS

University of California Press
Oakland, California

Cataloging-in-Publication data is on file at the Library of Congress.

ISBN 978-0-520-39388-2 (cloth)
ISBN 978-0-520-39389-9 (pbk.)
ISBN 978-0-520-39390-5 (ebook)

GPSR Authorized Representative: Easy Access System Europe, Mustamäe tee 50,
10621 Tallinn, Estonia, gpsr.requests@easproject.com

34   33   32   31   30   29   28   27   26   25
10   9   8   7   6   5   4   3   2   1

A mi mami, Verana Argelia, por darme tu amor y apoyo incondicional, porque es un honor ser tu hija.

To my husband, Josh, because I love loving you and being loved by you.

Contents

Figures

Foreword

"TENGO MIEDO" (I am afraid), Dolores messaged me only ten days after Trump took office for a second term in 2025. I had not heard from her in more than four years. I met Dolores when I lived in Kansas and was a graduate student conducting the research that is presented in this book. "Here in [Kansas] everything is difficult," Dolores continued. "They took one of my *paisanos* [comrades] in the downtown, and I still don't know anything. I am afraid. I can't even go buy food; I almost never leave." Her words were almost identical to the words she had shared with me when we first met in late 2016 in the aftermath of Trump taking office for the first time. I could picture her sitting at her dining room table and peeking out the window through the blankets that served as curtains. Dolores is not her real name. I chose this pseudonym because I thought it reflected her life. The Spanish term *dolores* means "pains." As you will read in the pages to come, Dolores has had a life of

painful moments—which are reflective of the structural colonial legacies that reproduce harm across the life course, particularly for Indigenous women—from her childhood in a poverty-stricken Indigenous community of southern Mexico and an early teen marriage to a much older man, to a violent journey across the border, violence after arriving in the United States, discrimination in the health care system, and a continuous roller coaster of fear of deportation. Yet Dolores's life is also one of strength, resilience, and joy. "I just turned thirty-five," she told me in the same message exchange to remind me of her birthday that had recently passed.

Only seventy days after the Trump administration took office in 2025, an avalanche of 216 immigration-related actions including policies and rule changes were enacted.[1] For comparison, the first Trump administration enacted 164 immigration actions during the first *year*. The pace and potency of these actions reflect much of the overall administration's strategies in areas beyond immigration, using a shock-and-slash approach. Shock politics involve the government use of crises to create a sense of urgency to pass policy changes fast so as to solve such perceived crises.[2] These "crises," however, can easily be manufactured by government doctrine and propaganda without real evidence, as has been the case with the creation of the "immigrant invasion" and the depiction of immigrants as criminals and terrorists in Trump's second administration.[3] Shock politics tends to reshape government control by shrinking state welfare systems and expanding privatization while simultaneously extending authoritative powers to control, manipulate, and discipline the governed population.

Utilizing a securitization alarmist rhetoric and depicting immigration flows as uncontrollable and certain immigrants as criminals and terrorists, Trump's immigration policies follow the shock doctrine while expanding the immigrant bureaucracy in authority and capital gains.[4] These tactics, however, have quickly stretched beyond the border into everyday communities and attempt to dismantle any type of previous protections that immigrants once had, even if these were limited, thus reproducing a state of panic that has impacted not only immigrants but also entire communities. Experiences such as Dolores's of feeling afraid to leave her home to even go grocery shopping were common during Trump's first seventy days in office in 2025, paralleling experiences of fear and hostility documented in this book during the first Trump administration.

MANUFACTURING PANIC: INVASIONS, CRIMINALS, TERRORISTS, AND THE UNDESERVED

The rhetoric that paints certain immigrants as criminals (e.g., Venezuelans seeking asylum as violent gang members)[5] or as terrorists (e.g., pro-Palestine student activists as enemies of the state)[6] generates fear of immigrants among residents. Likewise, the constant and growing threat of deportation, family separation, and denial of safety increases fear and panic among immigrants and their loved ones. While some of the actions that Trump has implemented are not new, many are harshly shaking what little constitutional protections immigrants once had. By the time this book comes out, many of the issues I consider here may have changed due to immigrant rights advocacy groups challenging actions in the courts.[7] However, some of the issues will be solidified and even further expanded, with frightful consequences for immigrants and transnational communities.

Inside the country, policy changes attempt to hypercriminalize immigrants, expand surveillance in the communities where they live, and decrease any existing safeguards. Since day one, Trump 2.0, under two executive orders (14165 and 14159),[8] reinstitutionalized and expanded 287(g) programs nationwide, which mandate cooperation between federal and local policing agencies to enforce immigration priorities. Thus, police and sheriffs' agents are charged with apprehending and detaining immigrants whom they deem undocumented regardless of actual immigration status or lack of criminal behavior. This is not new. Other administrations have used 287(g) agreements, which typically increases apprehensions and deportations.[9] However, these executive orders were accompanied by many more strategies that further expand the surveillance and criminalization of immigrants across the country. Places that were previously agreed upon as "protected areas" from immigration enforcement are no longer protected, including schools, churches, medical facilities, and courthouses.[10] The Department of Homeland Security issued an order to the Internal Revenue Service requesting identifying information of potential undocumented taxpayers, knowing that most undocumented workers pay their income taxes and thus could potentially be located through tax records.[11] Additionally, nongovernmental organizations that serve undocumented immigrants and receive public funds were threatened with audits and faced funding freezes and threats to repay already allocated funds. This included organizations receiving Federal Emergency Management Agency support for disasters (such as the wildfires and hurricanes experienced across the United States in late 2024 and early 2025).[12] These efforts to expand the surveillance of immigrants inside the country have been met with workplace raids and immigrant apprehensions in public spaces across all states.[13]

Sanctuary cities, those that publicly have made commitments to support immigrant rights, have been especially targeted. Under Executive Order 14159,[14] sanctuary jurisdictions have been threatened with denial of federal funds. Under Operation Take Back America,[15] resources from task forces that typically used to surveil and punish organized crime have been redirected to assess and apprehend potential undocumented immigrants, with sanctions for jurisdictions that refuse to collaborate. There have also been several attempts and strategies to increase detention and deportations, including the expansion of immigrant detainers in local jails and prisons and of expedited removal, which denies immigrants the limited due process rights they once had.

Claiming an "invasion" at the southern border has allowed the expansion of military strategies to surveil and control the US-Mexico border and repurpose military detention facilities. On day one of Trump 2.0, the president declared a national emergency at the southern border, which gave the executive office powers to utilize militarized personnel and equipment along with other resources without the approval of Congress, aiming to "seal" the border, as stated by a joint task force under the Department of Defense working in partnership with the Department of Homeland Security, Customs and Border Patrol, and Immigration and Customs Enforcement (ICE) to surveil the region.[16] The militarization strategies only in January included a Stryker brigade combat team and an aviation battalion team, totaling 6,600 military personnel, as well as geospatial satellites.[17]

The military strategies and denial of human rights has been best observed by the repurposing of a military prison camp as an immigrant detention facility in early 2025. Guantánamo Bay, although in Cuban territory, is occupied by the United States and has been used as a military prison camp for decades, best known as the holding cite of prisoners during the "War on Terror."[18] In a place where the US Constitution is silent and where the rule of law is unseen, nine days into Trump's second presidency, a memorandum directing the Department of Homeland Security to expand immigrant detention to Guantánamo Bay was signed. Close to three hundred immigrants, most of Venezuelan nationality, were sent to the Guantánamo Bay prison camp without any information shared to their families of their whereabouts and with detainees being denied access to council.[19]

The hypercriminalization of immigrants has also targeted students who were previously deemed part of the "good immigrant" narrative and for the most part have historically been left out of hyperpolicing tactics. The Trump 2.0 administration pressed ICE to target and apprehend students and faculty who supported the 2024 protests against the Palestinian genocide, including students with visas or permanent residency (Green Card), many of whom are Muslim, Palestinian, or nonwhite and are labeled as threats to national security.[20] The Department of Homeland Security also proposed adding social media as a tool to screen visa applications and individuals in ports of entry.[21] Plans to reinstate the 2017 Muslim ban were in progress with visa cancellations of immigrants from many Muslim-majority countries.[22]

Paradoxically, the Trump administration's efforts are resulting in the expansion of the undocumented population, whether on purpose or as an unwanted result. Studies have documented that when border crossings become more difficult due to militarization of the border, migrants are still likely to try to cross the border even if at higher risk of death and end up staying in the United States even if they remain undocumented.[23] Many of the semilegal statuses that gave liminal protections to certain immigrants, such as those under Temporary Protected Status, Humanitarian Parole, or Deferred Action for Childhood Arrival, were being shrunk or dismantled completely. Legal permanent resident (Green Card) applications were also suspended and paused.[24] Likewise, directives to asylum courts have complicated considerations for asylum, a process that had very slim chances of success in the first place. And for immigrant refugees who had been waiting years, even decades, for a refugee status, many of their chances were ripped away as refugee vetting and caps were reinstated along with slashes in funding for resettlement programs.[25]

The Trump 2.0 administration's immigration tactics have gone as far as attempting to change the US Constitution and enacting wartime policies without Congress approving of any war. With an attempt to end birthright citizenship on day one, Executive Order 14160 aims to take away citizenship from children born in the United States to parents who have undocumented or semilegal status.[26] The Trump 2.0 administration also enacted an almost never used law, the Aliens Enemies Act of 1798, which gives the president the authority to detain and deport any immigrant of an "enemy nation" without a hearing based solely on the immigrant's country of birth or citizenship. This has been used three times in history, including during World War II to support the internment of mainly Japanese Americans.[27] However, this power can only be enacted in times of war, which is decided by Congress. In March 2025 Trump, relying on the Aliens Enemies Act, deported approximately three hundred Venezuelans to a megaprison in El Salvador, falsely claiming that the immigrants were gang members even though a circuit court ordered a pause to their deportation.[28] The administration has also reenacted the Alien Registration Act, first used during World War II and later during the "War on Terror." Using the Alien Registration Act, immigrants over the age of fourteen and parents of minors who do not have a visa or have overstayed their visa are ordered to register with the US government. Failing to do so can be punished with criminal and civil penalties, fines, and even imprisonment.[29] The tactics used by the Trump 2.0 administration have direct and indirect consequences on the well-being of immigrants, their loved ones, and entire communities in the United States as well as immigrants' families abroad.

CONSEQUENCES AND REACTIONS

Jocelynn Rojo Carranza, an eleven-year-old girl, was taunted and bullied by her sixth-grade classmates in the days following the inauguration of the Trump 2.0 administration. Classmates threatened and mocked Jocelynn, telling her that ICE would deport her family and that she would be left alone in the United States. She died by suicide on February 8, 2025.[30] This type of anti-immigrant bullying is not new; I documented similar moments in the heartland during the first Trump administration. However, Jocelynn's end of life is devastating. Her pain leading to suicide and her family's and community's hurt of losing her reflect some of the severe consequences of the Trump 2.0 immigration policies. As research presented in the pages to come will show, immigration policies have direct and indirect harmful conse-quences that impact not only immigrants but also their entire commu-nities whether it is physical, emotional, social, or economic.[31]

Based on existing research,[32] we know that the fear of possible family separation, immigrant incarceration, and being returned to unlivable circumstances has direct consequences for immigrants' well-being, generating a state of *chronic fear* that is detailed in the pages to come. Chronic fear has detrimental consequences especially for chil-dren who are still developing, as was the case of Jocelynn, and for all individuals, with conceivable chronic health outcomes and long-lasting socioemotional impacts.[33] The consequences of fear of deportation are felt by entire families, including mixed-status families, that is, immi-grant families with undocumented, citizen, and semilegal status fam-ily members.[34] Bilingual, culturally sensitive mental health services are already limited across the country, especially in rural areas and places where immigrants are a smaller share of the population, as is the case for immigrants in the heartland, so children and families in these cir-cumstances must cope on their own with living with chronic fear as a result of a hostile political climate.

Many immigrants, such as Dolores presented earlier, experience isolation because they fear possible apprehension when leaving their homes and participating in public spaces. Given the dismantling of pro-tected spaces, this will likely increase isolation by decreasing participa-tion in schools, churches, health care facilities, and everyday spaces. Only days after the change to "protected spaces," schools across the country saw decreases in attendance along with increased concerns among immigrant students.[35] Likewise, given the possibility of appre-hensions in health care facilities, we can expect health care utilization to decline among immigrant families, including those who have citi-zen family members and are entitled to state benefits.[36] Social isola-tion also means less interactions in public settings and recreation areas such as parks, shopping malls, and grocery stores.[37] And as immigrant neighborhoods become hyperpoliced and hypersurveilled due to mandatory 287(g) programs and increased ICE presence, Latino communities more broadly become targeted due to the racialization of illegality,[38] causing relationships between Latino/a/x immigrants and the police to decline,[39] increasing crime victimization among Latinos,[40] and Latinos in general becoming more likely to be in contact with policing agents even if they are citizens and regardless of lack of criminal behaviors or activities.[41]

The hypercriminalization of immigrants is racialized and gendered, and thus Indigenous Latinos and Latino men who are more likely to fit the physical stereotypes of who is deemed "illegal" bear the harshest consequences.[42] As a result, it is not surprising that many immigrant Latinos enact strategies to distance themselves from stereotypes such as "criminals" and "illegals." This includes distancing oneself from criminalizing narratives and changing behaviors and appearance to fit into an imagined "good immigrant" ideal.[43] However, as we will read in the pages to come, this may also mean not seeking help when experiencing workplace violence, not standing up when experiencing discrimination in health care settings, and not seeking safety when experiencing violence in private and public realms. This distancing can generate divides within immigrant communities instead of building spaces of support while also creating room for interethnic exploitation especially between Indigenous and mestizo groups, as we will read in the pages to come.

The consequences of immigration raids and immigrant apprehensions are devastating at all levels: individual, family, and community. The forced separation of families and the detainment of immigrants have severe harmful impacts on immigrants' well-being, ranging from low birth weight among pregnant immigrants undergoing raids[44] to health impacts for individuals undergoing detentions.[45] The loss of a family member to deportation impacts everyone in the family, bringing family reconfigurations and socioeconomic challenges and increasing barriers toward social integration. And communities and workplaces will be impacted too by the loss of immigrants' contributions, including cultural gifts, spending power, and labor shortages.[46] Transnational communities will be affected as well with the loss of remittances that sometimes keeps families afloat and the reconfiguring of family, community, and employment as they receive deportees.

The immigration tactics implemented in the first seventy days of Trump 2.0, with more to come by the time this books is read, serve the state in many ways, including strengthening the immigration bureaucracy by expanding its profits and authority capacities, generating a state of fear and panic, and ultimately growing and maintaining a malleable, exploitable, and disposable workforce composed of undocumented immigrants.[47] The expansion of this immigrant surveillance and control follows a period in US history when—due to the COVID-19 pandemic and labor shortages—worker rights, union strikes, and labor union support were starting to make a comeback in the United States.[48] Likewise, these changes come with an increase in the gap between the richest and the poorest in the United States through legislation that cuts welfare and state-funded medical programs while increasing the wealth of the rich.[49] Thus, the of diminishing worker rights and the cutting of the welfare system, which have been other realms of policy changes in the Trump 2.0 administration,[50] demands a surplus of an exploitable and disposable labor force and a group to blame for social suffering, which is being expanded by the existing changes to the immigration bureaucracy.

Although the picture for immigrant well-being remains worrying due to the sociopolitical climate, the reality is that immigrants and their loved ones continue to live their lives. Even in the face of potential apprehension and the possibility of coming home to an empty bed after a loved one has been detained, most immigrants nevertheless go to work, go to school, celebrate birthdays and kindergarten graduations, mourn the loss of loved ones, get sick and heal, fall in love and form families, care for their neighbors, and have *carne asada* cookouts in the backyard. Immigrants *siguen adelante* (continue to move on, to get ahead) and find ways to navigate places of hostility and violence.

Communities, immigrant leaders, and allies have united to demand rights and protect their immigrant neighbors and loved ones. Immigrants have been flooded with "Know Your Rights" educational social media campaigns. Communities have organized "Protect Your Neighbor" groups, where allies provide support to immigrants during encounters with ICE and police officers. Mutual aid funds are created to provide financial assistance in case of an apprehension or deportation of a loved one. Free legal clinics are offered for immigrants to create family preparedness plans with which immigrants can designate a caregiver for their children and assets in case of deportation. And legal advocates as well as scholars are taking these challenges to the courts and lawmakers to demand the maintenance of the (although limited) rights that immigrants once had in the United States.

A CALL FOR SOLIDARITY

During the 2024 election a dramatic shift occurred within the Latino electorate. Forty-three percent of Latina/o/x votes went to Trump in 2024 compared to 19 percent in 2016.[51] This weighty increase is telling of a growing divide within Latina/o/x voters in the United States, emphasizing the complexities of Latinidad as the intersections of race, immigration, gender, sexual identity, socioeconomic status, and politics materialized in the election results. In 2004, Eduardo Bonilla Silva published an article in which he mapped what he thought would become the new racial order in the United States: a triracial system going beyond the historic Black and white divide of the United States. In this reconsideration of race, Bonilla-Silva categorized Latinos in two broader groups: "Honorary Whites" included "light-skin" Latinos. "Collective Black" included "dark-skin" Latinos, and the category

"White" included other immigrant groups including Asians but not Latin Americans. [52] Bonilla-Silva attributed these changes to cumulative transformations in society, including demographic shifts, whitening nation-building strategies, and global capitalist relations of labor. The shift in support to Trump signals a strong divide among Latino voters with tough considerations for Latinidad. Lessons from *Illegality in the Heartland*, however, will show that complexities tied to centuries of ongoing colonial divides are solidified in the immigration-racial nexus in the United States especially during times of hate and hostility, as is being experienced under the Trump 2.0 administration. Thus, *Illegality in the Heartland* will hopefully provide an opportunity for the reconsideration of Latinidad and its consequences for governing, policymaking, and organizing.

As Dolores's fears and Jocelynn's tragic loss to suicide tell us, immigration policies have life-changing consequences. Yet while the spillover effects impact both immigrants and their nonimmigrant loved ones, due to the racialization of illegality some immigrants are affected more than others, in particular Latinos and especially Indigenous Latinos who tend to fit the stereotypes of who is deemed "illegal." Solidarity building has been happening within immigrant communities and across Latina/o/x groups in the heartland and throughout the country. Yet this is a critical time in history for our communities to take a deep dive into the complexities of Latinidad and for us to disrupt the colonial legacies that continue to divide us. I only hope that even amid darkness and uncertainty, *Illegality in the Heartland* helps with solidarity-building efforts to create a better future.

Acknowledgments

THIS BOOK would not be possible without the trust and support of the immigrant families I met during my time as a graduate student at the University of Kansas. Thank you to the immigrants for trusting me even during a time of fear and hatred. Thank you for opening your homes and your hearts to me and for sharing your *testimonios* of hope and resilience, fear and violence, and undeniable strength. I truly hope that the pages in this book interrupt depictions of criminalized immigrants and instead show the humanity in who undocumented and mixed-status immigrants are, who Indigenous and mestizo Latinos are, their human experiences, and the many contributions they bring to our communities. I will always be grateful for your trust and confidence in my work. *Espero que estas páginas representen las luchas y logros de los inmigrantes que hacen que el corazón de este país siga latiendo día a día, gracias por confiar en mí.*

There have been many changes in my life both professional and personal from the time I began the fieldwork for this study to the completion of this book. This book is a tribute to the support I have found along the way. Throughout this time my intellectual mentor, Cecilia Menjívar, has guided me with compassion and care while always keeping high expectations of my scholarship and my career. Cecilia has been a mentor to many Latinas and first-generation scholars and has inspired many more through her work. Thank you for helping me reach the academic potential I did not know I had. Time with you in the field as your student and mentee taught me how to truly see the world sociologically and about the power of the sociological imagination to create real transformative change whether it is for one person, a community, or our society. *Es un honor ser su estudiante, gracias por guiarme y apoyarme, en lo personal y profesional, siempre.*

This book began during my time in Kansas. I am grateful to my mentors and teachers and the friends I met at the University of Kansas, especially in the Sociology Department. My deepest gratitude to ChangHwan Kim for your guidance through the complexities of graduate school, for teaching me statistics, and for your continued honest and humble support throughout the years. My sincere thanks to my dissertation committee members, Joane Nagel, Mehranghiz Najafizadeh, and Ben Chappel. Thanks to Bill Staples for research contributions and feedback. Thank you to Shirley Hill for your support in the beginning period of my academic path. I was lucky to find a second intellectual home at the university's Institute of Policy on Social Research (IPSR), where I learned about the possible impacts of social science research. Thank you to Steven Maynard-Moody, Hannah Britton, Nancy Cayton Myers and Jenna Gunter, and the IPSR fellows cohort 2016–2017. I appreciate my peers at the University of Kansas, especially David Cooper, Alex Myers, and Erin Adamson. I also appreciate my Sister Scholars, Marcy Quiason and Tamy Hardy; our writing sessions helped write the skeleton of this book. And thank you to Byeongdon Oh for your friendship and support over the years and inspiration through your brilliant work. I am especially thankful to the many immigrant leaders, community organizers, immigration attorneys, educators, social workers, medical providers, religious leaders, and allies I met in Kansas whom I cannot name to maintain their confidentiality. Thank you for the work you do every day to safeguard immigrant rights in the heartland.

I appreciate the intellectual communities I have been a part of since graduate school to becoming a professor. These spaces helped me in many ways small and big to develop this book. When I was a graduate student, ideas and inspiration for the book emerged during the IMISCOE PhD summer school in 2016 at Princeton University, led by Marco Martiniello, Maurice Crul, and Doug Massey. This was my first dive into immigration scholarship and where I met fabulous young scholars, many of whom over the years have become my friends and whose work I admire. I was able to do the fieldwork presented here thanks to the financial support of the Ford Foundation, the American Sociological Association Minority Fellowship, the Sociologists for Women in Society, the National Science Foundation, and internal grants from the University of Kansas. I am especially thankful to the Minority Fellowship Program cohort 44 and mentors, especially my friend San Juanita García, who took me by the hand and showed me how to "do" academic conferences and over the years has generously provided advice on how to navigate academia, *gracias amiga*.

During my brief time at the University of California–Los Angeles under the University of California President's Postdoctoral Fellowship Program, I wrote the initial drafts and workshopped many of the chapters. Thank you to my postdoctoral mentor Leisy Abrego for teaching me how to be a kind and thoughtful teacher and scholar and for providing a space of compassionate intellectual growth during the peak of the COVID-19 pandemic. There is no other scholar as heartfelt and grounded as you; *gracias por enseñarme que está bien llevar el corazón en la mano al escribir este libro y los que vendrán.* Thank you to Iris Ramirez, Briceida Hernandez-Toledo, Leighanna Hidalgo, Lucy León, and Joanna Perez for creating a writing community during this time of anxiety, uncertainty, and pain. I appreciate the working-groups led by Rubén Hernández León and Vilma Ortiz in the Department of Sociology at UCLA. I am especially grateful to Subini Annama, who created a virtual space of solidarity and coexistence during the shutdowns, quarantines, and isolation of the COVID-19 pandemic. Your yoga sessions kept me sane, and your academic work is transformative.

I received support from colleagues at Wake Forest University, especially Amanda Gengler, who created a welcoming and supportive space when I began my first job and gave advice on book writing. Thank you also to my colleagues Joseph Soares, Hana Brown, and David Yamane. I appreciate the book-proposal writing group including Alex Brewer and Derek Lee. I could not have completed this book without the financial support from the Institute for Research on Poverty (IRP) at the University of Wisconsin–Madison, the National Endowment for the Humanities, the Wake Forest University Humanities Institute, and internal awards from Wake Forest University. I am especially thankful for the emotional and intellectual support I received in completing the final stride of this book under the IRP fellowship with the generous and intellectually motivating *consejos* of Katherine Magnuson and the warmth of IRP staff, including Becca Schwei. I am especially grateful to the 2023–2024 IRP cohort, where I found a passionate interdisciplinary group of scholars with intense commitments to social change and where I built new friendships. I am thankful to my undergraduate research assistants at Wake Forest University who helped with different aspects of the book revisions, especially Kat Caesar, Monica Hernández, and Dani Fernandez.

I am grateful to the many conversations, discussions, and feedback provided throughout the years at conferences and invited talks, especially to Anthony Peguero, Elizabeth Vaquera, Dan Martinez, Cristina

Mora, Emir Estrada, Lisa Martinez, Jennifer Jones, and Nicole Novak. Thank you to my academic amigas who provided chapter feedback and writing accountability over the years, especially to Casandra Salgado and Sylvia Rodriguez Vega. I have special thanks for Stephanie Canizales for your feedback over the years, your motivation, and your generosity in editing support. *Gracias por tu amistad y apoyo.* I am thankful to my amigas near and far who have been patiently waiting for this book to come while cheering me on along the way. *En especial gracias a* Erica Dalman *por tu amistad todos estos años,* Maru Castro Bernardini *por ser la motivadora número uno,* and Annie Nahn for all the years of friendship. Gracias to my Sigma Lambda Upsilon/Señoritas Latinas Unidas *hermanas,* especially to Delia Fernandez whom I have always admired.

The University of California Press has always been my dream press. Thank you to Naomi Schneider for believing in my work and for your compassion and patience. Thank you to the First-Gen program at the press for providing financial support and guidance on the ins and outs of publishing, especially Raina Polivka, and to all the press staff for turning my pages into a real book. Thank you to my developmental editor, James Macmillen, and to the copyeditors. I am grateful to have received powerful and detailed reviews, helping me create a stronger manuscript. Thank you to the blind reviewers and to Nilda Flores and Elizabeth Aranda for your time, *consejos* over the years. The work you do that has always inspired me.

I am in deep gratitude to my family, including my chosen family. *Gracias a toda mi familia en México, España, EEUU, y otras esquinitas del mundo, a los que están y a los que nos cuidan. A mi papá, Manolo, por apoyarme desde lejos, sin importar tan grande sea la distancia, ni mis sueños. A mis abuelos Maruja y Samuel por colmar mi infancia de alegría y sabores inolvidables. A mi abuelita Julieta, te extraño siempre. A mi abuelito Waldo, que no daría por platicar hoy contigo. A mi familia Gómez Crespo que siempre me apoyan desde el otro lado del charco. A mi querida familia Cervantes—tías, tíos, primas, y primos—gracias por inspirarme cada día con su cariño y por ser siempre un refugio de amor y alegría. Tía Jaca y tía Mariana, gracias por apoyarme en los momentos más difíciles. Tía July, por tus palabras inspiradoras. A mis primas Ale y Vale: de cada una aprendo algo valioso que guardo con amor. A mi hermana Nata, gracias por ser siempre mi apoyo en todo momento de lejos y cerca. A mis sobrinos, que llenan mi vida de alegría a distancia, en especial a mi niña hermosa, Fernanda, la más luchona de todos. A Inés, que, aunque no llegué a conocerte, dejaste en mí una huella imborrable. Y a Fer, el hermano que siempre quise tener y me dejó muy pronto.*

To my chosen family, I never would have imagined that my academic path would bring me two sisters. To Brittany P. Battle, I am thankful for your friendship, your enormous kindness, and your passion for social justice. Thank you for your support at work and at home, for sharing both the darkest days and biggest accomplishments, and for being a mentor and *amiga* as we navigated our first jobs, first big grants, first homes, first time parenting, and many more firsts. To Jesús Pereda, *mujer gracias por tu apoyo todos esto años, por las charlas, por escucharme, por creer en mi trabajo, y por crear la portada más bella.* Thank you for sharing your creativity and artistry with me and for making the cover of this book that reflects the lives, struggles, and hopes of immigrants in the heartland. I am beyond grateful to the amazing team of loving and nurturing caregivers, nursing assistants, nurses, medical staff, therapists, daycare and pre-K teachers and assistant teachers and volunteers who have cared for Gael. Without your labor, support, and love for my son I would not have been able to finish this book (or continue my career). Special thanks to Lily Godfrey, Justice Nails, Jalisa Glover, Diane Adams, and especially to Brithany Teran-Boza—you make a big impact in this world.

This book is dedicated to my mom. *Gracias a mi mami, Verana Argelia, la mujer que me enseñó a nunca darme por vencida y sobrepasar cualquier obstáculo para alcanzar mis metas.* Thank you for your unconditional support, your cheers and jokes when I needed to laugh, and for always listening when I felt like giving up. Thank you for reading the drafts of my chapters and for being my biggest cheerleader. Thank you for teaching me to love books and to love learning. Thank you for turning princess stories into feminist truths. Thank you for teaching me to care deeply and humbly for others and for the way you have quietly supported so many immigrant women who survived gender violence over the years. Thank you for sharing a life with me without ever asking for anything in return, for your generosity, for loving me unconditionally, and for loving my son even more. *Este libro es tanto mío como tuyo.*

This book is also dedicated to my husband, Josh. This book would not be possible without your support, patience, enthusiasm, and motivation. You have supported me every day on the making of this book, whether I was in the field or in the library. Thank you for believing in my work, for brainstorming ideas, for listening to my presentations, and for your feedback and intellectually rich conversations at the dinner table. Thank you for the roses and the words of encouragement. Thank you for lifting me up when life gets hard and for bringing me so much joy. Thank you for staying with me through unexpected struggles and through the ups and downs of academia, for being my life partner, and for loving me.

And to my son Gael, *eres mi todo. Cambiaste mi forma de ver la vida. Por el simple hecho de existir me das la esperanza y fuerza para luchar y seguir adelante, tal como lo hacen las familias en este libro.*

INTRODUCTION

ON A COLD FEBRUARY MORNING in Kansas, Jenny hosted a Bible study group in her kitchen. Three other women sat talking around the table, their contrasting Spanish accents indicating their diverse nationalities. They were about to finish, Jenny explained, as she introduced me to her friends. She had not forgotten about our interview. Shortly, she informed the group, she would be telling me the story of her undocumented life. Jenny's friends chuckled nervously, looked at each other, avoided eye contact with me, and continued their reading. Half an hour later, the women said their goodbyes. Jenny gestured for me to take out my recorder. *"Ahora sí, ¿qué quieres saber?* (Now, what do you want to know?),"[1] she said.

Jenny was a confident and cheerful mestizo Mexican woman who had lived in Kansas for over a decade, most of that time undocumented. She arrived in Kansas with the help of her father, who had been living and working in the

United States for some time. Via her father's social networks Jenny found work at a fast-food restaurant, where she eventually met her husband, Vicente, who was also an undocumented mestizo Mexican immigrant. Together, Jenny and Vicente formed a blended family with their six children. One of the most difficult aspects of living undocumented, Jenny explained, was the worry she felt each time she or Vicente left their home. She said, "You wake up every day praying that they [immigration enforcement] will not take him, that they will not take me. Afraid that they will grab you, that is what I think. Insecurity all the time." Later, Jenny noted that at least her husband looked güero,[2] which had helped him avoid encounters with *la migra* (immigration enforcement).

Eventually after a long process and many ups and downs in her personal life, Jenny was able to "fix" her immigration status and obtain legal permanent residency. But she had never forgotten how living undocumented felt. Without papers and unable to speak English, she had been vulnerable to workplace exploitation, housing abuse, and medical neglect. It was only through learning English, she said, after working alongside English speakers for years at a restaurant and meeting other more established Latino immigrants in her community, that she had been able to navigate all the obstacles that undocumented immigrants face.

Months later I met Carolina, an Indigenous Tlapaneco Mexican woman who had also lived in Kansas, undocumented, for over a decade. Unlike Jenny, however, Carolina was still undocumented when we talked. We sat on Carolina's pistachio-green couch, which she had bought at a discounted price from a hotel where she had worked as a housekeeper. The room was dark, the window shades were down, and the lightbulb in the ceiling flickered with a thin yellow light. Carolina looked at me nervously. She was ready to chat, she said, but could only spare an hour because this was her break between two jobs. "My idea was always to come [to the United States], but we have no family here," she began and told me her story. Without any contacts in the United

States besides the moneylender who had funded her travel, it had been challenging to find a job—which she needed in order to repay the loan that covered the costs of her journey to the United States and to begin sending remittances to her oldest son in Mexico, whom she had left in her mother's care. After a month and through the lender's contacts, Carolina found a job at a fast-food restaurant. There, she worked alongside both Indigenous and mestizo immigrants, most of whom communicated in Spanish, which was not her first language. It was at work too where Carolina met Miguel, her husband. The couple soon had a son, Mateo, born a US citizen. Then, one evening, Carolina received a phone call from an unknown number. It was Miguel. He had been arrested, charged with driving under the influence, and placed on an immigration hold—meaning he was ineligible for bail and was being processed by the immigration authorities. "They punished him," Carolina told me as their period of separation approached one year. After some months in jail, Miguel had been sent to a detention center outside of Kansas, likely in Louisiana. "Since he went inside, I haven't seen him," Carolina continued. "My son cries and cries. He wants to see him [Miguel], but I can't take him." Because she remained undocumented, Carolina could not drive her son to either the local jail where Miguel was first held or the immigrant detention center where he was moved to. She could not enter the buildings without risking her own deportation. As a result, Mateo would not see his father again for the foreseeable future. "My boy is the one that is suffering a lot," she said, getting ready to leave for her second job. "I spend my time working because there is nobody else to bring money to support us."

Jenny's and Carolina's accounts reflect the diverse trajectories that immigration policies produce in the United States and reveal the varying resources that mestizo and Indigenous immigrants can access to navigate life undocumented. Existing scholarship on the experiences of Latin American immigrants in the United States has generated valuable insights about immigration policies' consequences and immigrants' reactions to such conditions. Much of this literature, however, tends to homogenize Latin American immigrants under the monolithic category "Latino/a," "Latinx/e," or "Hispanic."[3] By contrast, this book follows the lead of Critical Latinx Indigeneities scholars[4] and Indigenous immigrant scholars[5] seeking to highlight the differing experiences of Indigenous immigrants from those of mestizos and other non-Indigenous groups.[6] Indigenous immigrants originate from communities that maintain a historical continuity with the precolonial societies that experienced colonization. Indigenous communities persist through the maintenance of linguistic, cultural, political, social, and interpersonal practices. Mestizo immigrants, by contrast, do not have ties to such communities and blend into Latin America's broader nation-state identities. Indigenous immigrants I met during the period of this study, such as Carolina, negotiate multiple overlapping histories of colonialism before, during, and after their migration journeys—making their experiences different from their mestizo counterparts. Additionally, the racialization of illegality—how perceptions of "Mexican origin," "Hispanic," and "Latino" are tied to criminality in the public imagination—renders some immigrants more vulnerable to policing and surveillance and accentuates existing social hierarchies among Latino immigrants in the diaspora.[7] This book sheds light on the experiences of Indigenous and mestizo Latin American immigrants in the heartland so as to learn about how their lives and lived experiences illuminate the (re)production of colonial legacies within contemporary immigration policies and their enforcement.

THE HEARTLAND: WHY PLACE MATTERS

Until recently, most immigrants in the United States settled largely in "traditional destinations," places with long histories of coethnic migration and well-established mutigenerational immigrant communities, such as California, Texas, and New York. Since the 1990s, however, driven largely by criminalizing immigration policies, increasingly dispersed demand for immigrant labor, and expanding immigrant networks, immigrants have settled in "nontraditional" or "new" immigrant destinations, places such as Kansas that lack continued and well-established migration patterns.[8] Immigration scholars agree that the context of reception—that is, the place where immigrants arrive to—deeply shapes immigrants' experiences in their new communities.[9] Various levels of governance shape the context of reception, including government policies at the federal, state, and local levels. Societal reception matters too—how the established community receives immigrants and the institutional support (or lack thereof) immigrants encounter in schools, health care, housing, work, and the broader community.[10] Compared to their peers in traditional destinations, Latino immigrants living in new immigrant destinations tend to be recent arrivals and have lower socioeconomic status and limited English skills and are more likely to be undocumented.[11]

Studying immigrant life in the heartland thus presents an opportunity for understanding the complex context of reception mechanisms in a nontraditional destination. I am reluctant to view Kansas as a truly "new" destination because Latin American immigrants, particularly Mexicans, arrived in Kansas as early as the 1900s.[12] Yet as Thomas Jiménez noted in his examination of Mexican multigenerations in Kansas, this migration has followed periodic waves of labor demands in the state.[13] It was not until the 1990s that Latin American immigrants' arrival to Kansas has followed a continuous flow. Furthermore, with growing established Latino communities, Latinos in Kansas made up the largest nonwhite group in an otherwise white-majority state by 2020.[14] *Illegality in the Heartland* therefore offers a critical case study through which to examine the intersection of immigration policies and racialization mechanisms in a context of reception where immigrants are not yet an established part of the public imaginary, despite their essential contributions to their communities and their growing share of the population. Kansas is a good reflection of the heartland more broadly, as the state exposes the region's politics, demographics, and geographic composition.

To appreciate Latinos' experiences in Kansas, I employ a *colonial legacies* lens. This approach yields an understanding of how enduring colonial logics and structures still shape the lives of Indigenous and mestizo immigrants—from their decision to leave their home countries to their harrowing migration journeys and their settlement in the heartland. In particular, the colonial legacies lens allows us to disentangle the similarities and differences between Indigenous and mestizo immigrants' experiences, as the case with Jenny and Carolina. Furthermore, the analysis in this book aims to foster conversations within the Latino/a, Latinx/e, and Hispanic community—including students, scholars, and organizers—to rethink our relationships to each other and to reconsider how internalized colonial legacies may shape our understandings and exercises of Latinidad and immigration in hopes of fostering solidarity for future change.

COLONIAL LEGACIES

Colonial legacies are maintained in contemporary social structures and institutions, perpetuated via state powers that (re)produce social divisions, including ethnoracial and gender divides. These processes are shaped and strengthened through the enforcement of laws and cemented through everyday social norms and practices. For immigrants, this manifests in multiple forms of violence—structural, legal, symbolic, and interpersonal—that they face throughout their lives. These forms of violence occur in the places they leave behind, the spaces they travel through, and the communities they finally reach and make their homes. Colonial legacies reflect the various fusions and contradictions that materialize in Latin American *coloniality*[15] and in *settler colonialism* in the United States.[16]

In Latin America, colonial projects varied by country and context, generating diverse forms of social oppression and resistance.[17] Colonial relations were primarily sustained through resource extraction, labor control, and land dispossession.[18] Across the region, colonial powers engaged in a racialization processes in which the normalization of social hierarchies, tied to observable physical characteristics, was key to labor extraction and capital accumulation.[19] The idea of race, Quijano argued,[20] was created to legitimize the power imbalances that served the global expansion of capitalism.

Colonial rule also enforced the heterosexual nuclear family and naturalized patriarchal gender roles tied to sex categories and reproductive capabilities.[21] Colonized women were both racialized and gendered as inferior, transformed into functional labor for globalizing capitalism. Women of European descent were characterized as fragile and sexually passive, while colonized women, both Indigenous and enslaved Africans, were dehumanized, hypersexualized, and framed as physically strong for performing strenuous labor. These heterosexual notions of the family and the construction of gender and sexuality into binaries have been maintained via state powers, policies, ideologies, and values across Latin American nations.[22]

After gaining independence from European rule, Latin American power elites relied on *mestizaje* to forge the nation-state. *Mestizaje* represents a set of ideologies and practices that force Indigenous- and African-origin groups to assimilate into Eurocentric norms and worldviews.[23] *Mestizaje* is reliant on two processes: (1) *blanqueamiento* (whitening), in which white European physical appearance, languages, worldviews, and political practices are favored over Indigenous and African-origin alternatives,[24] and (2) *indigenismo*, which cemented Indigenous and mestizo divides by stereotyping Indigenous and Afro-descendant people, languages, culture, and worldviews as inferior.[25] *Blanqueamiento* and *indigenismo* politics have shaped dynamics that continue to affect Latin American nations, institutions, and people today, such as in Mexico and Guatemala where most of the immigrants I met during the period of this study are from.

In Mexico, for example, *mestizaje* has been woven into laws and policies aiming to assimilate Indigenous and Afro-descendant groups into a "Mexican" national identity. For instance, the Mexican government only counts people as Indigenous based on language ability. Thus, Indigenous Mexicans who do not speak Indigenous languages are not recognized as such. And for Mexicans who are Afro-descendants, their assimilation to *mestizaje* and Mexican identity has been more complex. It was not until 2017 that Afro-Mexicans were recognized as a group with protected rights.[26]

In Guatemala's colonial racial hierarchy, unlike Mexico's attempt at racial homogenization, Ladinos—a group considered neither Spanish nor Indigenous—emerged as the ruling elite after colonization.[27] Ladinos enforced segregationist policies that isolated Indigenous communities and erased their power and autonomy. Overall, the projects of *mestizaje* and *indigenismo* across Latin America reflect settler colonialism's logic of elimination, perpetuated through structures that deliberately disempower racialized groups via inescapable poverty and violence.[28]

In the United States, settler colonialism reflects the long-term settlement of white Europeans and the attempted elimination and land dispossession of Native Americans.[29] The early racial structure in the United States was largely based on a Black-white divide; white people and whiteness were associated with rights to ownership and ultimately freedom, while Black people were associated with slavery. Citizenship rights and notions of freedom were synonymous with whiteness, notions that were cemented under the first naturalization laws.[30] Native Americans were constructed as "Indians" who blocked colonizers' access to the territory and thus became targets of colonial regulation and attempted elimination. The racialization of Native Americans as Indians, of Black people as slaves, and of non-Western European immigrants as the "other" ultimately counterposed these groups as inferior to whites—those descendants of Protestant, Anglo Western Europeans—and implied that their oppression through violence was justifiable.[31]

Unlike European colonies in Latin America, where colonial settlers were typically male, British colonization in the United States involved family-unit migration, a dynamic that fueled the genocide of Native Americans.[32] British settlements followed a heteropatriarchal family system, enshrined in law, that shaped not only family patterns but also wider social norms and values.[33] Gender roles were aligned with white Protestant values, while enslaved African women, Native American women, and non–Western European immigrant women, in particular Asians, Muslims, and Latin Americans, were racialized and hypersexualized. These settler colonial dynamics continue to the present—maintaining social structures and institutions that reproduce racial and gendered oppression.

I thus use the colonial legacies lens to consider the multiple and transversal aspects of colonization that continue within contemporary social structures—especially the policies and institutions that shape Indigenous and mestizo migration experiences in a nontraditional destination. This involves investigating how immigration policies and their enforcement maintain and reinforce colonial hierarchies of power and how these impacts accompany migrants across geographical contexts. I use the term "colonial legacies" to connect studies of *settler colonialism* in the United States with Latin American understandings of *coloniality*. As Indigenous and mestizo immigrants flee land dispossession, resource depletion, and state violence, they encounter additional colonial systems during their journeys and upon arrival in the heartland—which all serve to reify colonial taxonomies.

LATINIDAD

Understanding the history of how Latin Americans have been racialized in the United States can deepen our appreciation of Indigenous and mestizo migrants' experiences in the heartland. Following the Treaty of Guadalupe Hidalgo in 1848, Mexico lost considerable territory and natural resources to the United States, stretching from what is now southwestern Kansas to the coast of California. Later in 1898, the United States extended its governance over the colonies of Cuba, Puerto Rico, and the Philippines.[34] During the acquisition of Mexican and Puerto Rican territories, two racialized hierarchies merged. The Spanish colonial stratification—designating Spaniards and mestizos as landowners and Indigenous and Afro-descendant groups as laborers—fused with the US settler colonial system that comprised a dominant class of white Protestant settlers and the colonized class of Native Americans and enslaved Africans. This US imperial expansion granted citizenship to conquered Mexicans and later to Puerto Ricans.[35] These new citizens were classified as "white," following the 1790 Naturalization Law that granted citizenship only to *free white men*. Racial classification of whiteness, however, did not equate to social classification or acceptance. Leaders of southwestern states argued that Mexicans' Indigenous origins made them ineligible for full citizenship rights and that the new population should be classified alongside Native American groups—in other words, denied citizenship and exposed to anti-Indian legislation.[36]

Until the 1970s, the US Census collected statistics on Latinos using the Spanish language and Spanish surnames as proxies for ethnic and national backgrounds. By the late 1970s, the terms "Hispanic" and "non-Hispanic" appeared in the census alongside four racial categories: white, Black, Asian or Pacific Islander, and American Indian or Alaskan Native.[37] In 2024, the census combined the race and ethnicity category to offer "Hispanic or Latino" alongside the other racial categories.[38] In her investigation of how "Hispanics" developed as a political group, an ethnoracial identity, and a categorization, Cristina Mora has found that the Hispanic category materialized from collaboration between government institutions, community organizations, and the Spanish-language media industry.[39] Political organizers with predominantly Puerto Rican, Mexican, and Cuban origins formed Hispanic advocacy groups to take advantage of Spanish-language media's popularity in the United States. Together, these groups emphasized "Hispanic" to represent commonalities of culture, Spanish language, values of hard work and familism, and a source of pan-ethnic political representation.[40] Highlighting in-group differences and the intersections of nationality, language, class, sexuality, gender, race, ethnicity, and immigration status—as *Illegality in the Heartland* does—thus attempts to view the complexities, tensions, and spaces of unity of a Hispanic pan-ethnicity.

The "Latino/a," "Latinx/e," and "Hispanic" categories act as an umbrella term that, Critical Latinx Indigeneities scholars argue, obscures "Indigenous identities, unique histories, and sociohistorical context that shape their movement" across borders.[41] Likewise, the experiences of Afro-descendants are also veiled by this category. Such pan-ethnic labels thus act as an ongoing form of *mestizaje*, blurring the heterogeneity and the various genealogies of violence and resistance to such violence that different Latin American immigrant groups face in their home countries and the United States.[42] Although the early Chicano mobilizations of the 1970s claimed ownership of a romanticized Indigenous past—through narratives of a *reconquista* of Aztlán—Indigenous immigrants were also homogenized under the "Chicano" identity, one that was specifically tied to Mexican American histories in the Southwest. From this perspective, the "Latino/a," "Latinx/e," and "Hispanic" categorization conceal the racial discrimination and inequality that migrants face in their countries of origin and that often trigger migration in the first place. Furthermore, notions of Latinidad may obscure interethnic conflict and tension between Indigenous, mestizos, and Afro-descendant groups in the diaspora. At the same time, without such categories of pan-ethnicity, measures of the Latin American experience would be difficult. *Illegality in the Heartland* interrogates Latinidad by closely examining Indigenous and mestizo experiences in Kansas.

ILLEGALITY

Illegality is legally and socially constructed; that is, actions, behaviors, and groups that are deemed "illegal" are shaped by laws and reinforced by our social perceptions. An examination of immigration policies helps us understand the complex relationship between laws and colonial legacies—in their reproduction of racial, economic, and gender power divides.[43] Between 2004 and 2020, 90 percent of deportees from the United States were men originating from Mexico, Guatemala, El Salvador, and Honduras.[44] Given that these nationalities comprised 65 percent of all undocumented migrants in the United States and that half of all undocumented migrants were women during the same period, these deportation rates are highly disproportionate.[45] Legal and social factors concentrate immigration enforcement on Mexicans and Central Americans, making them more likely to be apprehended and deported and thus creating the *racialization of illegality*.[46]

The 1965 Immigration and Nationality Act ended the quota system that had given preference to Western European immigrants since the 1924 National Origins Act and the 1929 National Quota Law—in addition to legislation that excluded migration from most Asian countries from the mid-1800s into the early 1900s.[47] The 1965 Immigration and Nationality Act created the immigrant and nonimmigrant visa trajectories that remain in use today.[48] Immigrant visas pertain to family reunification and can lead to permanent residency, while nonimmigrant visas allow temporary admittance for work, study, or short visits. However, these visas have been historically difficult to obtain. The criteria for visa selection has been based on class symbolism, which is not only tied to economic advantages but is also gendered and racialized.[49] For instance, salary and diploma requirements for a visa automatically disqualify applicants who do not have bank accounts or college degrees. Employment requirements leave out labor in the informal economy, which tends to be predominantly female labor such as care work.

After Ronald Regan declared undocumented migration at the US-Mexico border to be "a threat to national security," the 1986 Immigration Reform and Control Act (IRCA) marked the beginning of the criminalization of undocumented immigration and the hypermilitarization of the border.[50] Aiming to decrease undocumented migration, the IRCA gave amnesty to an estimated 2.7 million undocumented immigrants, mostly Mexican temporary farmworkers.[51] However, the IRCA also criminalized undocumented labor by penalizing employers who knowingly hired undocumented workers. Employers could avoid penalties simply by showing that they verified an employee's status, which then placed any subsequent blame on the undocumented migrant.[52] As De Genova noted, this indirectly fueled a market for counterfeit documents among immigrant workers, exposing them to further criminal charges.[53] The criminalization of undocumented labor under the IRCA also rendered workers deportable, as employers could alert immigration authorities to undocumented workers' presence in order to avoid sanctions themselves.[54]

The IRCA also expanded the US Border Patrol budget, targeting enforcement at the busiest border crossing sectors.[55] Rather than preventing undocumented crossings, however, these initiatives have pushed immigrants toward more dangerous terrain at the border, with life-threatening consequences for immigrants. These initiatives, known as "Prevention through Deterrence" tactics, knowingly put immigrants lives in danger with the hopes that this will discourage attempts to cross the border.[56] Border Patrol officers tacitly use "Mexican appearance" to apprehend *potential* unauthorized border crossers.[57] Most people apprehended at the border and most people who have died in the Sonora desert trying to reach the United States are Mexicans and Central Americans—reflecting the border enforcement system's criminalizing and racializing practices.

Immigration policies in the 1980s and 1990s followed the War on Drugs–era policies that expanded incarceration and policing in Black and Latino communities. The "aggravated felony" charge, introduced through the 1988 Anti–Drug Abuse Act, further intensified deportation punishments for immigration offenses—justifying additional policing in Latino immigrant communities and merging the immigration and criminal legal systems.[58] In 1996, the Illegal Immigration Reform and Immigrant Responsibility Act (IIRIRA) blurred the lines between immigration enforcement and the criminal legal system even more. First, the IIRIRA imposed criminal penalties—including fines, up to two years of incarceration, deportation, or a combination of these—on immigrants who entered the country without inspection, defined as an "illegal entry."[59] Second, the IIRIRA created an "illegal reentry" offense for immigrants who reentered the country without a visa or a permit after having already been deported, carrying a sentence of up to ten years in prison. Both charges entailed a ban on subsequent lawful entrance, from three years to as much as a decade or more. Third, the IIRIRA transferred authority from judges to immigration officers for deciding immigrants' deportability.[60] Finally, the IIRIRA ended "waiver of removal" for legal permanent residents convicted of a crime and simultaneously introduced "expedited removal," giving immigration officers the authority to deport any immigrant apprehended at the southwestern border without a hearing.[61] Unlike criminal statutes, immigration laws pose no statutes of limitation on deportability, heightening this state of illegality.

Immigration enforcement and consequently the production of illegality has been extended beyond the border region. Under section 287(g) -of the Immigration and Nationality Act added through IIRIRA 1996, local policing agencies that entered into agreements with Immigration and Customs Enforcement are authorized to screen immigrants' status, issue detainers for potential offenders, and issue documents for initial removal proceedings—sometimes wrongfully including US citizens profiled as undocumented migrants.[62] As Coleman and Kocher find, "'Mexican appearance' has been at the core of 287(g)" programs.[63] Local police have used traffic stops or any "reasonable doubt" as grounds to apprehend suspected undocumented immigrants. However, because officers can document reasonable suspicion on the most minor infractions, race becomes a "mostly inaccessible and hypothetical void of subjective decision making by officers once a civil or criminal violation, however minor, has been observed." It is not surprising, then, that traffic offenses have ranked among the most frequent bases for deportation, behind "no conviction," "driving under the influence," and "illegal entry"—none of which are considered high-level offenses.[64] The use of 287(g) programs was initially optional for most jurisdictions, and after findings of racial profiling, the Obama administration diminished its use to focus on high-level offenses only. However, under Trump's first administration these were reinstituted nationwide.

The racialization of illegality is rooted in colonial systems of power, where racialization processes are utilized to surveil, control, and punish unwanted populations. US policies and immigration enforcement initiatives have long discussed "illegal immigration" as a "Mexican problem"[65] and, more recently, a "Central American" one.[66] Unsurprisingly, then, racial profiling of Latino immigrants as "illegal" has been a common thread within immigration enforcement at the US southwestern border and in the US interior. Given the ethnoracial differences within Latinos, however, it is possible that not all Latinos are racialized in the same ways and that mestizos and Indigenous immigrants have different experiences.[67] The criminalization of Latinos as "illegal" is further cemented in society through political and media narratives.[68]

Gender also plays an important role in the (re)production, enforcement, and surveillance of illegality. On the one hand, the exceedingly high rates of detentions and deportations of Latino men compared to women points at gendered mechanisms that are underpinned in immigration law and its enforcement: Latino men are criminalized and targeted as "illegal."[69] Gender is also entangled with illegality in asylum processes, as women who are most often fleeing gender violence have limited possibilities to successfully claim and gain asylum relief in the United States.[70] Central American women are often viewed as deceiving of the asylum system, and Mexican women are seldom viewed as credible and are blocked from the possibility to try to file an asylum claim.[71] Likewise, gender mechanisms—which have been rooted in colonial legacies—shape how men and women experience and navigate illegality and its repercussions, whether it is in the home, with their families, at work, or participating in their communities.

During the 2016 presidential campaigns, which coincided with the period of this study, Donald Trump referred to Mexican immigrants as "bad hombres," criminals, drug dealers, and rapists, thus heightening the image of perceived Mexicans as a danger to US communities.[72] These anti-immigrant and anti-Latino political narratives shaped immigration laws and their enforcement once Trump reached his first presidency. In 2017, days after gaining control of the executive branch, Trump signed nine executive orders that further criminalized Latino communities and amplified immigration enforcement at the border and inside the country.[73] Among other things, the executive orders reestablished the 287(g) program across the country, increased funding to expand immigrant detention facilities, slashed refugee and asylum budgets, terminated semilegal provisions such as Temporary Protected Status and Deferred Action for Childhood Arrival,[74] added eligibility restrictions for visas and legal permanent residency status, established a denaturalization office, and created penalties for localities that did not comply with the 287(g) policies.[75] Trump's first administration created profound changes to the immigration system. With over one thousand actions solely on immigration reform, the

US immigration system was transformed with changes that would last into future presidencies.[76]

While immigration policies and their enforcement mechanisms have contributed to the racialization and criminalization of undocumented immigrants—tying perceived "Hispanic" and "Mexican" origin to illegality—enduring colonial legacies also influence how these racialization mechanisms are experienced by the Latino community. *Illegality in the Heartland* investigates how mestizos and Indigenous migrants experience the trickle effects of such policies in their everyday lives, in their attempts to gain social mobility, and in their efforts to make Kansas their home.

NAVIGATING ILLEGALITY

While all undocumented Latino immigrants face the same legal exclusions due to their lack of immigration status,[77] immigrant groups rely on differentiated resources and social ties to navigate the barriers and exclusions they encounter. Sociologists have long noted the importance of social connections among immigrants, as it is through such contacts with family members, friends, and friends of friends that immigrants obtain resources for their journeys and assistance in establishing themselves at their destination—such as accessing housing and food and information about employment, schooling, and health care. The size of immigrants' social network depends on their individual social locations—that is, nationality, immigration status, race, gender, socioeconomic background, and educational level—as well as the context of reception.[78] Immigrant networks and their capacity to provide access to the resources immigrants need are further complicated by sociopolitical structures and institutions in the sending and receiving countries.[79] Influential too are the power relations that shape individuals' social positioning, and community and family relationships—all of which are prone to change over time.[80]

Gender is a vitally important factor shaping power dynamics within social networks and for determining resource access.[81] Immigrants are entrenched in gendered networks that offer varying access to opportunities and resources. For example, in the 1990s Mayan men in Texas were able to gain higher-paying jobs than women because their social networks connected them to out-group, male-segregated workplaces in growing industries such as construction.[82] Mayan women also worked in gender-segregated jobs, mostly as domestic housekeepers or nannies. These women, however, were often isolated and had limited access to the sort of valuable mobility-enabling information and resources present in male networks.[83] Schmalzbauer found similar gendered divides within Mexican immigrant families in rural Montana in the 2000s. While immigrant men in Montana were more frequently detained and deported, they were also able to access a wider network of social ties, enabling greater work opportunities and financial stability. Immigrant women in Montana, meanwhile, remained socially isolated and struggled to keep their families afloat after a partner's deportation.[84]

Menjívar in her work on Salvadoran immigrants in California argued that immigrant networks do not always provide a "buffer to the hardships that immigrants encounter."[85] Due to social structures—such as immigration policies and rules within institutions—immigrant ties cannot always deliver the resources that new immigrants need to survive and thrive, and these conditions can even dissolve social ties. Similarly, Rosales's study of street vendors in Los Angeles showed that although immigrant networks facilitate access to jobs and migration trajectories, social ties can also create exploitative relationships—driven by arrival contexts that are made hostile by criminalizing immigration policies.[86] And in Canizales's observations of immigrant youths in Los Angeles coming of age without parents, peer support is integral for their success but is limited, given the existing anti-Indigenous and anti-immigrant contexts.[87] Finally, in Del Real's investigation of interpersonal ties among mixed-status families, the uneven distribution of legal rights—both within immigrant families and throughout broader networks—generated exploitative conditions that reduce immigrants' trust, reciprocity, and mutual aid.[88] These so-called toxic ties reproduce power imbalances within romantic relationships, labor relations, and friendships between undocumented and documented immigrants.

Studies examining ethnoracial hierarchies in Latino communities in the United States also find an absence of mutual aid in social ties between mestizo and Indigenous immigrants. Instead, these ties reproduce social division, usually placing Indigenous immigrants in exploitative conditions.[89] By applying a colonial legacies lens to the investigation of Latin American immigrant networks, *Illegality in the Heartland* explores how access to these unevenly distributed social ties leads to diverse experiences of illegality, especially in a context of reception where immigrants are a smaller share of the population (even if growing). Ongoing colonial projects of *mestizaje* maintain social structures and everyday relationships in Mexico and Guatemala, and these do not simply disappear with migration to the United States—despite perceptions of a collective "Hispanic," "Latino/a," or "Latinx/e" diasporic community.[90] The book thus aims to better understand how Indigenous and mestizo immigrants use their social ties to survive and thrive in the United States. Some immigrants face similar circumstances but have differing resources to navigate and overcome struggles. Others are united in solidarity against an oppressive immigration system. What is certainly clear, however, and revealed through immigrants' accounts and ethnographic observations is that colonial legacies endure in the heartland.

VOICES FROM THE HEARTLAND

This study began in 2016, coinciding with the US presidential campaigns, and continued throughout Trump's nativist and white supremacist first presidency. To learn the experiences of Indigenous and mestizo immigrants alike, I became immersed in the Kansas communities in which they lived—undertaking ethnographic participant observation and conducting in-depth interviews. For several years prior to and continuing throughout the study, I also volunteered to teach English to newly arrived immigrants in a free program sponsored by a local church. I attended religious events and gatherings in multiple churches with Spanish-language services and, when invited, attended get-togethers in immigrants' homes. For six months I also attended an immigrant women's support group that was run by two health care professionals. I participated in cultural events, such as the annual Mexican fiesta and the Latin American festival, as well as pro–immigrant rights protests in the wake of the 2016 election. I offered free Spanish/English interpretation support to help immigrants communicate with schools, health clinics, and dentist offices and in public spaces as often as I could. I met with leaders of Latino-led community organizations and grassroots movements that aimed to uphold immigrants' rights. All of these spaces allowed me to gather and document interactions between immigrants and public institutions, learn about immigrants' experiences in intimate and private settings, and understand the enduring complexities of colonial legacies in the diaspora. Participating in community gatherings and public settings enabled me to meet immigrants who connected me to their friends, family members, and neighbors, thus allowing me to use snowball sampling as a technique to invite immigrants to share their experiences via interviews. Many of these additional connections were with immigrants who were uninvolved in community organizations; thus, they provided many diverse perspectives on Kansas life.

After interviewing two Indigenous Mixteco families, whom I met through a religious leader, it was evident that their experiences in navigating illegality in the heartland were vastly different from the experiences of the mestizo immigrants I had met. I therefore sought out more Indigenous immigrants in the area, finding that while their experiences sometimes varied, Indigenous accounts were similar to one another, although there were important cultural and linguistic differences given various Indigenous origins. With the help of the religious leader and a health worker who provided support to immigrant women in the community, I was introduced to several Mixteco and Tlapaneco immigrant women. These women then connected me to their friends and family members. Building relationships with Indigenous families was not easy. My social position as a Mexicana *mestiza*, with fair skin and light eye color echoed the same colonial divides that I aim to illustrate in the pages of this book. Given the deep colonial legacies of violence and racial hierarchies this represented, Indigenous immigrants were often apprehensive, mistrustful, and doubtful of my true intentions. To assuage their concerns, I met with Indigenous immigrants multiple times before conducting an interview. Besides providing car rides and interpretation free of charge, I also helped Indigenous families fill out or translate documents and made phone calls on their behalf to social institutions, including to the police, courts, the Internal Revenue Service, immigration enforcement, health clinics, schools, and stores. I made myself available at most times of the day, knowing that immigrants' shift work often occurs late at night and early in the morning.

Through these interactions, I built trust with Indigenous immigrants. In turn, they generously showed kindness and support for my research. I was invited to conduct interviews in their homes and to spend time with families in intimate gatherings and celebrations, including Christmas, kindergarten graduations, birthdays, and quinceañeras. On the other hand, it took less time to build rapport with mestizo immigrants. Although all immigrants were initially wary of who I was, given the context of heightened immigration enforcement and heightened surveillance, the support of trusted community leaders helped mestizo immigrants trust me with their experiences. I also made myself available to support mestizo immigrants with any translation and interpretation needs and with rides. However, this group had a stronger network of support to achieve such needs and seldom reached out to me for things other than sharing their personal life experiences.

I conducted the interviews and conversations mostly in Spanish and a few in English—in English only with some of the second-generation immigrants who were born and raised in the United States. The interviews and conversations with Indigenous immigrants were conducted in Spanish, although Spanish was not their first language. When we first met, Indigenous immigrants were quick to apologize for their Spanish accents or poor grammar—a signal of the devaluing of Indigenous languages that I further discuss in Chapter 5. However, language was not a barrier when interviewing Indigenous immigrants in Spanish. I sometimes asked for clarification during our conversations to make sure I was not misinterpreting their words, and I also did this with immigrants from nationalities whose Spanish accents or slangs I was unfamiliar with, such as the Ecuadoran and Salvadoran interviewees. I showed Indigenous immigrants my appreciation for the Indigenous languages they spoke, and in some cases families I spent more time with taught me basic phrases such as "how are you doing" in Chuj and "see you later" in Tlapaneco.[91] In a few cases, some of the Indigenous immigrants I met used their Indigenous names with me instead of their Spanish names. Mexican and Guatemalan Indigenous people often take on Spanish-language names for documentation and formalities, but many also have Indigenous names that they use with their families and loved ones. Thus, sharing such intimate aspect of their identity with me was a true honor.

Illegality in the Heartland illuminates the voices of sixty-four first-generation immigrants (thirty-five Indigenous and twenty-nine mestizos) and six second-generation immigrant mestizos. All immigrants I interviewed lived in Kansas during the Trump administration's era of heightened anti-immigrant hostility. The Indigenous immigrants were of Mixteco, Tlapaneco, Maya K'iche, and Maya Chuj origins. The countries of origin for all the immigrants were as follows:

Mexico (thirty-six), Guatemala (twenty), Honduras (three), El Salvador (two), Ecuador (one), Chile (one), and Venezuela (one). The six second-generation mestizo immigrants were born in the United States and are the children and siblings of first-generation immigrants. On average, the mestizo immigrants had spent fourteen years in the United States, while Indigenous immigrants had lived in the United States for an average of ten years, spending most of this time in Kansas. Some immigrants were the mothers and fathers of children born in Kansas, while others migrated to support their children who remained in their countries of origin in the care of their trusted family members, usually their mothers. While their immigration statuses varied, all had been undocumented at some point in their lives while living in Kansas. Significantly, however, every Indigenous immigrant I met during this study was undocumented and remained so for the duration of my fieldwork, which ended in 2019. Among mestizo immigrants, immigration statuses included undocumented (nine), Temporary Protected Status (one), Deferred Action for Childhood Arrival (seven), legal permanent residency (five), and naturalized citizen (seven).

The immigrants I met worked in restaurants, housekeeping, hotels, gardening, retail, grocery stores, food processing, construction, agriculture, nonprofit organizations, and higher education. Most lived in urban areas of Kansas, although sixteen Mayan Guatemalans and two mestizo Mexicans lived in a small town.[92] Their living circumstances varied and changed over time. Some families lived with roommates and coworkers, while others lived with their nuclear or extended families. Educational levels varied widely. While mestizo immigrants held high school diplomas and some had graduate degrees, Indigenous immigrants had only six years of schooling on average—a product of the exclusionary educational systems in their countries of origin and the limited opportunities for schooling upon arrival in the United States.

During our conversations I asked about their lives before migration, their migration journeys, their lives in Kansas, and their hopes for their futures. We also discussed the heated topic of immigration enforcement in a time of significant US immigration policy reform. During and after my fieldwork, some of the immigrants I met were detained and deported, while others had family members undergoing deportation or had been deported in the past and had since returned to the heartland. Immigrants' emotions during our conversations ranged from worry and frustration when we discussed political and media narratives surrounding crime and immigration to a mixture of fear and hope when we talked about the future. On other occasions we laughed at their anecdotes of life in a new country, sharing stories of trial and error that I could relate to. Some immigrants told me that our conversations were the first time they had spoken freely about their immigration experience with a stranger. I hope the stories I present in the following pages reflect their realities, worries, joys, struggles, passions, and hopes.

BOOK OVERVIEW

Illegality in the Heartland investigates how colonial legacies and structures are maintained through racialized and gendered governance mechanisms, and how these affect immigrants' lives in Kansas. Chapter 1 examines colonial legacies in immigrants' home countries, primarily Mexico and Guatemala where most of the immigrants I met originated. It also explores immigrants' motivations to migrate, their journeys north, and their forms of entry into the United States. In Chapter 2, I investigate the sociopolitical climate that made Kansas a hostile context of reception and immigrants' reactions to the first Trump administration.

Aguantar—in English, "to endure, to hold out, to bear, to put up, to weather, to suffer"—was a common theme among undocumented and semilegal immigrants when talking about their lives in Kansas and is the main theme of Chapter 3, where I explore mestizo and Indigenous experiences navigating social institutions of work, housing, and driving. Chapter 4 then explores ethnoracial differences in immigrants' use of language including Spanish, English, and Indigenous languages when building community in Kansas.

Although all the immigrants I met were undocumented at some point in their lives, most mestizos were eventually able to shift their immigration status, while every Indigenous immigrant remained "stuck" as undocumented. In Chapter 5, I investigate how immigrants interpret and react to these possibilities (or lack thereof) for changing their immigration status and the consequences of this for their family relationships. Chapter 6 highlights Indigenous and mestizo migrants' strategies to *salir adelante* (get ahead). Through immigrants' accounts, I pay particular attention to how intersections of race and gender shape their internalization of both success and failure.

The Conclusion returns to the implications of colonial legacies' entanglement with US immigration policies and how this intersects with mechanisms of place. Given the enduring colonial hierarchies, Indigenous and mestizo migrants arrive in the United States on an unequal footing in a hostile environment and encounter differing experiences of racialized and gendered exclusion and violence. I thus position my conclusions in a broader sociolegal framework, grounding the case of the heartland in a wider context of concern.

1

"VENIMOS POR NECESIDAD"

Migrating North

AS WE SAT in the open living room in front of the TV, Suzy, a little girl around age eight, played on the coffee table with dolls while looking back at me every few minutes, hesitant as to why I was in her house. After bringing me a glass of water, her mom, Luz, sat down next to me and promptly started talking, "We are here because of necessity. That is what I think," she said right away. "If there was money there, in my country, I would go [back]. But because of necessity, there is no work there, not for us; there is no work." She went on to talk about her life in Guatemala. "I can't buy anything, not even a soda, or a bread to eat. Nothing, because there is no money."

On a different day, sitting in a lively Christmas-decorated living room next to an elaborate nativity set and rainbow Christmas lights, Amelia, a mestizo Mexican woman, recounted her motivation to leave Mexico. "I was studying. I only studied two years because I had to pay rent."

Remembering her college days, she went on. "I made the graphics in the computer and more things." After a deep breath, Amelia looked at me and said, "But unfortunately in Mexico money is not enough." So, she left her agronomy engineering college life due to the high costs and only months later decided to migrate north, following her husband who was already working in Kansas. "Well, it was never my idea to come to this country," Amelia said. "All of a sudden, he called. 'You know what? The person that will bring you is ready.' So, from one day to the next, I came."

Like Luz and Amelia, most immigrants I met left their countries in search of economic stability, yet differences in their backgrounds were rooted in enduring colonial structures. Coloniality planted a seed that grew deep roots and has proved difficult to eradicate, making Latin America the most unequal region in the world.[1] Colonial legacies are present in the control of land, labor, economy, culture, and governance across the region—from territorial displacement to the creation of a racialized, classed, and gendered state power. Indigenous and Afro-descendant groups and those living in rural areas face the harshest forms of poverty and state violence, and women in these groups are especially vulnerable. In the contemporary era, colonial legacies are maintained via neoliberal capitalism—with ideologies, policies, and institutions that cause direct and indirect harm and displacement throughout the region. In this chapter, I examine how such colonial legacies—manifested in exclusionary migration policies and frequent acts of violence—intersect with Indigenous and mestizo migration processes.

BEFORE MIGRATION: LIFE IN MEXICO AND GUATEMALA

Across Latin America, Indigenous groups continue to fare worse than their non-Indigenous counterparts.[2] In Mexico, Indigenous groups accounted for 19.5 percent of the population in 2020.[3] These groups face economic and social well-being challenges. In 2018, 69.5 percent of Indigenous Mexicans lived in poverty compared to 39 percent of non-Indigenous Mexicans.[4] In Mexico, the larger proportion of Indigenous groups live in the southern region of the country, which is also the region with the worse mortality outcomes, the worse access the health resources, and the worse literacy rates and less access to quality schools.[5]

Mexican women have fared worse than men. Women earn less than men across all occupations, hold lower-paid jobs, and undertake the majority of unpaid childcare, elder care, and household labor. Over half of Mexican women between the ages of twenty and twenty-four do not seek work outside of the home because they already performed unpaid domestic labor full-time.[6] Indigenous women, as Maya-Kaqchikel scholar Aura Estela Cumes has noted, are frequently depicted as "naturally apt" to work in nonremunerated labor positions.[7] As a result, and reflecting oppressive patriarchal and colonial systems, Indigenous women in Mexico have been pushed out of the paid labor force and encounter additional barriers to educational and economic advancement.

In Guatemala, although Indigenous groups made up 43.75 percent of the population in 2019, they also fared worse than their non-Indigenous counterparts.[8] Due to centuries of violence and exclusion, Indigenous Guatemalan communities have continued to experience the highest unemployment rates and the lowest incomes in the nation. In 2015, 75 percent of Indigenous Guatemalans lived in poverty compared to 36 percent of non-Indigenous people.[9] Over three million Indigenous people in Guatemala lacked access to basic living conditions, such as clean water, plumbing, basic housing, education, and health care.

Guatemalan women have also been more likely to be responsible for unpaid domestic and care labor, pushing them out of the paid labor force. Women have experienced significant disadvantages compared to Guatemalan men, with reduced educational attainment, and when they do participate in the paid labor force, they receive lower earnings.[10] And as in Mexico, Guatemalan Indigenous women have faced even greater oppression and socioeconomic barriers. Over 90 percent of Indigenous adult women were illiterate in some rural areas in 2015.[11]

While violence rates have continued to be excessive throughout the region, women experience gendered violence perpetuated and veiled by patriarchal social structures and norms.[12] Women face torturous violence with little to no support from government agencies and civil organizations. Throughout the region *feminicidios* have continued to be on the rise,[13] even in places where laws are supposed to protect women.[14] Again, Indigenous women have the least resources to cope with such circumstances.

Indigenous Experiences: *"Nos llaman campesinos,"*
They call us peasants

In the spring of 2016 I drove to the home of Dolores, an Indigenous Mixteco woman to whom I'd been introduced by a community health worker. The front yard of Dolores's small two-bedroom house was scattered with tricycles, toys, and dolls, and when I knocked on the door, it was cracked open by a small boy with piercing brown eyes. Dolores invited me inside, offered a fresh *café con leche*, and, seated at the dining table, recalled her former life. "In my town there is nothing," she said of her Mixteco community in the mountains of southern Mexico. "The town has about fifty houses. It is very small, and there is a lot of poverty and there is no work. My parents don't even have anything to eat, for shoes, or for clothes." Dolores's parents were campesinos, peasant agricultural workers. "There is nothing," she said. "People used to grow mango, but now it has an owner." The new owner that Dolores inferred to was a foreign agribusiness company. After the North American Free Trade Agreement (NAFTA) was signed in 1994, foreign investors took over agricultural sectors across Mexico, pushing Mexican campesinos and many Indigenous people, such as Dolores's family to lose their small plots of land and their main source of income. To help her family make ends meet, Dolores left school very young to sell tacos in the street. Then, at age thirteen and lured by the prospect of a life without poverty, Dolores married a man more than twice her age who helped her migrate to the United States. "We came," she said, "for necessity."

Jazmin, an Indigenous Maya woman, told me similar stories about her childhood in rural Guatemala. We met in her apartment after being introduced by Pastor José, a religious leader in her community in Kansas. Now, sitting on a wooden chair in her empty living room with the Kansas sun highlighting her long, sleek ponytail, she remembered her parents. "They just work. They have one job, only one. There they go to work; they work in a [coffee] roaster. If they have some free time, they go to work for another person." Jazmin clarified, "We plant coffee, care for the fields; sometimes you go to work in the forest, bring firewood, that's how you spend the day. There they have no money; it is very poor. That is why I don't want to be there."

The Guatemalan agricultural landscape is largely privatized, with transnational agribusiness as the main employers. Campesinos' earnings are meager and barely enough to survive on, even when working long hours. In some regions of Guatemala, campesinos are not renumerated and live as indentured servants.[15] "My mom works a lot," Jazmin told me. "She goes fishing, cuts [crops]; that is all she does, my mom. And we don't have money; we don't have anything to eat." To contribute to her family needs, Jazmin did not go to school. "My mom sent me to work to take care of the house, take care of my brothers. So, I did not study anything." Besides taking care of her siblings and household chores, Jazmin sometimes sold vegetables grown by the family in the nearby market.

During one market outing, Jazmin was abducted by a taxi driver. "He took me on a different route," she recalled. "I told him, 'This is not the way.' He said, 'No we are just going for a ride.' But I knew. He was acting odd. He asked me if I have family in the United States, if my dad has money, if I have family here [in the United States], if my dad has a herd, if my dad has a business. He asked me all of that. And I told him no because my dad doesn't have anything. He said, 'That is fine, *vamos a aprovechar* [let's take advantage].' I felt sick. But thanks God, I started praying and praying in the car. It was all mountains, and lots of rocks [fell] in front of his car; it was blocked. I opened the door, and I ran, I hid." Lost in the mountains for hours, Jazmin finally made her way back to her hometown by hitching a ride with a truck driver. It was this harrowing experience, combined with her family's poverty and lack of economic opportunities in her hometown, that motivated Jazmin to leave Guatemala for the United States. "I realized that this cannot be my future," she told me. "That is why I came here, *a luchar* [to work hard to get ahead]."[16]

Mexican and Guatemalan campesinos—many of whom are Indigenous—have fought continually for land rights since the colonial era. After the 1910 Mexican Revolution, the Mexican Constitution determined that land was communally owned. In 1992, however, influenced by neoliberal ideology, the Constitution was altered—public lands became private property, and Mexican territory became available for sale on the private market.[17] Two years later, the North American Free Trade Agreement further complicated small land owners' and campesinos' ability to compete against foreign agribusiness and land developers.[18] This hindered campesinos and rural farmers the most, since they sold produce in local markets and relied on state subsidies to support their farms.[19] These land reforms were accompanied by a simultaneous cut in social welfare programs, further compounding campesinos' plight. In the decades since, Mexico's ruling mestizo elites have instituted numerous laws that further opened the country's territory to privatization and resource expropriation.[20] These macrolevel changes have led to the local vulnerabilities and hardships that Dolores described, with transnational agreements eradicating the small-scale mango production that her family depended on for their livelihood.

In Guatemala, slightly more than 46 percent of the population live in rural areas,[21] and conflicts over land are endemic to the nation's peasant history. The unequal distribution of land was a central feature of Guatemala under colonialism, through the postwar Guatemalan Revolution, and into the decades of the 1960s US-backed armed conflict and beyond.[22] Guatemala's civil war (1960–1996) was especially devastating for Indigenous Maya groups, with at least 626 massacres of Indigenous villages, 1.5 million displaced people, 150,000 people fleeing to Mexico, and more than 200,000 killed or disappeared.[23] The 1996 Guatemalan Peace Accords marked Guatemala's turn toward neoliberalism,[24] with the Agreement on Socio-Economic Aspects of the Agrarian Situation in particular moving the country toward a "market-assisted land reform" strategy, guided by the World Bank, and creating a private sector, strict property rights, and a credit-based lending system for poor peasants.[25] A decade after the accords, however, only 4 percent of the total agricultural land in Guatemala was redistributed,[26] and 72 percent of Guatemalan land was owned by the top 2 percent.[27] Campesinos—many of whom, like Jazmin's family, are Indigenous—have found it very difficult to own land and suffer from extreme poverty and indebtedness. The long-standing colonial erasure of Indigenous peoples is thus perpetuated through neoliberal tools of financialized land reform and global capitalism.

Alejandro, an Indigenous Maya Guatemalan man, described his childhood to me and explained his motivation to migrate. Instead of attending school, he had started working in the fields at age eleven. "We work a lot, but we don't earn anything," Alejandro shared. "We don't have anything. Around the house, it is not good; you don't feel good. You need something more to help the family. That is why we decide to come." Like Alejandro, Indigenous campesinos in both Guatemala and Mexico often lack basic domestic infrastructure, including *techo y piso* (a concrete roof and floor), electricity, and running water. In Guatemala, although poverty conditions and access to resources also vary within ethnic groups and across regions, 44 percent lacked basic services in their homes, compared to 19 percent of the general population.[28]

Alejandro said, "My dad doesn't have money; put it simply, we are poor. When he wants something, we have to borrow, and sometimes they don't lend us. They think we will cheat them. And seeing how my dad . . ." Alejandro took a deep breath and looked out the window before continuing. "Sometimes we go to bring wood, and I see my dad carrying the wood. He is older, and sometimes I feel like crying and I think, 'Why are we like this?' I decided to come to help my dad and my mom too, my sisters, my brothers, to be better so that they don't have to worry so much. They worry because we don't have anything."

Likewise, Catia, an Indigenous Maya woman, also talked about the food insecurity she experienced growing up in rural Guatemala. It was a hot, muggy day in Kansas, and Catia and I were sitting on her porch eating homemade frozen chocolate-covered bananas and watching her children play. "When I was little my mom gave me warm water with salt," Catia said, remembering the countless nights she went to bed hungry. "That was the soup."

The extreme inequities faced by Indigenous communities in Mexico and Guatemala reflect the continued presence of colonial legacies, political disenfranchisement, and the reproduction of structural violence. Indigenous communities' lack of resources—such as housing, health care, educational opportunities, living wages, and access to nutritious food—reproduces suffering, with long-term, multigenerational consequences.[29] Almost all of the Indigenous immigrants I met in Kansas described a former life of extreme rural poverty.

Mestizo Experiences: "I always had a house like here"

The mestizo immigrants I met in Kansas had more varied backgrounds and experiences. At a restaurant, for example, Rita, a mestizo woman, described her childhood in El Salvador, where she'd lived with her parents and her sibling:

> In El Salvador, we lived, like, all the areas are ugly, they are dangerous, but I lived in the city, so it wasn't that bad. I lived in a gated community. It was a normal house. So, we moved here, it wasn't a big change. In terms of housing, it hasn't been a large change. Maybe just in the environment because there [in El Salvador] you always had to be cautious, careful.

Paloma, a mestizo Mexican woman, also noted how her former living arrangements were comparable to those in the United States. "We are from [Mexico]. But to tell you the truth I always had a house like here," she told me. "We never suffered. I never knew what it was like to not have water or electricity."

Like Rita and Paloma, mestizo immigrants, particularly those who grew up in urban areas, distanced themselves from extreme poverty—illustrating the pervasiveness of urban/rural class, socioeconomic, and ethnoracial divides across Latin America. Nevertheless, while the region's wealthier residents are mestizo and tend to live in urban areas,[30] Latin American cities are also the site of deep inequities, power imbalances, and many forms of violence. Rural destitution, described by the Indigenous immigrants above, has caused significant rural-to-urban migration, transforming 80 percent of the Latin American population into urban dwellers and thus supplying cheap labor for (often foreign-owned) manufacturing plants in urban free trade zones.[31] These structural conditions illustrate the enduring influence of colonial legacies, as Latin American cities were originally established to facilitate the export of natural resources and agricultural products while also administering and controlling colonial territories.[32] Thus, contemporary cities reflect long-standing power relations and structures of colonization, creating strong class divides between elite neighborhoods and poor enclaves.

Reinalda, a mestizo Ecuadorian woman, exemplified this point. Reinalda and I met in an old musty church. "Well, first of all, I come from middle-upper class," she began our conversation.

We used to come regularly on vacation to New York, because my mom's family is very big, so half of my mom's family lives in New York and the others in Florida and the other part in Ecuador. There are only a few left in Ecuador. So, we came to New York on vacation. The two months of vacation we went to Florida to visit Disney World and things like that.

Emphasizing her class standing in Ecuador, Reinalda continued:

I worked for a bank in Ecuador. I was the supervisor. I was in charge of reviewing people's credit reports. It wasn't bad for the age that I had. I started working at age seventeen and by then I was twenty. I came here when I was twenty-two. I was doing well, but then the bank went bankrupt. . . . For my husband it was more complicated to find a job. My family helped him find work, but in reality he didn't need it. We were mom's and dad's kids; they helped us economically.

Besides Reinalda, other mestizo immigrants described growing up in middle-class families, heavily reliant on parental support for their economic needs. However, many stressed that college degrees and highly skilled professional jobs were poorly remunerated in their home countries and that their families struggled financially. In El Salvador, for example, Rita's parents were both college graduates, but opportunities to develop their professional careers were scarce. "My mom, her job laid her off," she explained. "I mean, they fired her, without a reason. She was a manager of [the company], and she used to give conferences and everything. She traveled outside of the country for this company." As for Rita's father, "In El Salvador, he had a lot of jobs. At first when I was little, he distributed gas. . . . He is an agricultural engineer; he had a nursery. He would go to Guatemala to get the plants to sell them during Christmas; that was the last thing he did before coming [to the United States]." As Rita's experience reveals, even for families with high levels of educational attainment, financial stability in their home countries proved elusive. Although minimum wage rates have increased slightly in countries such as El Salvador,[33] income returns on educational attainment have decreased steadily across Latin America since the 1990s.[34]

Some mestizos also grew up in working-class and low-income families and struggled to make ends meet. Linda, for example, grew up in Mexico with her parents and siblings. A family medical episode quickly forced Linda and her sister out of school and into the labor force:

> I wanted to keep studying. I wasn't very good at school, but I wanted to keep studying. But my mom had an embolism when I was in sixth grade, almost out of elementary school, and she had the embolism. So there was no money; besides it was a lot of us. There was no money for her disease. So, we left elementary school. We started to work cleaning a house.

Gerardo, a mestizo man who also grew up in a working-class and low-income family in Mexico, remembered a teenage conversation with his father about social class and politics. Sitting beside his wife in their Kansas living room, Gerardo shared what his father told him: "The rich don't have anything to do; that is why they are in politics. They are not thinking only about what they will be eating tomorrow." Gerardo reflected, "We are of the band of the poor."

As these accounts demonstrate, the mestizo immigrants I met in the heartland were mostly raised in urban areas and had varying socioeconomic backgrounds prior to migration. Clearly, then, mestizo immigrants had left behind a very different set of socioeconomic circumstances in Latin America when compared to Indigenous immigrants—a division largely shaped by enduring colonial legacies.

CROSSING BORDERS

Indigenous and mestizo immigrants' lives before migration also determined their resources for their journeys and strongly influenced how they entered the United States. Nineteen of the mestizo immigrants I met in Kansas entered the United States with a visa. The remaining ten and all of the thirty-five Indigenous informants entered the United States via "unauthorized" means. Colonial legacies are visible here too. Immigration policies involve the militarized enforcement of borders and territories, international and local cooperation, and extensive bureaucracies. These processes operate under the continuing logic of coloniality, reproducing power divides and gendering and racializing immigrants. Focusing on one key aspect of migration—crossing borders, whether entering a nation-state or encountering a border en route—allows us to delve into the mechanisms that reproduce colonial differences in contemporary migration processes.

Authorized Travel: Visas

As outlined in the Introduction, there are two main US visa categories. Immigrant visas usually involve family or employment sponsorship, offering the possibility of long-term residency and a path to citizenship. Nonimmigrant visas—including those granted for tourism, business, athletic travel, work, and study—are temporary and do not provide a path to residency or citizenship. Because the family sponsorship program involves a classed and racialized vetting system matched with long waiting periods, sometimes decades long,[35] most of the mestizos who entered the United States with a visa did so using nonimmigrant visas.[36] Eligibility requirements for nonimmigrant visas manifest various intersectional exclusions pertaining to class, gender, and race that mark who is considered eligible for US admission. These map onto colonial ethnoracial hierarchies, reflected in the fact that none of the Indigenous immigrants I met in Kansas had ever received a US visa.

I visited Victoria and her husband, an Indigenous Tlapaneco Mexican couple, during the Christmas season holiday break. Over tamales, we discussed the emotional toll of being separated from loved ones during the holidays. Weeks earlier, Victoria had telephoned me to ask for the contact information of someone in Mexico who could help her mother apply for a tourist visa to visit Kansas. Victoria had not seen her mother or her eldest daughter since leaving Mexico over a decade earlier. Years prior, the couple tried to get a tourist visa for Victoria's father-in-law, a Tlapaneco *campesino*, but it was denied. Now, they worried that the US consulate would also deny Victoria's mother's application. The couple emphasized that neither his father nor Victoria's mother wanted to live permanently in the United States. They simply wanted to visit their children whom they had not seen in years and meet their grandchildren.

At the time of the study, US tourist visa requirements for Mexican nationals included a Mexican passport, work and educational history, a lengthy application in English, a $185 fee, and proof of economic standing. Victoria's mother had worked her entire life in the fields as a *campesina* as well as washing and cooking for families in a nearby city. She was always paid in cash, making it difficult to provide employment documentation. Victoria's mother had not attended school and so lacked an educational history. She could not read or write in either Spanish or English and would need to pay someone to fill out the application. Additionally, she would have to travel several hours to the nearby consulate, where she would have to wait for a slot to even be considered to apply. Clearly, therefore, Indigenous families such as Victoria's mom could not easily meet US visa requirements for temporary nonlabor visas.[37]

In contrast, mestizo immigrants were more likely to meet temporary visa qualifications, in keeping with their broader range of economic and educational backgrounds. Reinalda, whom I'd met at the church, had only minor difficulties gaining a tourist visa. Her social position—including class background, educational attainment, previous travel experience, and ties to family in the United States with recognized immigration status—positioned her as an eligible. Rita too came to the United States from El Salvador, at age thirteen, on a tourist visa with her parents and sibling. "So, my dad came at the beginning of 2007. He stayed until holy week, which is more or less in March, and he came back. Once he returned, they told us we were all coming."

Obtaining a visa was not so straightforward for all mestizos, however. Carlos, a mestizo Honduran man, recounted how ties to his citizen brother were instrumental in gaining the tourist visa him and his mom used to enter the United States:

> Every time we would go to get the visa, they would always come up with an excuse. You don't have enough funding, you don't have this, you don't have that, just excuse after excuse, and we would always go back with the requirement they were asking, and yet they would always have new requirements every time we would go. Finally, in 2001 I don't know what happened; they were probably getting tired of my mom going every year. They finally gave us a [tourist] visa. It was through an invitation that my sister did. She sent a letter saying "Hey, I haven't seen my mom for over so many years, I want her to be part of this ceremony; it would make my dreams come true." And then my brother, who was just a citizen at that time, wrote a letter saying you know, can they just come for a few weeks so they can be part of the wedding? Me as a citizen I will be in charge of any expenses, and all that stuff. . . . And it was a pretty long process for us. But for them too here, they had to come up with letters of recommendation. They had to fill out all these documents from here, send it back to Honduras. My mom had to open a bank account and put a lot of money in one account so they could think we had like so much more money, when in reality it was just an effort to have everyone help out, you know. So, we could get the visa. And that is how we were able to get the visa. And we came here.

Unauthorized Travel, I: "It is very difficult to cross Mexico"

For immigrants who could not fulfil US visa requirements, reaching and entering the United States involved a long and treacherous journey. Esperanza, an Indigenous Maya Guatemalan woman, described her experience. She left home at age sixteen, and it took her twenty days to reach the US-Mexico border. "It is very difficult to cross Mexico," she said. "The coyotes brought me from [Guatemala]. They asked for around ten thousand Quetzales; that is around $1,500. Then we got to the border, and then they asked for more." Francisca, a young Indigenous Maya woman, had a similar story. She left Guatemala at age nineteen. As we chatted in her Kansas trailer home, with her son watching cartoons, Francisca recalled their journey across Mexico. "The boy was crying a lot, crying and crying," she said. "What am I going to give him? It was almost around twenty days that we were [traveling through Mexico] walking, [taking] buses and taxis. That is how we came."

During my fieldwork in Kansas, I met fourteen Indigenous Maya Guatemalans and two mestizo Hondurans who traveled across Mexico en route to the United States. Mexico is considered one of the most dangerous migrant transit routes in the world.[38] Besides the risk of detention and deportation—initiatives spearheaded by US-backed funds—immigrants encounter kidnapping, sexual violence, physical assault, extortion, and other forms of human rights abuses such as threats, discrimination, and xenophobia. As with the United States, Mexican immigration policies are influenced by colonial legacies that make Indigenous and Central American immigrants especially vulnerable to violence, expulsion, and criminalization. Mexico has been a transit country since the early 1970s primarily to Central Americans, when especially Salvadorans and Guatemalans fled their homelands following US-backed civil conflict.[39] Economic crises, political instability, increased violence, and several natural disasters have also pushed many to flee the region.[40]

Migrating from Central America first entailed securing sufficient funds. As crossing Mexico became more dangerous—due to Mexican immigration policies that criminalized Central American immigrants—these costs increased. Alejandro, the Indigenous Maya Guatemalan man who described above the pain he felt watching his elderly father collect wood, secured his migration funds after his cousin—who'd already worked in the United States—introduced him to a US-based lender. "There is a gentleman that lives in Tennessee; he is legal here," Alejandro explained. "He did the favor to pay the money for my passage, and sometimes I ran out of money at the border, and he sent me money. If I don't pay him, he takes the land and kicks us out. They are even capable of harming us." Alejandro's impoverished family thus used all their collective resources, including their small plot of farmland, as collateral for Alejandro's loan. If Alejandro had been unsuccessful in his journey, he would still have had to repay the moneylender or his family would have lost everything.

This is a pattern that occurred across ethnoracial backgrounds: immigrants became indebted as soon as their travels began. Luz, for example, an Indigenous Maya Guatemalan woman, left for the United States at age twenty-two. Lacking funds to pay for the journey up front, she asked two men from her hometown—known as coyotes for serving as travel guides across Mexico—for a loan, which she promised to repay upon reaching the United States. "I told them, 'I am not going to go to do bad things, but because I have necessities, I'm going to work, and around three months later, I can give you the money.'" The men agreed to cover the cost of Luz's trip, with the expectation that she would repay them with interest once she reached her destination.

Once their funds are secured, immigrants undertook the two thousand–mile journey across Mexico. Depending on their resources, they traveled in buses, trailers, trucks, cars, cargo trains, or on foot.[41] Most of the Indigenous Guatemalans I met had traveled by bus and on foot, guided by coyotes (also known as *polleros* among migrants). Jazmin, who left Guatemala at age seventeen after being abducted by the taxi driver, recalled her journey: "In my country [Guatemala] I traveled in small cars; then I went to the Mexican [southern] border. There I took the bus. Then I traveled like five days, day and night, to come to a place that is called Chihuahua." Luz too traveled through Mexico in buses. "I came with them [coyotes]," she said. "And nothing happened; I came directly." Luz's phrase "nothing happened" is telling. Most immigrants traveling through Mexico experienced dangerous encounters, as I would soon learn from listening to the story of Ofelia's family.

In the winter of 2018 I visited Ofelia, an Indigenous Maya Guatemalan woman who lived in a small trailer in rural Kansas. Sitting at her kitchen table beside the window, Ofelia recounted that some of her relatives had been journeying through Mexico with the hope of reaching Kansas. They were part of a large group of immigrants traveling inside a trailer truck, guided by a *pollero*, when armed Mexican nationals raided the vehicle. Ofelia wasn't sure whether the aggressors were police officers, gang members, or drug traffickers, but they robbed the immigrants and fired at the group with machine guns.[42] Two men from Ofelia's town were killed. Ofelia's breath quickened as she showed me pictures on her cell phone of a small room in her hometown with gray cement walls and a dirt floor. Men and women, dressed in traditional Mayan clothing, kept vigil over a purple and yellow casket that awaited the body of one of their loved ones. According to the International Organization of Migration, 556 immigrants were reported as dead in Mexico and Central America between 2014 and 2019.[43] However, thousands more have gone missing.[44]

Erica, a mestizo Honduran woman, left her country at age twenty-two, pregnant and fleeing a violent relationship. Without money or support, she first crossed Guatemala and then Mexico's southern border by foot. In Chiapas, southern Mexico, a man assaulted her. "When I saw the sixteen stitches," she told me, "I started crying, but I said, 'No, even like this, I keep going.'" With a strong will to reach the United States, Erica traveled in one of the most dangerous transports immigrants can take, hopping on and off the top of cargo trains. In Erica's words, "And well, I kept going. I kept going, and I came by the trains. And when I threw myself to the trains . . . Yes, I went through a lot of difficulties because, well, pregnant you get cravings, and I was pregnant with my son, and I said, 'Oh my God, don't let my son be born bad,' because I came starting a pregnancy. It was easy to lose him throwing myself from the trains, enduring hunger and cold."

Erica reflected on the dangers of the journey and the need motivating her migration. "Even if I die, even if I stay in the line [at the border], one is very conscious, but superconscious, that you can lose your life, that they can do to you *barbaridad y media* [terrible things]. But well, one takes a chance for . . . I mean, hunger and necessity are bigger than your life." As Erica's words indicate, immigrant women must physically navigate sociopolitical contexts where patriarchal norms target women and make them vulnerable to gendered violence, in addition to the many aspects of the migrant journey. Like Erica, many women flee the gender-based violence of their homes and communities, only to encounter further gendered violence on their journeys.[45]

Violence against immigrants crossing Mexico is legitimated through xenophobic, racialized narratives promoted by Mexican media and politicians. During the period of my research, these were mainly directed against Central American immigrants but also toward Indigenous groups more broadly. Mexican news and political rhetoric portrayed Central American immigrants as "invaders," claiming that immigrants brought crime and public health concerns to the country.[46] Such tactics have been a clear attempt to evade accountability for the violence generated by Mexico's own neoliberal policies, rooted in colonial divisions and control mechanisms. The racialization of Central American undocumented immigrants in Mexico is also tied to colonial ideologies of *indigenismo* and ongoing anti-Indigenous discrimination. In 2015, Mexican immigration officers detained four Indigenous Mexicans aged fifteen to twenty-four. The officers targeted the Mexican Indigenous youths based on their physical appearance, clothes, and limited knowledge of Spanish and claimed that the youths were Guatemalan immigrants. One of the youths was tortured until he signed a deportation order. While the chief of the Mexican National Institute of Migration apologized, the six officers who targeted and tortured the Mexican Indigenous youths were never charged.[47] The racialization of undocumented immigrants in Mexico, rooted in the control of Indigenous mobility, thus demonstrates the legacies and structures of colonialism in current immigration policing. Indigenous immigrants' ethnoracial backgrounds thus further expose them to violence, as colonial legacies in Mexican immigration policies and militarized surveillance strategies legitimize violence toward Indigenous groups.[48]

Unauthorized Travel, II: *La frontera*, the US-Mexico Border

Once Central American immigrants successfully traversed Mexico, they joined hundreds of other immigrants attempting to cross the US-Mexico border: *la frontera*. Regardless of ethnoracial distinctions, all immigrants here had to maneuver between multiple human actors while navigating the dangerous ecological terrain of deserts and rivers. Illicit routes enrich multiple actors in the migration industry, ranging from cartel and criminal affiliates to guides and smuggler organizations and even to state-sponsored surveillance groups.[49] Immigrants encountered multiple forms of violence on these border crossing attempts, yet racialization and colonial legacies produced different circumstances for different immigrants.

Gerardo, a mestizo Mexican man, migrated at age eighteen with his father and brother. He once explained to me how multiple actors tried to profit from the precarity of their undocumented crossing. "The mafia is there, so if you are crossing and if you don't pay the quota, you get kicked around, and they send you back," he said. "So now you don't just have to watch out for the *migra* [referring to US Customs and Border Patrol officers], but now you must watch out for the mafia and everything." Gerardo went on to explain the "quotas" that immigrants must pay to these various actors, whether it is cartel territory or to pass the Mexican officials as they transverse the border. "If they cross people, they pay a quota for every person that crosses." While most immigrants are aware of these quotas and include this in their journey financial planning, some are unable to pay, and they must try to avoid these various actors or face violence and possible death. As Paco, an Indigenous Mixteco Mexican young man who migrated at age fourteen, told me, "You must hide if someone comes, or if someone sees me, you hide. That is all you can do."

The surge in border surveillance has increased the likelihood of apprehension. As a result, immigrants attempt to cross the border multiple times, increasing the associated costs and dangers.[50] As was the case for Alejandro, many preferred to take their chances alone in the desert rather than face the possibility of apprehension by Border Patrol agents and deportation to their home country. Alejandro went on to explain:

> We had been walking for five nights, and the *migra* [Border Patrol] found us, so we ran. We were like ten people. They grabbed the rest, and I ran a lot, like a half hour, and that is where I stayed. By sunrise there was nobody there, in the middle of the desert. Sometimes it was very hot. Sometimes I went under the trees; the coyotes [animals] walked by looking at me, thinking I was dead. I came to a highway where immigration [officers] drive by. I was standing, and there was nobody to take me—but nobody. When you need help there is nobody.

Stranded in the desert for days, Alejandro ran out of water. "I couldn't walk," he recalled. "My knee swelled up. I couldn't walk, everything was dry, and I couldn't talk. I couldn't scream. I wanted to scream so someone would hear me, but I couldn't. It was like a nightmare." Alejandro eventually stumbled upon a ranch, where he found help. "It was a miracle from God; it was not my destiny [to die]," he said. "They even took me to a store and bought me a soda. I had no money." Alejandro had been stranded in the desert for days but did not make it to the United States. The Mexican ranchers took Alejandro to a house, where a man offered to help him cross the border because the man would be guiding a group of people the following day. Following the new guide and adding costs to his already growing debt, Alejandro eventually made it across the desert into the United States.

During conversations in Kansas with Maya and Mixteco men, I frequently heard similar stories of immigrants getting lost in the desert because they tried to avoid Border Patrol or physically could not keep up with the rest of their group. Domingo, for example, chatting on the porch of his cousin's aging trailer home, told me how he'd tried to hide from Border Patrol and became separated from his companions. Domingo wandered the desert for days until he collapsed from dehydration and heat exhaustion. Luckily, he was saved by volunteers from a charity that searches for missing immigrants. While exact figures are difficult to establish, scholars and advocacy organizations believe that immigrants are dying at increasing rates at the US-Mexico border—rising in tandem with heightened surveillance and militarization of the area.[51] Border enforcement "deterrence strategies" have made immigrant life valueless due to immigration policies that seek to "secure" the border while inflicting pain and even death on immigrants. Most immigrant deaths at the border go unnoticed and unresolved.[52]

Immigrant women, as we have seen, encounter additional risks of gendered violence during border crossings, and sexual violence is part of many women's journeys across *la frontera*.[53] "At the border . . . there are robbers. They abuse everything; they take even your shoes," Dolores told me. "I never want to go back there," she said as she took a deep breath while tensing her shoulders and frowning before continuing. "You see, they robbed us there. They put the gun to our head, and in front of you they rape your *compañeras* [women travel companions]." Dolores recalled that after only two hours of walking in the desert, a group of men approached her travel group. The men took the immigrants' money and jewelry and gang-raped two women in front of the rest of the group. Dolores believed that the only reason she wasn't raped was because she was traveling with her husband, an experienced immigrant more than twice her age. But she sometimes wondered if she just got "lucky." Fifteen years later, these memories still troubled her. Immigrant women are systematically targeted for sexual violence and have no state protection. While sexual assault and rape have occurred throughout history in conflict and border zones, these forms of violence nevertheless illustrate the gendered mechanisms under colonial legacies that allow the dehumanization and violation of women's bodies without consequence.[54] Colonial legacies, combined with undocumented immigrants' extralegal vulnerability, leave immigrant women facing extreme violence with no room for redress.

While immigrants of all backgrounds faced similar forms of violence en route to the United States, their positionality and access to networks and resources shaped how they navigated these circumstances. The cases of Luz, an Indigenous woman, and Jenny, a mestizo woman, illustrate this point. Both women were kidnapped shortly after successfully crossing into the United States. Luz, after crossing the desert, was taken by coyotes to a house in California. Luz had no family or friends in California and had previously arranged with the coyotes that she would repay them for the trip after working for a few months in the United States. The men demanded $3,000 in exchange for her freedom. "They asked the phone number of my family members. I have my ex-husband; maybe he can receive me. They called him, my son's dad. They told him, 'I have your wife here. Can you receive her?' And he said, 'No, I don't have money, only $500.'" Luz's ex-husband sent $500, but the guides wanted more and refused to let her go. They also called Luz's father, who complied with their request and sent $3,000. After receiving the money, however, the men demanded even more. "They started saying that the money wasn't complete. So, they called my dad again. They told him, 'You know what? This money is not enough.' My dad told them, 'No, you told me that it was $3,000. I am very sorry for her, but I cannot give any more.'"

The men then forced Luz to work as a housemaid until the rest of her spurious debt was paid off. "As a servant, I was afraid because I didn't know the people or where I was," she confided. Luz cooked and cleaned the house for several weeks but could not remember exactly how long she was held captive. Eventually she managed to contact her brother, who lived in the US heartland. She had not seen him in years. Her brother paid the remaining ransom, and Luz was released. As Cecilia Menjívar's work has shown, while new immigrants to the United States tend to rely on their undocumented peers, the structural barriers and marginalization associated with undocumented status often limits their peers' ability to provide help.[55] In Luz's case, while help was eventually possible, she was left further indebted to her male relatives while facing the severe trauma of being kidnapped for weeks.

Jenny, a mestizo Mexican woman, was also kidnapped after she crossed the border. A group of men took Jenny and her siblings, whom she was traveling with, to Colorado, where they were extorted and threatened with forced return to Mexico if they did not pay:

> When we crossed the border, we had to go through the river; we didn't have a visa. We crossed, and then they put us inside a car's trunk until [New Mexico]. It must have been . . . And from there, well, they let us sit on the car seats; we weren't in the trunk anymore. We could sit up like this [motioned sitting up straight in her chair]. We arrived at [Colorado], and there we couldn't leave; we couldn't look outside, nothing. And then the coyote that brought us didn't want to let us go until we paid.

Jenny's father lived in the United States and was in the process of changing his immigration status to legal permanent resident. Jenny and her siblings reached out to him for help. "My dad didn't have money to pay, and they told us they would return us to Mexico," Jenny went on. "So, then my dad said, 'No, if you take [them] back to Mexico, I will call the police.' My dad ended up paying half of the money, and they let us go. We never paid the rest." Unlike Luz, Jenny had ties to a person with semilegal status who felt comfortable confronting the kidnappers—going to the police if necessary—because his own presence in the United States would not be compromised, something Luz could not do because all her contacts in the United States were also undocumented.

Finally, Indigenous and mestizo border experiences were shaped by the racialization of illegality. Racialization processes within US immigration policy and law enforcement tie perceived Mexican origin to illegality, making some immigrants around the border more conspicuous than others via racial profiling.[56] For instance, Jenny's husband Vicente, a mestizo Mexican man, self-categorized himself as white, *descolorido* (colorless), and *güero*,[57] and he described how his physical appearance once helped him escape a close encounter with US Border Patrol agents. As we ate freshly made quesadillas and red rice that Jenny had prepared, Vicente described the episode in detail:

> It is really funny because I ran all night to be able to get around the [Border Patrol] checks. . . . And when I was on this side [the United States] where there was information about transport, well, I went and I told the guard, I told him, "Hey I will pay you money if you leave me in Houston." "No," he [the guard] said. "I don't do that. I won't turn you in, but I don't do that." Okay, and then there was a big rock, and I was so tired. The rock was like from here to where that car is [pointing out the window, across the street]. I was so tired that I fell asleep beneath the rock. And then, there, in the desert it is so cold, and in the day it is so hot and at night very cold. And I said, "Okay, oh well." And I was discouraged because a group of young guys passed by running. I tried to join them, but they didn't let me. They left me. So, since they saw me white and since I was wearing American clothes—because when I crossed the border I went to the store and I bought new clothes—I said, "I am going to dress like people from here [the United States] dress, so I don't 'stick out too much.'"

Jenny jumped in and clarified how Vicente's appearance helped him "to blend in." Vicente continued, "It helped me because I am white, when I was crossing." He went on to explain how he avoided Border Patrol thanks to his appearance: "They saw me." Vicente said.

> They stopped the traffic, and I was walking, like this [Vicente stood up and walked across the room with a tall posture]. They saw me, and they just said "goodbye" [waving goodbye with his hand]. There was a trailer [truck] on the other side, and they [Border Patrol officers] thought that I was the driver of that [trailer truck]. So, I got up the stairs of the truck, and I saw the guy was Mexican. He [the actual driver] was Chicano, and I told him, "You know what? I will tell you the truth. I am a person that jumped the line, and I want to go up, north." He said, "I cannot do that." Then his wife, she was a German migrant woman, she opened the door and said "get in."

This was not Vicente's first border crossing experience. He had crossed once before and lived in the US heartland for some time before returning to Mexico to see his aging, dying parents. On this second crossing, however, Vicente used his physical appearance and knowledge of American dress to "blend in," as Jenny put it, and outmaneuver Border Patrol enforcement.[58]

Unlike Vicente, Indigenous immigrants and other Latinos who fit the physical stereotypes of illegality—which are broadly tied to "Mexican" stereotypes—are frequently unable to avoid policing, apprehension, or deportation. "Looking Mexican" is tied to perceptions of darker skin tones, short stature, dark eyes, limited English ability, strong accents, and Spanish names.[59] Between 2015 to 2020 at least seventy US citizens were wrongfully deported, with many more apprehended and incarcerated in immigrant detention facilities who were profiled as "undocumented" on their physicality and ties to "looking Mexican."[60] In a video obtained by National Public Radio, a US Border Patrol agent and a Mexican agent are seen attempting to detain and deport an injured man. The US agent said, "I think he's Mexican. He's going to return to his country." The Mexican agent asked, "You don't know if he's Mexican or not?" The US agent replied, "He looks like it."[61]

La linea: Seeking Asylum

Esperanza, who left her home in Guatemala at age sixteen, entered the United States seeking asylum. She had fled violence and poverty in Guatemala, survived the violent journey through Mexico, and now hoped to start a new life. In broken Spanish, holding back tears, she recalled,

> When I came here, the most difficult that I suffered was the border. When I got to the [detention] center, I felt it was difficult. My mom was sending my documents. My mom was worried. Sometimes she was sad, and I was sad. I did not feel well there. Sometimes I felt *incomoda* (uncomfortable, out of place). It was difficult in the [detention] center where I was. I suffered at the border and *luché* [worked hard, struggled] to be here.

Besides Esperanza, four other Indigenous Maya Guatemalan women whose stories are told in this book were asylum seekers. Most, like Esperanza, entered the United States through what they called *la linea*, the line in which prospective asylum seekers waited to turn themselves over to Border Patrol officials upon reaching the US-Mexico border to request asylum. While their cases are processed, asylum seekers are incarcerated in detention centers, following mandated detention rules in US immigration law. The immigration detention system is thus emblematic of colonial legacies and structures of racialization and domination. As Lytle Hernández argued, incarceration is an active strategy, advancing capitalistic goals of cheap labor and human control rooted in colonial ideation. Colonizers historically relied on criminalizing tactics to exclude certain groups from decision-making and power.[62] Indigenous immigrants experience further anti-Indigenous discrimination and human rights abuses.[63]

Jazmin, the Indigenous Maya young woman who was abducted by the taxi driver in her hometown in Guatemala, also entered the United States seeking asylum at age seventeen with a fellow family member who was also a minor at the time. She discussed her experience with me in detail. "When I entered in Arizona, there no one could speak my language. There is a lot of Spanish [language], and sometimes I understand some [people] and others I don't. So I don't bother anyone, so I don't talk a lot, I am just listening to learn." Jazmin went on to share how she was mocked by other Latina, Spanish-speaking immigrants while in detention. "There is a girl, we couldn't speak well in Spanish, and she made fun of us. She made fun of us who could not speak Spanish. And she would say, 'Why are you talking if you can't speak Spanish? We don't want anyone to be gossiping here.'" Jazmin felt isolated. "No one wanted to speak with us because we could not speak any Spanish. I felt very *incomoda* [uncomfortable/out of place] there." Jazmin continued: "There are some [people] that are mean. There they do bullying."

After being detained for several weeks near the US-Mexico border in an adult detention center, Jazmin was then transferred to an unaccompanied minors' shelter. She should not have been placed in the adult detention center in the first place, since she was a minor. Once she was moved to the minors' shelter, she again encountered discrimination and isolation:

> When I went to the center for minors, there, yes, no one speaks Spanish. They speak English, and the ones from Africa speak the language that they have. And I don't understand anything. I wanted to talk, I wanted to communicate with someone, and I couldn't. I tried to speak Spanish. "I don't understand what you are saying," they would tell me.

As Jazmin's words illustrate, racial, ethnic, and linguistic hierarchies of power among Latino immigrants—entrenched through colonial rule—are transferred and exacerbated in places of overt social control such as detention centers. Jazmin experienced anti-Indigenous discrimination from both her peers and detention officers. And because US immigration officers did not provide an interpreter for her native language, Chuj, Jazmin was detained in an adult center while she was still a minor, violating her rights and prolonging her detention—circumstances that resonated with the plight of other Indigenous immigrants who speak neither Spanish nor English.[64] Asylum seekers in adult detention centers have fewer rights than immigrants held in youth detention centers. Adults, unlike youths, do not have access to free phone calls and pro bono legal representation; if a detained adult wishes to telephone their family or find a lawyer, a person from outside the detention center must provide phone credit for that person to use, which can be extremely expensive.

The lack of adequate Indigenous-language interpretation services can also mean the difference between receiving asylum relief and being deported. In order to apply for asylum at the US border, immigrants must participate in a "credible fear" interview with an immigration officer and demonstrate that there would be a credible threat to their well-being if they were returned to their home country.[65] Without proper interpretation services, Indigenous immigrants have difficulties explaining such circumstances and create misunderstandings in both the initial claims of credible threat and during asylum proceedings.[66] Immigration officers have the discretion to deny or accept a person's story as credible, making these initial encounters crucial for the possibility to receive asylum later on.

CONCLUSION

This chapter highlighted the ongoing pressures, tensions, and violence that colonial legacies reproduce throughout the migration journey. From the inequalities within countries of origin to the multiple forms of violence of the immigration policies that govern cross-border migration pathways, colonial legacies are maintained via neoliberal capitalist practices, ideologies, policies, and institutions across Latin America and the United States. The experiences of Indigenous immigrants from rural campesino communities as well as those of mestizo immigrants from urban areas highlight how neoliberal capitalist policies extended original colonial struggles over land and territory. The practices and politics leading to land privatization and export-oriented agriculture have pushed for the mass migration of peasantry and regional urbanization, reproducing class and ethnoracial divides often obscured by the project of mestizaje governance.

Furthermore, increased border control and surveillance across the region reflect colonial structures that produce criminalized and vulnerable conditions for racialized and criminalized immigrants, with Indigenous groups particularly vulnerable. From the US visa system to the US asylum process, Indigenous immigrants are formally excluded, and de facto segregated and discriminated against when attempting to navigate these systems. While similarities were apparent in immigrants' border crossing experiences, gender is a particularly vital aspect to understand. Immigrant women encounter patriarchal structures that reproduce, veil, and legitimate violence against them in ways that are reminiscent of colonialism. And while every immigrant's experiences were challenging, the resources they had available to cope with struggles and the violence they faced varied along ethnoracial lines.

2

"UN AMBIENTE HOSTIL"

Kansas during Trump's First Presidency

ON NOVEMBER 10, 2016, the front page of the bilingual Kansas newspaper *Dos Mundos* outlined what the incoming Trump presidency might mean for the local Hispanic community. The newspaper report included an interview with several experts on immigration law who warned readers about worst-case scenarios in the months and years ahead. "I am telling people two things that they need to do," one immigration attorney was quoted as saying. "Number one, pray; and number two, act."[1] *Dos Mundos* also ran a political cartoon showing Donald Trump holding the Statue of Liberty by the neck. A thought bubble hung in the air above the statue's head: *"Qué susto! Esto se ve muy oscuro"* (How scary! This looks very gloomy).[2] In February 2017, a month after Trump's presidential inauguration, the front page of *Dos Mundos* featured two headlines: *"ICE genera miedo, infórmate"* (ICE Generates Fear, Get Informed) and *"Los efectos del temor"* (The Effects of Fear).[3] These were accompanied by an image of a woman holding her hands to her mouth and looking frightened. Similar headlines appeared in national Spanish-language news outlets, such as Univision and Telemundo. In Univision news, for example, one headline in the same month read *"El miedo invade a la comunidad inmigrante por los informes de redadas en al menos seis estados"* (Fear Invades Immigrant Community with Raid Information in at Least Six states).[4]

These media headlines reflect the fast-changing immigration environment under the first Trump administration and its rippling effects on immigrant communities across the country, including the heartland. Many of the immigrants I met in Kansas, across ethnoracial lines, first described the state as a desirable destination, as a place where economic stability was achievable and as *un lugar tranquilo* (a place of tranquility). However, because my ethnographic fieldwork coincided with the 2016 presidential election and the aftermath of Trump's first presidency, I was able to capture how immigrants' perceptions about Kansas changed. In contrast with the tranquility they had hoped to find in the heartland, immigrants instead found an increasingly hostile place to live and experienced chronic fear, which impacted their well-being and interactions with the broader community.

UN LUGAR TRANQUILO

When immigrants depicted Kansas as *un lugar tranquilo*, a calm place to live, they alluded to the state's perceived job opportunities, lower housing rents, and low crime rates as well as ideals of lax immigration enforcement. These observations were typically made in relative terms—comparing Kansas to long-standing immigrant destinations in the United States that have larger immigrant and Latino populations, places such as California and Texas. Elena, a mestizo Mexican woman, for example, shared how she arrived in Kansas: "My mom's husband had a brother here in Kansas, and the brother told him that here in

Kansas there is a lot of work, 'Come over!'" Elena explained the difference between Kansas and California. "There in California it was very hard. There were a lot of people; rent was expensive." Coming to the heartland, Elena said, gave her family economic stability. "We came here, and everything changed. I think that it is like if we would have arrived at the US for the first time, because here there were more opportunities. Here one could live a lot better, with less money but a lot better."

As we continued to talk, Elena's husband, Gerardo, chimed in, explaining how several of the couple's extended family members had also moved to Kansas for similar reasons. "We are all here now. Like my wife says, California is more expensive. I told my aunt 'It is better here.'" Reflecting on his previous experiences in California, he went on. "There [in California] we were poor, and here we are poor, but it is not the same. Even like this, we are living well. Maybe we don't have luxuries and all that, but we are healthy, and we have a good time." As Elena and Gerardo explained, living costs in Kansas allowed the couple to reach some economic stability.

León, a mestizo Mexican college student, told me how his family came to Kansas fleeing crime rates in other states when he was a young child. "We lived in California for a while," he began, as we talked in his apartment. "We lived there for a year, then we moved to Michigan for another job that my dad got offered over there." While living in Michigan, however, León's father was robbed. "So that was when he [León's father] was like, 'Okay! Looking for a job in another state!' He [Léon's father] has a brother, and he lived in Kansas. . . . And so, he [Léon's father] contacted him, and he [Léon's uncle] got him a job there. So, we moved. And that's how we ended in Kansas." Like León, Jaime, an Indigenous Mixteco Mexican man, appreciated Kansas for its perception of low crime rates. Jaime had lived in Kansas for over a decade, arriving directly from Mexico with his brother's help. Jaime had never lived in another state during his time in the United States. "We like [Kansas], *es muy tranquilo,*"

Jaime said, looking out of the window, "Because they say in other places there are criminals, but not here." The *tranquilidad* of Kansas was also contrasted with migrants' former lives in their home countries. "It is hard living there," Alejandro, an Indigenous Mayan Guatemalan man remarked, comparing his life in Kansas to the struggles of extreme poverty of his childhood in Guatemala.

Tranquilidad was also connected to perceptions of community in Kansas. For instance, Celestina, a mestizo Mexican woman whom I first met in a Latina women's support group, described her community. "*Mi barrio es muy tranquilo* [my neighborhood is very calm]. I have good neighbors. I have shops nearby; the clinic is not far. There are programs that I can attend." Celestina, who did not drive due to fears of apprehension and the risk of possible deportation, shared that her community had most of what she needed within walking distance. She concluded that she enjoyed living in the heartland because, "I think the place is *muy tranquilo*." Indigenous migrants too said that they enjoyed their communities in relation to the services they could access. Alejandro told me something similar: "It is *tranquilo* here. The shop is nearby; we are fine."

Most immigrants I met had lived in the heartland on average fourteen years for mestizos and ten years for Indigenous immigrants, with Indigenous immigrants having more recent arrivals, including the asylum seekers I introduced in Chapter 1. However, immigrants across racial lines who had been in the heartland longer described some of the changes they had observed and felt over the years. "When I got here, I felt uncomfortable," Reinalda, a mestiza woman, told me once. "It was hard to communicate well. But now society and the community has adapted. We have Hispanics, and they find the way to communicate. But at first, I would say it was very hard." Anglo white people, she said, "Would get frustrated or mad." Since her arrival, over a decade prior to when we met, Reinalda had witnessed considerable changes in Kansas, reflecting the state's demographic shifts. "When

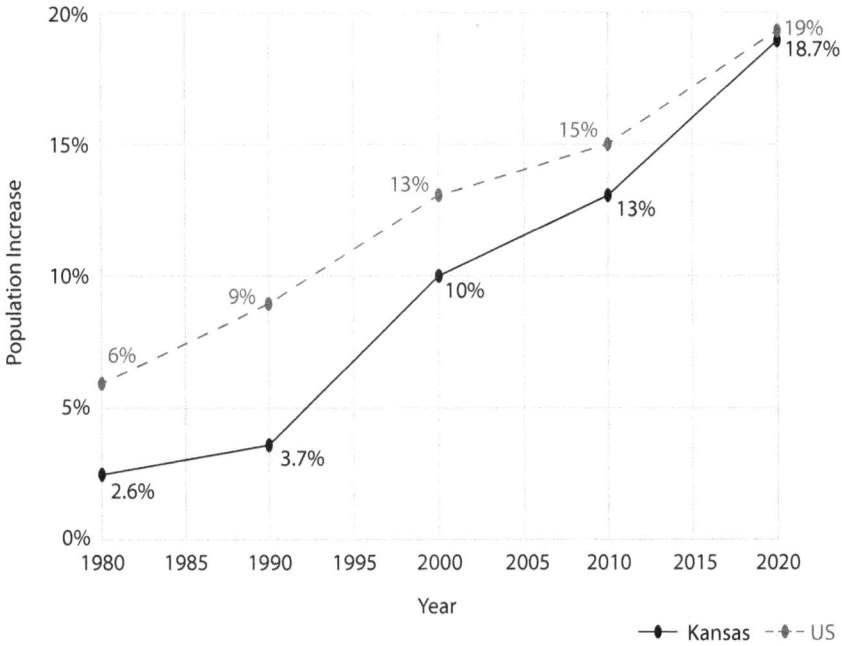

Figure 1. Hispanic origin population trends in Kansas and the United States, 1980 to 2020. SOURCE: Data for Kansas comes from the US Census (US Census Bureau 2020) and the Institute for Policy and Social Research at the University of Kansas (Institute for Policy and Social Research 2023), and the data for the United States comes from the Pew Research Center (2022).

I got here, in Kansas, there were not a lot of Hispanics. You could count Hispanics with the fingers of your hand," she told me. "You saw two or three, no more."

Kansas has experienced a steady increase in its Latino population (see Figure 1), reaching 18 percent of the state's total population in 2020.[5] Most Latinos in Kansas were born in the United States. The composition of foreign-born Latinos has changed too. While most foreign-born Latinos were Mexican for most of its history, by 2022 Central Americans made up a growing share of the foreign-born population in the state.[6] Latinos collectively accounted for 54.8 percent of all immigrants in Kansas in 2022. While estimates of undocumented immigrants vary, various sources show that undocumented immigrants comprised about 3 percent of the total Kansas population—a number that has remained steady across estimations.[7] Echoing national trends, most undocumented immigrants in Kansas have been there for a decade or more, also paralleling the experiences of mestizo and Indigenous immigrants I met during my fieldwork.

Another prominent reason why immigrants considered Kansas to be *un lugar tranquilo* was the belief that contrary to US states with a higher immigrant concentration, immigration enforcement, or *la migra*, was less present and that apprehensions occurred less frequently. Some Indigenous immigrants even told me that they had deliberately moved to Kansas in order to avoid encounters with Immigration and Customs Enforcement (ICE) or the police in other states. Contrary to their expectations of safety and *tranquilidad*, however, undocumented immigrants soon realized that Kansas was not exempt from *la migra*—as Renata's story illustrated.

Renata and her husband, both Indigenous of Tlapaneco Mexican origin, first arrived in North Carolina, joining Renata's younger brother who lived and worked there. In North Carolina, however, the couple worried constantly about *la migra* because reaching their workplace involved a long highway commute, and without driver's licenses, Renata and her husband risked apprehension daily. Renata's husband had a friend in Kansas who mentioned employment opportunities there in the restaurant industry. Drawn by these social ties, related job prospects, and accounts of Kansas as *un lugar tranquilo*, the couple moved to Kansas hoping that it would be a place with limited immigration enforcement, Renata told me. However, after living in Kansas for just a few years, Renata's husband was apprehended while driving and soon after deported. Renata became anxious when she shared this story and did not want to talk more about her feelings or happenings during or after her husband's deportation.

Furthermore, despite immigrants' perceptions of Kansas as *un lugar tranquilo*, the realities of living undocumented or in semilegal status, coupled with the looming prospect of an extremely anti-immigrant president, meant that life in Kansas was rarely as calm as they had hoped. Broader changes in anti-immigration legislation, enacted in recent decades at the federal level, had also trickled down to local communities across the country,[8] amplifying fears among immigrants living in the heartland.

MIEDO, FEAR

When I first met Liliana, a mestizo Mexican woman, she had been living undocumented in the United States for eight years and in Kansas for five of those years. Liliana's husband was also mestizo Mexican and undocumented. The couple had a daughter, age three, who was born in Kansas. Our meeting took place in December 2016 shortly after Donald Trump had been elected president. Sitting in her Christmas-decorated living room with colorful lights and a lively Christmas tree, Liliana shared some of her worries and concerns about what would be Trump's first presidency: "Everything is difficult," she said about living life *sin papeles* (without papers). "But now with the president that we are going to have, the situation is going to be more difficult for all of us. At work, here at home, or the fear of going out to the street." Liliana's concerns about how Trump's campaign promise to deport undocumented immigrants could affect all aspects of her life felt closer than ever. She explained about Trump, *"No nos quiere* [he doesn't like us]; he doesn't want us here." Liliana took a deep breath and concluded, "We are afraid of everything; it's very difficult. And yes, this is very difficult to not have papers and to go out into the street, and everything is very difficult, but well, let's see how it goes."

Undocumented life in the heartland had never been easy for immigrants, requiring constant vigilance against the threat of deportation and navigating the many exclusions that complicated their everyday activities. Trump's election, however, marked the beginning of what became a period of extreme fear for immigrants and for many other minority groups across Kansas.[9] As Liliana predicted, everything did become "more difficult"—going to work, going out in public, and even domestic life in the family home. Indeed, Trump's reinstatement of Secure Communities programs and the expansion of 287(g) initiatives exacerbated immigrants' fears of apprehension, detention, and deportation in all spheres of life. The reinstatement of Secure Communities programs and 287(g) meant that policing localities that previously were not collaborating with ICE were now having to do so. This meant that local policing agents across the state had to collaborate with federal level immigration enforcement. 287(g) initiatives also involved using local jailing facilities for ICE enforcement purposes. Thus, jails could hold undocumented immigrants—even those who did not have any criminal charges—who were waiting for ICE officials to pick them up and transfer them to an immigration detention facility for further processing. These expansions, along with the severe anti-immigrant rhetoric during the first Trump administration, increased fears among the immigrant community in the heartland.

Like Liliana, many immigrants I met discussed the 2016 election and the Trump administration during our structured interviews and informal conversations and in moments of participant observations. These conversations always emerged organically, without me prompting immigrants to discuss their feelings or reactions. At the beginning of my study, coinciding with the 2016 presidential campaigns, I was concerned that discussing these topics would make immigrants feel uncomfortable and that this would diminish our rapport. However, the 2016–2017 election cycle—including Trump's campaign, election, and presidency itself—was a topic that immigrants openly wanted to discuss regardless of ethnoracial background. Both Indigenous and mestizo immigrants highlighted their concerns and reactions to the political climate we were facing. Sometimes these conversations were accompanied by jokes and sarcasm, a common tool of resistance among disenfranchised groups.[10] Most often, however, these conversations were accompanied by anxiety and tension—with migrants talking to me with tightened faces, fidgeting hands, and heavy or fast breathing and sometimes through tears. Before the election, they shared their *preocupaciones* (worries) with me and talked openly about what the outcome might bring. After the election, many discussed their fears and the consequences of the first Trump administration.

I once talked with Sofia, an undocumented Indigenous Tlapaneco Mexican woman, who was also the mother of a US citizen. Our conversation occurred just weeks before the 2016 election, and Sofia shared her *preocupaciones* with me. "I am afraid that they will kick us out, with this president, Trump," she confided. "What if he wins? They call him the '*trompas*' [nervous giggles]. They say that he is going to take our children, all the people without papers." Sofia's concerns regarding family separation were well founded—expressed only weeks before Trump's subsequent zero-tolerance policy that separated asylum seekers from their children and other policies that deported immigrants who had lived in the United States for years. Like Sofia, immigrants I spoke to managed their anxiety and fear through humor, calling Trump "El trompas" and "El trompudo." To explain, *trompudo* colloquially means a person who talks a lot, and *trompas* can also mean someone who is deceiving.

Like Sofia, Liliana, the mestizo Mexican woman who worried about the 2016 election, shared with me her worries about the many Kansans who voted for Trump and these voters' revealed stance on immigration. "A lot of people voted for him," Liliana noted nervously while fidgeting with her hands. "Hopefully he does something good for the US." However, she admitted that Trump ignited insecurity especially "for us that we are immigrants." Likewise, other immigrants worried about Trump's supporters. "There are a lot of people that are racists," Sofia said of Trump's supporters. Ordinary Kansans' support for Trump's candidacy and his election victory thus signaled a broader anti-immigrant climate in the heartland.[11] All but two counties in Kansas voted for Trump in 2016, which is not surprising given that Kansas has been historically a Republican state in almost all presidential elections.[12] Yet given Trump's strong anti-immigrant rhetoric, his win signaled a much broader environment of hostility to immigrants in the heartland.

Elena, the mestiza who moved to Kansas from California a decade earlier, shared her thoughts with me about Trump supporters and how the election of an openly racist and nativist president had unlocked a space for ordinary people to share their anti-immigrant sentiments. "The environment is hostile," Elena shared with a deep breath. "The people took out what they had inside, what they had repressed inside them. They, the people, are letting it out, and that is in all aspects. One aspect is against immigrants." Later while trying to hold back tears, Elena gave an example of how such sentiments had already trickled down to her children at school:

> My youngest daughter who is in kindergarten came home very worried because someone at school told her that she had to go back, and all her family, to Mexico. We are in a school that is 40 percent Anglo, 15 or 20 percent Hispanic, and another 20 percent African American. So, in her class there are only Anglos. She is the only Latina. So, they told her, 'You know that you all have to go back; you and your family have to go back.' That hate and that hostile sentiment is passing from the parents to the children, and I see it in my kids. They are taking it to the schools, and in the schools the kids are receiving that hate.

Reinalda's children had endured a similar experience. With a tightening face and sitting up straight, she said, "[My son] came crying because, just like that, someone told him that he looked like a Mexican donkey. I told him, 'Why do you feel bad?' First, you are not Mexican. You were born here, and you are not a donkey. You are a boy." Similarly, reports of children chanting "build the wall" were documented across the United States following a viral video recorded days after Trump's election in 2016.[13] These chants were directed toward classmates perceived to be immigrants or of Mexican origin.

The hostile environment also heightened immigrants' fears of family separation. Several undocumented immigrant women, both Indigenous and mestizo, expressed these *preocupaciones*. "I am alone with my son," Carolina, an Indigenous Tlapaneco woman, told me. "It is very difficult." She feared being deported and separated from her son. She had already lost her husband to deportation, and she wondered who would take care of her son if she too was deported. Likewise, Esperanza, an Indigenous Maya Guatemalan woman, told me,

> Well, I am a bit afraid also. They say that maybe, I don't know who is the person that will enter in the new government. The president says that we all have to leave; he will take our children. I don't know if that is true if they were born here. He said they will take them, and you just go back just like that. I don't like that at all. I just think, I am used to being with my children.

While the fear of deportation is always present for undocumented immigrants, regardless of presidential administration,[14] the extreme nativist rhetoric that flourished under Trump increased immigrants' fears, altered their everyday behaviors, and affected their plans for their future.

After Trump was elected to his first presidency, he implemented swift changes to the immigration system that amplified migrants' anxieties. Across ethnoracial lines, immigrants worried more and more about the possibility of deportation when conducting everyday activities. Many immigrants told me that they opted to stay at home instead of spending time in public spaces including parks and shops, and this was especially true for Indigenous immigrants. Many described this state as being *encerrados* (locked inside their homes).[15] Renata concluded, "We don't go out. We are *encerrados*. I am afraid to go out." Renata feared the possibility of being deported, she shared nervously.

"Lots of fear," Luz, an Indigenous Maya Guatemalan woman confided. "They started saying that if someone knocks [at the door] in your house, don't open. In the news they say that when they knock at your house, they [immigration enforcement officers] come to your house to search. They told us that if they knock [at the door] in your house, do not open. If you open the door of your house, it is because you are turning yourself in." Luz took some deep breaths. "How scary," she whispered. Luz went on: "For about one month we didn't go to [the larger grocery store in town]; we were afraid to leave."

Renata's and Luz's fears reflected the tenor of campaigns aired on the Spanish-language news channel, Univision, as well as the advice of pro-immigrant advocacy groups regarding how immigrants could protect themselves from ICE raids and apprehensions during the first Trump presidency. However, these materials often generated even greater fear and further encouraged immigrants to stay indoors and be suspicious of anyone knocking at the door, thus shattering their perceptions of *tranquilidad* previously associated with their communities. A repeated interaction during my fieldwork, for example, involved me casually asking immigrants what they were doing on the weekend or on their days off. I thought this would be a good conversation starter but quickly realized that the question was annoying. Immigrants' responses were often similar, something like *"¿Que vamos a hacer? No podemos salir"* (What are we going to do? We can't go outside). Immigrants reported feeling afraid of spending time outside their homes.[16]

The threat of deportation felt so real following Trump's election that some undocumented immigrants with US-born children made arrangements for its eventuality. Amelia, a mestizo Mexican woman, told me

The thing we are worried about now, because of the president that is now, and what I tell my husband is that we have our plans now. We want to go fix their [the children's] papers so they can have their passport from here [the United States] and also so they can have their papers so they can be citizens of Mexico. That is what I tell my husband: 'Just in case, I want to have every-thing in order.' That is what I tell him: 'If they deport us or if they want to do something to us, if we have to go.' Because we don't know with this gentle-man; this president has said a lot of bad things, a lot of ugly things.

In the event of her or her husband's deportation, Amelia planned to fol-low the advice publicized in Spanish-language news media, including Univision Noticias and local bilingual newspapers. Following the lead of immigrant rights organizations, these news sources advised immi-grant parents to make a family preparedness plan, which involved deciding whether their children would remain in the United States or accompany their deported parents out of the country. Parents were advised to prepare proper documentation for each of these paths. Days after Trump signed various anti-immigration executive orders in 2017, for example, Univision Noticias advised undocumented parents that "one of the most important steps is, without doubt, to have custody documents prepared so that if needed, a person can take care of your children."[17] While such advice offered a strategy for mitigating the impacts of enhanced immigration enforcement on immigrant families, it also amplified immigrants' fears.

Ximena and Valentina, two mestizo Mexican sisters who had De-ferred Action for Childhood Arrival when we met, shared their worries about their parents, who remained undocumented. Ximena told me about "their [Ximena's parents] situation and the fear that they're liv-ing in right now, which I often forget because it seems like everything's fine. My sister can drive. I can too, but my dad, he could be pulled over at any moment, and anything could happen, so it's scary." Valentina had similar worries. Trying to catch her breath and with tears rushing down her cheeks, she said,

Now, with everything that's happening, my parents are making plans if anything happens. We recently got a house. My parents are like, 'If any-thing, just sell everything, and try to get as much as you can out of it.'

Sometimes I think they're just kidding, but it's not, and it's just sad because they put it in a way that they think they're gonna go first.

The period of heightened deportation fears that followed Trump's initial wave of 2017 executive orders also generated rumors among immigrants about potential apprehensions in the workplace as well. Rita, a mestizo Salvadoran woman, explained:

> Well, now because of the raids and all that, it is not just people that don't have papers but everyone around them. They can end up searching for a group, and if you are there they are going to grab you and take you. So that is the biggest fear we have now. I mean, before we didn't have it, but now I know they have started. [That is] what gives us a lot of fear.

These rumors that Rita described in her community were based in national-level operations. In February 2017, ICE announced a nationwide raid that led to the apprehension of 680 immigrants in several major cities, including Los Angeles, Atlanta, Chicago, New York City, and San Antonio. This marked the beginning of targeted workplace immigration raids across the country, including apprehensions in rural and urban Kansas, that took place in the subsequent years of the first Trump presidency.[18] The fear and anxiety of the possibility of deportation, enhanced by Trump's first election and presidency, created significant mental and physical harm for undocumented immigrants and mixed-status families, mestizo and Indigenous alike. The fears that immigrants disclosed under the first Trump administration, however, was long-lasting, since the "threat" of possibly being deported or losing a loved one to deportation was ongoing. The rumors of deportation and the ongoing hostile political context (which I outline below) made immigrants live in a constant state of fear.

When we are scared our bodies respond; most have heard of this as the "fight-or-flight" response. When we perceive a threat, our brains turn on an alarm and send a message to the endocrine system, which then connects to other parts of our body—the heart, muscles, and sweat glands—and also affects our breathing. This is known as "sympathetic arousal."[19] When we are scared, our brains automatically hyperfocus on the threat, making concentration on other things difficult. Usually after the threat passes our bodies return to their baseline. However, when we are scared over a long period of time or when fear comes too frequently, our bodies can also experience *chronic fear*.[20] This means that the alarm never gets turned off. Living with chronic fear can yield physical concerns (impacting the immune system, the endocrine system, the autonomic nervous system, sleep, and eating) as well as emotional effects. The description of immigrants' *miedo* (fear) and *preocupaciones* (worries) they felt during the presidential campaigns and consequently after the elections throughout my fieldwork, reflect an ongoing state of fear—reproducing *chronic fear* in the lives of immigrants, across ethnoracial lines.[21] This fear of possible deportation anytime and anywhere, however, was generated through political rhetoric and the expansion of criminalizing anti-immigrant policies of Trump's first administration.

CREATING HOSTILITY: TRUMP'S FIRST PRESIDENCY

Immigration policies targeting undocumented immigrants and promoting the racialization of illegality—linking illegality to Mexicans and Hispanics in particular—have a long history in the United States, as summarized in the Introduction. Politicians have especially utilized immigration policies to divert voters' attention from social ailments and Trump's 2016 campaign followed this trend. However, Trump's rhetoric was particularly distinctive—perhaps because he employed overtly racist speech following a period of modern history that has since been described as "color-blind."[22] After the 1960s civil rights movement ended Jim Crow–era segregationist policies, race and racism in the United States was largely veiled in society, cloaked by neoliberal tropes that blamed individuals for situations created by colonial legacies and systemic racial violence. This phenomenon was most apparent under the two-term Obama administration, when conversations surrounding racial systemic inequities all but disappeared from political platforms.[23] In 2016, however, Trump and his team openly blamed minority groups, especially immigrants, for the country's social ailments, speaking without any indirect "racially coded language."[24] It is not surprising, then, that his presidency was endorsed by leaders of white supremacist groups.[25]

By making immigration central to his 2016 campaign, Trump cemented the links between undocumented status and criminality—tying criminal labels to Mexican and Central American stereotypes. On social media, at campaign rallies, and in presidential speeches, Trump continuously referred to Mexican and Central American immigrants as criminals, as threats to American safety, as risks to American wages, and as threats to overall national interests.[26] In a campaign speech, Trump referred to Mexican migrants as drug dealers and rapists: "They're sending people that have lots of problems, and they're bringing those problems with us [sic]. They're bringing drugs. They're bringing crime. They're rapists. And some, I assume, are good people."[27] After becoming president, Trump referred to Central American immigrants as "animals" during a cabinet meeting. "You wouldn't believe how bad these people are," he said. "These aren't people, these are animals, and we're taking them out of the country at a level and at a rate that's never happened before."[28] This type of political rhetoric generates fear of immigrants among US residents, depicting immigrants as a dangerous threat to the United States and its communities. Additionally, rhetoric of this kind had direct consequences for immigrants and other targeted groups, bringing about the *preocupaciones* and *miedos* shared by immigrants above along with increased hate crimes documented nationwide, including in Kansas.[29]

One week after Trump took office, fast changes were introduced to US immigration policy via presidential executive orders and thereafter

via hundreds of informal rule changes across the immigration bureaucracy. This included the reactivation and enhancement of 287(g)
programs, such as Secure Communities (Executive Orders 13767 and
13768), which encouraged local policing agencies to surveil, apprehend,
and detain *suspected* undocumented immigrants regardless of immigrants' activities or past criminal history. Other executive orders expanded the expedited removal of immigrants apprehended inside the
country—a practice previously limited to border apprehensions. In the
months following implementation of the executive orders, immigrant
apprehensions inside the country rose by 30 percent compared to 2016
levels.[30] And not surprisingly, only a day after the election results were
announced, the stocks of private companies such as CoreCivic and Geo
Group that run and own immigrant detention facilities as well as private prisons and jails rose substantially.[31]

Besides the use of executive orders, the Trump administration created and enforced a vast web of immigration transformations beyond
those that were formalized, archived in the Federal Register and view-
able by the public. This involved hundreds of policy changes made via
memos, bulletins, and internal communications—removing the details of immigration enforcement practices from the public eye. Guttentag and fellow researchers documented 1,064 immigration-related
actions during the first Trump administration, spanning both formal
and informal policy changes.[32] These encompassed the following nine
areas: (1) enforcement strategies, both at the border and inside the
country, including the separation of children from their parents and
caregivers; (2) restructuring the asylum and refugee systems; (3) reducing legal avenues for migration, including the visa system; (4) curtailing protections associated with liminal statuses, such as Deferred
Action for Childhood Arrival and Temporary Protected Status; (5) reducing protections for vulnerable groups, such as unaccompanied minors and victims of violence; (6) reorganizing immigration courts to
limit immigrants' rights during hearings and to exclude due process;

(7) restricting access to subsidized programs, including housing and health care, for immigrants and their family members, including citizen family members; (8) curtailing immigrant workers' rights; and (9) denaturalization initiatives. What caused the most harm and generated the most fear among immigrants already living in the heartland was the ongoing threat of deportation, amplified by the extension of 287(g) programs and other efforts to enhance immigration enforcement inside the country.

Another impact that came in the middle of Trump's first administration was the restriction of asylum options particularly for immigrants fleeing their countries due to violence such as Erica, whose story we read in Chapter 1. Although the asylum process was already extremely limiting and rarely ever provided relief to those seeking asylum, in 2018 Jeff Sessions under the first Trump administration announced a rule change to the asylum process that practically banned victims of violence from being considered for asylum.[33] This policy change disproportionately affected women fleeing gender violence from their countries of origin particularly when gender violence and *feminicidios* were continuing to increase in Mexico and Central American regions with little to no redress from governing bureaucracies (as observed in Chapter 1). This change led to potential asylum seekers being deported through expedited removal processes without being able to share their asylum claims with asylum officers or be considered for asylum relief by an immigration judge.[34] The fast-paced policy changes trickled down to the communities where everyday immigrants lived, thus generating a hostile environment of reception.

The anti-immigrant political maneuvering of Trump's first presidency's had direct ties to the heartland, with Kris Kobach as one of Trump's major immigration policy advisers. At the time Kobach was serving the Kansas secretary of state, an office he held between 2011 and 2019. Kobach drafted some of the harshest anti-immigrant policies across the country,[35] such as the infamous SB1070 in Arizona, a state law that allowed and encouraged local police agents to detain anyone they deemed undocumented, encouraging racial profiling and having direct negative impacts on immigrants' well-being and entire Latino communities.[36] Kobach served as a guide to author similar laws in multiple states across the country in the early 2010s. In 2018 he ran for Kansas governor, bringing Trump's anti-immigrant promises to the state. However, Kobach lost. Yet, it was much of his initial works—during his time as Kansas secretary of state and as an adviser to other states and nativist organizations[37]—that advised Trump's crusade against immigrants during his first presidency.

Trump's immigration policy changes were far-reaching and trickled down to communities across the country, including in the heartland. Kansas has had a history of mixed compliance with immigration enforcement, perhaps in part because the state relies heavily on immigrant workers for some of its largest industries, such as meatpacking and agriculture. In 2018, immigrants comprised over 9 percent of the Kansas labor force.[38] However, with the 2017 signing of Executive Order 13768 and the reinstitution of Secure Communities programs as a mandatory federal policy, increases in apprehensions were seen all over the country, including in Kansas. Between 2017 and 2019, 2,952 immigrants were held on immigrant detainers, which means that immigrants were held in local jails without bail awaiting immigration enforcement to move them to an immigration detention facility.[39] This was a sharp increase compared to years prior (Figure 2).

Over 55 percent of immigrants placed on these detainers had no criminal convictions during the 2017-2019 period.[40] There was also a sharp increase in the number of ICE apprehensions in Kansas during this period: ICE arrested 449 immigrants in 2016 and 700 immigrants in 2017 in the state.[41] Additionally, following immigrants' fears, ICE apprehensions were enforced in the vicinity of places that were previously considered safe zones for undocumented immigrants and their loved ones, including schools, courts, and medical facilities. Reports

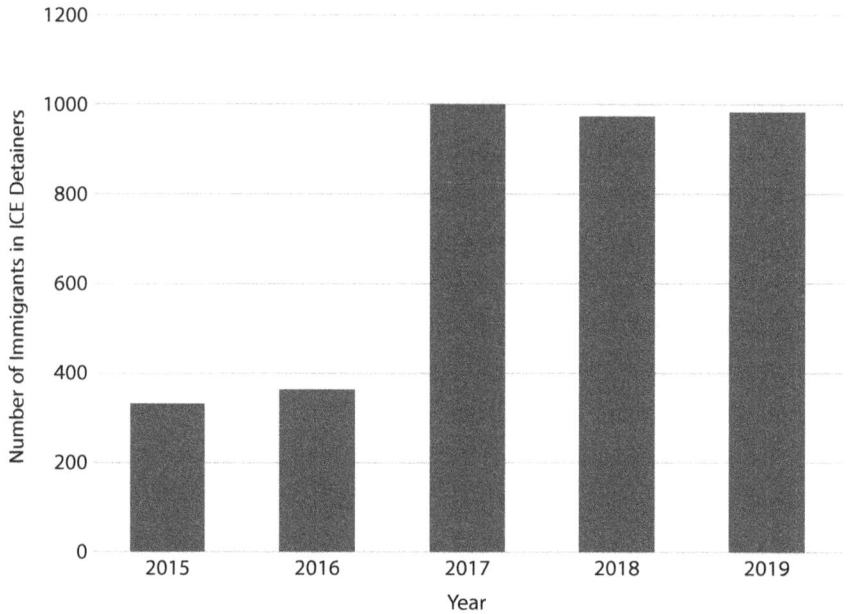

Figure 2. Immigrants held on ICE detainers in Kansas from 2015 to 2019. SOURCE: Data comes from the Transactional Records Access Clearinghouse (2023).

documenting immigrants' experiences in Kansas demonstrate that immigrants were being apprehended shortly after dropping off their children at school.[42] And rumors about ICE apprehending immigrants en route to hospitals and outside of medical settings were common.[43] These policies, in addition to media coverage of detentions and deportations in the national and local news, increased immigrants' fear of detention and deportation across ethnoracial lines, positioning Kansas as a hostile context to live.

The hostile environment generated under Trump's first presidency and the fears it caused among immigrants created what some scholars have termed the "chilling effects" of immigration policies,[44] that is, the secondary and tertiary consequences of immigration policies and their enforcement, which impact not only immigrants but also nonimmigrant family members and entire communities. In short, the fear of enhanced immigration policing trickled down to not only immigrants but also Hispanic/Latino communities more broadly not only in Kansas but also across the nation. In schools, for example, educators observed the educational impacts among students who feared their parents' deportation, with some students experiencing disengagement, missing classes, and receiving lower grades.[45] In some classrooms students became divided, with some nonimmigrant students perpetuating anti-immigrant rhetoric against their immigrant classmates, similar to what parents observed in this study. However, Rodriguez Vega's work with children in the K–12 education system demonstrates that while these chilling effects have direct consequences on children's well-being and perceptions of self, it is also these children who can bring immigrant communities hope by dreaming of better futures where their families can be safe and free.[46]

The chilling effects extended beyond immigrant students, affecting their classmates and entire schools. Examining the impacts of increased immigration enforcement on schools, Ee and Gándara found that Title I schools were highly impacted by increases of immigration enforcement.[47] The impacts included behavioral and emotional problems among the overall student body, increased absenteeism, academic performance, classroom climate, concerns for peers, decreased parent involvement, and increased bullying. While immigrant students, particularly those who are English-language learners, tend to be in Title I schools due to low income in their families, these impacts affected all students in the school, not only the immigrant students. Similar studies have found that the activation of Secure Communities programs impacts Hispanic student achievement overall and not only among immigrant students. And increases in deportations in a community are also associated with low achievement among Hispanic and Black students more broadly.[48] Because of the racialization of illegality, Latinos broadly—and not only immigrants—are impacted by the chilling effects of the hostile context. Latino citizens also experienced harassment and discrimination and were often targeted by immigration enforcement and policing agencies as "illegal" even if they were born in the United States.[49]

Other chilling effects of the hostile anti-immigrant climate that broadly impacted the communities where immigrants lived include health care access and the labor market. In Latino communities where immigration enforcement was increased, both immigrants and non-immigrants alike were less likely to access routine health care,[50] and there were significant decreases in public benefit use—including Medicaid and the Children's Health Insurance Program.[51] Likewise, citizen children in mixed-status families lost insurance coverage after the 2016 presidential election.[52] And not surprisingly, immigrant-led labor markets were also largely impacted. For instance, increases in 287(g) programs impacted the labor supply of farms, given that immigrants make up a large share of farmworkers.[53] Likewise, because immigrant women tend to support the labor of nonimmigrant highly educated women, working as nannies, caregivers, and housekeepers, their labor experiences were impacted. Increased exposure to 287(g) programs such as Secure Communities also led to reducing the labor supply of college-educated US-born mothers, particularly those with young children.[54] Thus, the chilling effects of the hostile climate under Trump's first presidency had consequences for entire communities, with particular impacts on Kansas given its unique geography, demographics, and history.

CONCLUSIONS

Indigenous and mestizo immigrants alike initially described Kansas as *un lugar tranquilo*. However, these perceptions of *tranquilidad* were heavily changed by the increasingly hostile political environment fueled by Trump's first administration. Considering the longer history of Latinos in Kansas, we see the roots of this hostility in decades of nativist politics, which strongly influenced the experiences of immigrants in local communities. The first Latino immigrants in Kansas were largely Mexican. During the early 1900s at the time of the Mexican Revolution and coinciding with anti-immigrant policies that blocked Asian migration to the United States,[55] Mexicans were called to fill cheap labor needs of the railroad industry—which was a major industry in Kansas.[56] Thus, most of the early Mexican immigrants arrived in Kansas as workers on the Santa Fe railroad. The Great Depression slowed most new immigration trends to Kansas during the 1930s. However, the growth of the meatpacking industry post–World War II in the state again called for new immigrants to fill employers' needs for workers. Early Mexican immigrants experienced the segregation and racism of Jim Crow, as they were denied housing and experienced open discrimination in public spaces, in schools, and at work.

By 1980, millions of immigrant farmworkers nationwide gained amnesty through the Immigration Reform and Control Act of 1986. While this policy aimed to decrease undocumented migration and maintain the existing farmworker population, the indirect effects led to an increase of Latin American immigrants to the United States broadly,[57] especially Kansas.[58] Since then, Latin American immigrants (mainly of Mexican origin) as well as other immigrant groups seeking work in the meatpacking industry have settled across the state and slowly reached many industries and areas of the state beyond meatpacking. These dynamics had made the steady population growth among Latin American immigrants relatively recent.

Thus, the Latino immigrant population in Kansas has both increased and diversified, a population change that some of the longer-term residents of Kansas observed. Mexicans have continued to be the largest group multigenerationally, with Central Americans, Puerto Ricans, and South Americans arriving most recently, including many of Indigenous origins. With the growth and diversification of the Latino immigrant population, changes in the heartland landscapes of towns and cities also developed. Immigrant enclaves, which began due to housing segregation, reclaimed their spaces and made communities their own, with growing businesses, *tiendas* (shops), restaurants, and cultural events such as the traditional Mexican fiesta celebrated in September in various cities across Kansas.

Although most immigrants thought that Kansas would be *un lugar tranquilo*, a tranquil place to live, immigrants across ethnoracial lines increasingly encountered a hostile environment in the heartland, which was amplified by Trump's first presidency. Certainly, it was not surprising that the majority of Kansans voted for Trump. Since 1920 (under the Harding administration) Kansas votes only went to a Democratic presidential candidate in three occasions: for Franklin Roosevelt in 1932 and his reelection in 1936 and for Lyndon Johnson in 1964.[59] The anti-immigrant sentiments that were used in Trump's campaigns and then established through various policies, however, veiled a much broader agenda of an authoritarian populist movement.[60] Scholars have called attention to Trump's win and first administration as a response to the unconsidered consequences that fell on everyday US residents resulting from neoliberal policies previously cemented during the 1980s and 1990s that pushed for a free market economy and limited government intervention in the United States. Yet the consequences of this neoliberal turn impacted people's well-being and included the housing crisis of 2008 that led to people losing their homes and their farms and going into debt along with a myriad of psychological and physical health concerns.

Furthermore, the anti-immigrant rhetoric and clear nativist ideologies present during Trump's first campaign and then in his time as president were rooted in settler colonial strategies, where the actual Indigenous groups to US territory were erased from public imaginary and the settler-colonizers became reimagined as the true native—in this case the "true Americans." Thus, Trump's immigration policies are rooted in colonial powers with the goal to "protect" Americans and "secure" the nation, which has further cemented divisions of race through an imagined "us" and an imagined "other"—tied to perceptions of illegality and Latinidad. Indigenous and mestizo immigrants both described living in a "hostile political environment" and being in constant fear of deportation of themselves or their loved ones, ultimately experiencing a state of chronic fear in the heartland.

The chronic fear that immigrants encountered and the chilling effects of the immigration policies are produced by the broader sociopolitical context that intentionally targets and criminalizes Latino immigrants, thus perpetuating a form of state violence. State violence, according to Torres, refers to the state utilizing violence to the "structure of governance, citizenship, and the quality of life of individuals and communities."[61] The production and maintenance of fear allows for control over the population and is grounded in colonial powers— instilling the fear of the "other" among colonizers while simultaneously creating a state of violence and terror that generates fear among the "colonized" population. Aldama further explains that "the propagation and internalization of fear in the social body attempts to keep people docile, numb, silent, and afraid to challenge the status quo."[62] Immigration policies and surrounding rhetoric reproduce such a dynamic. On one hand, the political rhetoric, particularly under the first Trump administration, promoted fear among US residents of potential "illegal'" immigrants, tying ideas of criminality and the potential threat of harm to their communities to an imagined "illegal" other. On the other hand, the hypersurveillance and increased enforcement practices and the criminalizing policies generated a constant state of fear among immigrants, generating chronic fear and a state of *encerrados* (locked inside). Yet these dynamics are further complicated under gendered and racialized mechanisms of "othering" the immigrant,[63] thus producing racialized illegality and uneven consequences that play out differently for Indigenous and mestizo immigrants and in particular locations, as we will see in the chapters to come. The immigrants who fit into stereotypes of "illegality" bear the harsher consequences of this state violence. Through immigrants' accounts of their *miedos* (fears) and *preocupaciones* (worries) associated with the first Trump presidency, it is clear that a hostile context developed in the heartland during the time of this study. In Chapter 3, I examine what life was like *sin papeles* (without papers) for Indigenous and mestizo immigrants as they made Kansas their home and as they lived through fast-changing and turbulent political times.

3

"AGUANTANDO SIN PAPELES"

Life without Papers

THE AROMA OF BEANS cooking on the stovetop made the small bare room feel cozy and warm. Laura, a young Indigenous Tlapaneco Mexican woman, was multitasking, tending the beans and handing small pieces of warmed tortillas to her three-year-old daughter. Exhausted, Laura recounted her day: rushing between work, childcare, and her daughter's medical appointments. "You know," she said, "everything is harder *sin papeles* [without papers]."

In a similar scenario, Jenny, a mestiza Mexican woman, stood in front of her stovetop. Her hands flipped quesadillas in a *comal* while red rice cooked in a pot as she shared her life story. She felt, similarly to Laura, that *"aguanta uno muchas cosas* [you endure many things]." She told me about life *sin papeles* (without papers), with its ever-present risk of deportation.

In Kansas, life *sin papeles* entailed navigating multiple spheres of institutional exclusion and legal violence. In this chapter, I delve into Indigenous and mestizo immigrants' accounts of going about daily life *sin papeles*, either undocumented themselves or with an undocumented loved one. While some of their immigrant experiences spanned across ethnoracial lines, their access to resources and strategies for addressing these challenges varied.

At the outset, it is worth considering what is "legal violence." Menjívar and Abrego introduced legal violence to uncover how immigration policies directly and indirectly (re)produce harm in the lives of immigrants, their loved ones, and their communities.[1] Legal violence thus results from laws and their enforcement, which generate practices that "harm individuals physically, economically, psychologically, or emotionally" in both the short term and the long term.[2] This is most visible in policies that intentionally exclude immigrants from certain rights and protections, such as the criminalization of work, the exclusion from safe and quality housing, and the denial of driver's licenses. While policies determine immigrants' legal participation in society, institutions in the communities where immigrants live can also mediate these policies and create avenues for engagement and decision-making to be shared with immigrants and their loved ones.[3]

By exploring immigrants' experiences with three social institutions—work, housing, and driving—I examine the ways in which the boundaries of illegality are established in the heartland, how legal violence is reproduced, and the ways in which immigrants cope with such conditions through the strategy of *aguantar*, that is, to endure and to survive. Importantly, the experiences of Indigenous and mestizo immigrants reflect the ways in which these mechanisms of illegality and legal violence are intertwined with colonial legacies in multiple ways, whether through exploitation at work, exclusionary housing practices, or the policing of driving and, by default, limiting their mobility and generating short- and long-term harm. Examining these areas of daily life reveals how undocumented Indigenous and mestizo immigrants employ different social strategies to navigate the challenges that legal violence imposes. Immigrants' social ties were separated along ethnoracial divides, providing different resources for Indigenous and mestizo immigrants to handle setbacks and harm. Additionally, women experienced added layers of discrimination tied to gendered social structures rooted in coloniality that produced gendered violence and harm, which generated particularly harmful outcomes for Indigenous women.

WORK

With passage of the Immigration Reform and Control Act of 1986, employers who knowingly hire undocumented workers can be penalized with fines and potential prison time.[4] As a result, employers commonly surveil immigrants' work eligibility. Employers can fire undocumented workers who lack a work permit, and, in order to avoid penalties, will sometimes turn them over to the immigration authorities.[5] Further intensifying such surveillance, in 1996 the Immigration and Naturalization Service, whose functions are now largely handled by the Department of Homeland Security, established various programs that allowed employers to check immigrants' work eligibility. One of these programs is E-Verify, which utilizes an online software program that enables employers to check workers' employment eligibility using Department of Homeland Security and Department of Motor Vehicles data.[6] During the time of this study, it was up to individual states whether to participate in E-Verify and whether penalties were given for employers that did not use this program. By 2018, although not mandatory in the state, over nine thousand Kansas employers were using E-Verify.[7] How, then, could undocumented immigrants find work when their labor was both criminalized and so heavily surveilled?

Rita, a twenty-two-year-old mestiza Salvadoran woman, had lived undocumented along her entire family in the United States since she was thirteen. She recalled her experience of finding her first job as a teen:

Well, my parents didn't want us to work. They said, "You should study; don't worry about work." But we didn't want to ask them for money, and I didn't feel good asking, so my mom worked in [a restaurant] and my brother started there when he was a junior [in high school]. And the manager also knew that I wanted to work; he had seen me. I went to eat there, and he asked [her mom], "Why don't you let her work here?" And my mom let me. She said, "He wants you to work here." So, then I started working there. So, you buy papers basically. That is how we did it. He [work manager] knows someone, and that person finds them [the documents] . . . \$300 and that is all. I only used them [documents] for work. Actually, my parents never . . . [Rita starts fidgeting with her hands and breathing heavily] You can't have those papers at hand or anything because they [parents] are afraid that if they [immigration enforcement or policing authorities] find them, they could get in trouble.

Vicente, a mestizo Mexican man, shared a similar story regarding his first job:

Because of my status, because I didn't have papers, I didn't have anything. So, he [a friend] took me with someone that he knew, and they made me some *papeles chuecos* [crooked papers]. And with that I took those to the company, because the company did not want to give me a paycheck even if I had worked hours, because I did not report my Social Security [number] and my Green Card. So, when he [the friend] took me there, he paid for me, but as soon as I got my first paycheck, I paid him [back]. That is where all my check went; I only had twenty dollars left. No more. Because I only worked about three days.

As Rita and Vicente demonstrate, undocumented immigrants relied on their social networks to navigate legal barriers and institutional exclusions within the workplace as early as finding work. The hypersurveillance of undocumented labor created an informal market for documents, transferring legal liability onto workers instead of their employers.[8] These strategies thus risked criminalizing undocumented immigrants even further. In 2020, the US Supreme Court ruled in *Kansas v. Garcia* that individual states could prosecute immigrants who use such work documents.[9] Furthermore, under the Kansas statute, this is considered fraud and can be charged as a felony, further penalizing immigrants and heightening their risk of incarceration, detention, *and* deportation. Without such documents, however, immigrants were unlikely to secure employment given the wide use of E-Verify in the state.

Indigenous undocumented immigrants went through a similar process to secure employment. As we stood on his front porch, Domingo, an Indigenous Maya Guatemalan man, told me he believed that Chicanos and Mexican Americans (largely mestizos) had monopolized the documents market—forcing Indigenous immigrants to pay a premium for the same service. Domingo further speculated that this explained why, in some instances, such documents did not pass employer screenings. In some cases, he clarified, a Social Security number (SSN) was sold to multiple people in the same region. Once the document was recognized through E-Verify databases, further attempts to use the document could cause employers to alert immigration enforcement or policing authorities, leaving immigrants without a job and at risk of apprehension. Like Domingo, Indigenous immigrants frequently discussed problems they encountered with the work documents they had acquired—much more regularly than did mestizos. Indigenous respondents reported paying between $1,000 and $1,500 for these documents, more than double the price reported by mestizo informants. Likewise, Juan Carlos, an Indigenous Maya Guatemalan man, explained to me during a car ride that newly arrived immigrants had to first find someone who had lived in the United States a long time; next, this person connected the newly arrived immigrant with another contact, who then, in turn, found a "Chicano" who sold the desired documents. To afford the documents, Indigenous immigrants borrowed money from their fellow Indigenous ties, which they then had to repay after finding work. This debt accumulated along with other debt acquired from their journeys to the United States. This added to immigrants' existing indebtedness, which typically took Indigenous immigrants longer to repay than the amounts borrowed by their mestizo counterparts such as Vicente and Rita.

Despite their considerable cost, these documents did not always pass the E-Verify screenings. Besides elevating deportation risk in the workplace, such "bad" papers greatly hampered immigrants' ability to secure a job, which caused additional stress, tension, and delayed debt repayment. Lorena, an Indigenous Maya Guatemalan woman, arrived in Kansas in 2018 with the support of her husband, Juan Carlos. As we spoke outside their home, Juan Carlos told me that he had spent over $1,000 on Lorena's work documents. But after only two weeks of work, Lorena was let go by her employer. The couple suspected that this was due to the acquired work documents not passing the screening. Some days after our conversation, Lorena asked me to accompany her on a visit to her former workplace to help her request her paycheck since she could not speak English. I picked up the couple and drove them to her job's main office, which was only minutes away from the trailer that Lorena, Juan Carlos, and their two children shared with Juan Carlos's extended family. Juan Carlos stayed in the car, and Lorena and I entered the office building through two glass doors. Behind a tall counter there were two Anglo white women managing paperwork and phones. We walked up to the counter. Lorena stood nervously behind me. I said hello, and one of the women asked what we were there for. I explained that we were there to collect a paycheck. The woman was unamused by my presence and only glanced quickly at Lorena. The woman asked Lorena for her name and then pointed us to a row of chairs a few feet away from the counter. Lorena fidgeted with her hands as we waited. A few minutes later, the woman called us to the counter. She handed Lorena her paycheck and said she'd need to provide additional proof of identity if she wanted to return to work the following week, signaling the use of E-Verify in this workplace. As we walked to the car, Lorena and I knew she would not be returning to that job anytime soon.

For women it was additionally tough to find work even when using their immigrant ties, with these networks segregated by both ethnoracial background and gender.[10] Many immigrant labor niches too, such as construction and housekeeping, are explicitly gendered. Victoria, an Indigenous Tlapaneco Mexican woman, highlights this point. Victoria and her brother were the first in their immediate family to migrate to the United States. They traveled with their female cousin, Mara. The trio first arrived in Missouri, staying first at Mara's ex-boyfriend's house. "We arrived with one of my brothers; he came with us. And for him they [the ex-boyfriend and his contacts in Missouri] found him work right away," Victoria recalled. "But for us [the women] it was very difficult. There was never any work there for us in Missouri. Then they brought us [to Kansas] because there was no work there." With the help of Mara's ex-boyfriend's contacts, both women moved to Kansas, where they eventually found work—at a restaurant and a hotel—with the help of a coethnic woman they met through a friend of a friend.

Mestizo immigrant women also relied on other women to find work. Amelia, a mestiza Mexican woman, migrated to the United States to join her husband, also mestizo Mexican and a construction worker. She only found work after meeting a woman at a local grocery store, who mentioned an opportunity at a fast-food restaurant. "I told her, 'But I don't have papers. I am illegal in this country. I can't [work],'" Amelia recalled. The lady helped her secure documents and a job shortly afterward. Across ethnoracial lines, women reported finding work through ties to other women. However, ethnoracial divides persisted in these networks; Indigenous women relied on other Indigenous women, and mestizo women relied on other mestizas.

Stolen Wages and Workplace Violence

Once employed, both Indigenous and mestizo immigrants told me that their wages rarely reflected the amount or value of their labor.

Denials of renumeration and stolen wages were a common form of legal violence that undocumented immigrants faced in the workplace. Esperanza, an Indigenous Maya Guatemalan woman who came to the United States as a minor seeking asylum, shared her experience at a fast-food restaurant.

> I try hard. Just working there and I cook everything, even burned my hand. Trying hard, and they pay me very little. And it hurts me because I am killing myself [at work]. I don't know what it is. I don't understand. Well, they only gave me $400 in one month. I went to train there, and then I started working there and they only gave me $400, but I am working so hard.

Esperanza shared that she worked around thirty hours per week, sometimes more. This means that she was paid approximately $3.33 per hour, well below the Kansas minimum wage of $7.25 per hour (at the time) and her supposed wage of $8.50.[11]

Wage theft can take several forms and afflicted undocumented workers of all ethnoracial backgrounds. Workers sometimes did not receive any pay after a day's labor. Other times their pay was withheld for an unreasonable period of time or—as Esperanza illustrated— received only partial payment. For those who lived in employer-owned housing, their wages could be excessively withheld for inflated housing or utility costs.[12]

Gerardo, a mestizo Mexican construction worker, experienced multiple forms of wage theft ranging from subtle ways of losing his paycheck to blatant unpaid labor. His wife, Elena, also mestiza Mexican, said, "Look, now, precisely what we have, since this house is the company's. He works like one would say, under the water, because he doesn't have a *seguro* (SSN). So, the houses that you rent are of $950 a month, and they discount that from his paycheck of the week. So, they take out $250 [per week]." The amount that was discounted on Gerardo's paycheck was more than half of his wages, which affected the family's ability to pay for other everyday needs since Elena worked odd and irregular jobs. The rental fee was the amount that was average for the city where they lived during 2016. Rental prices have since then increased in the heartland following trends in increased housing costs nationwide.

In addition, there were several occasions when after completing a multiday job, Gerardo would either be paid below what was initially agreed or receive no wages at all. "Here it has also happened that I have worked with a lot of people," Gerardo said. "You work some weeks; they pay you what they want, and then they disappear." Gerardo went on. "Yes, I have been discriminated a bit because of the pay; they pay little. Or one time they took us, like I told my wife, they took us to [a town in Kansas] to work for a few weeks, and they did not pay us." Like Gerardo, immigrants across ethnoracial lines experienced multiple forms of wage theft.

One cold winter morning Pastor José, a religious and community leader, called to ask if I wanted to learn more about immigrants' rights as workers and invited me to observe an important interaction that would happen that afternoon. About an hour later I met him outside his home, a modest house with a white-painted wooden porch. We hopped in his Suburban and drove to pick up Diego, an Indigenous Tlapaneco Mexican man, outside of a run-down apartment building. In the car, Pastor José introduced me as a student researcher and summarized my study. Diego quickly turned to me to share his story. Two years earlier, Diego had been unexpectedly deported to Mexico. Because of his deportation, he was unable to collect his wages, which were already past due, for three months working as a cook at a Japanese restaurant. His employer had agreed to send the money to Mexico, but Diego never received it. Now, Diego, again undocumented, had returned to Kansas and was ready to collect his wages, which he estimated should come to over $3,000.

When we arrived outside the Japanese restaurant, Diego called a friend who still worked there and asked to let us in from the back of the building. Diego's friend greeted him warmly with a hearty handshake followed by a hug. The owner, a Japanese immigrant woman, came out and was clearly surprised to see Diego but still greeted him. Pastor José said he was part of "the workers' coalition" that helped protect workers' rights and was there because Diego could not speak English very well. The Pastor then told the owner that Diego wanted his paycheck and that she had promised to send it to Mexico but Diego never received it. Speaking nervously, the owner explained that she'd sent the wages to the Department of Labor and that she no longer had the money. The pastor asked for the Department of Labor's telephone number so he could confirm her story, and the woman disappeared into a small alcove where a bulky computer sat on a desk surrounded by stacks of papers. Pastor José asked the owner for some documentation of the wage transfer, since, if that had been the case, it would surely be in her files. The owner replied that she had hired a new manager since Diego's departure and was unsure where the paperwork was. She said she would look for it on her home computer and told the pastor and Diego to come back in a few days. Even after this exchange and without giving him his overdue paycheck, the owner tried to convince Diego to come back to work for her, using Diego's friend as an interpreter. Diego, unsurprisingly, said no.

Back in the car, Diego shared that he had only been back in Kansas for one month. He had a wife and two daughters in Mexico who depended on the remittances he would send home for their household needs and school supplies. I learned some weeks later that the restaurant owner never provided any documentation to prove her story, and Diego never received his wages. This happened often, Pastor José confessed, with a defeated tone. Despite his best efforts at mediation, recovering immigrants' withheld wages was rare.

The laws that prohibit immigrants from receiving work permits, that criminalize their labor, and then further criminalize their use of purchased documents to work heighten the risk of workplace abuse, including wage theft. While unions could help mitigate such abuse, none of the immigrants I met during this study belonged to a union. Furthermore, given the outlined factors and detailed examples above, immigrants across ethnoracial lines endure such conditions due to the limits imposed through the law, their narrow social networks, and family responsibilities. The pastor's workers' coalition consisted of just him trying to mediate between immigrants in the community and abusive employers, with little success. This also reveals the role of place. Kansas was a right-to-work state, which weakened existing unions and made labor organizing difficult. Compared to regions with stronger labor rights, larger immigrant populations, or both, emerging immigrant destinations exhibit a combination of local labor policies, demographic changes, and anti-immigrant sentiments that hinder immigrant unionization and thus put at risk immigrants' worker rights.

Workplace Raids and Apprehensions

Immigrant raids are the most blatant form of legal violence in the workplace. Raids represent the direct enforcement of immigration laws, and their goal is to apprehend and deport undocumented immigrants regardless of immigrants' actual criminal backgrounds or how long they have lived in their communities. The immigrants I met in Kansas, both Indigenous and mestizos, all had stories about workplace raids, with some experiencing an immigration raid firsthand. Gerado, the mestizo construction worker, described how the fear of raids spread through immigrant networks and increased workers' sense of vulnerability—aware that deportation could happen anywhere and at any time:

> There was a person that, I did not work there but it was around 2000, that companies from Texas would come [to Kansas], and they were contracting painters. My friend and I went, but they were full; they didn't have space for us. They [the employer] told them [the workers] that they would not

get paid until the end of the month, and they worked for a month. . . . And when they were supposed to pick up their paychecks the güero [white American] sent la migra [immigration enforcement] to avoid paying them [the workers].

Although Gerardo did not experience the workplace raid himself, hearing about workplace raids from friends and coworkers sent a powerful message that deportation could happen anywhere and at any time. Deportability and the "illegal" label created a contradiction for undocumented workers. On the one hand, they were pushed to society's margins, with limited rights and protections from the state.[13] On the other hand, deportability worked only when immigrants were under the glare of state control.

Celestina, a mestiza Mexican woman, was packaging lettuce at a Kansas food-processing factory when she was apprehended and deported. This had happened almost eighteen years earlier, when her daughter, a US citizen, was only four months old. "They came at the time that we were switching shifts," she recalled. "They grabbed the morning group and the evening group. There were parents who worked there—la señora [the lady/mother] in the morning and el señor [the gentleman/father] in the evening—they were switching [shifts]. El señor would arrive with his girls, and she [the mother] would take them when she was leaving. There were even children." Celestina went on:

There were rumors, and sometimes the manager would call us: "Don't come to work; immigration [enforcement] is around." And they would call us and tell us, but that day just someone said . . . We were all working, almost about to leave, and they said, "Está la migra!" [Immigration enforcement is here!]. And we turned around, and we were surrounded. And some ran there, and nobody, no place to go. Only two escaped through the ceiling. There were a lot of immigration [officers]. And they said that there were [officers] up to the gas station. There was a gas station, and you would turn around, and from there on it was all factories, and they said that they blocked it [the street] so that people could not escape.

As a result of the raid, Celestina experienced severe trauma—not only from being apprehended by militarized immigration officers but also from the forced separation from her family, including her newborn baby girl who was still breastfeeding at the time. In tears, Celestina shared, "My daughter didn't drink formula." Catching her breath, she went on: "I just wanted to come back to see my baby girl. Because I was breastfeeding. I would ask my husband, how is my daughter?"

Immigration raids are a direct form of legal violence, adversely affecting immigrants' health and the health of their families. For example, Latina immigrant women in Iowa who experienced a workplace raid while pregnant had a 24 percent greater risk of low birth weight after the raid when compared with the same period one year earlier.[14] Immigration raids can also cause post-traumatic stress disorder.[15] Moreover, when people are apprehended en masse, they are processed quickly, with limited access to interpretation services, no access to legal representation, and no form of due process. Celestina estimated that about one hundred people—including immigrants who were fathers, mothers, sons, daughters, and friends—were deported alongside her, bringing chaos to their families and their communities.

In addition to workplace raids, immigration officials also conduct individual workplace apprehensions, searching for a specific person pursuant to a court order. Although officials are only supposed to apprehend the named individual in such operations, the reality is that they can apprehend anyone they suspect of being undocumented, especially in the wake of the various presidential executive orders from 2017 that enhanced immigrant apprehensions. One of these operations occurred during my fieldwork and involved two cousins: Jazmin and Blanca, both of Indigenous Maya Guatemalan origin.

On a wintery morning I received an urgent telephone call from Pastor José. Esperanza and Blanca's family had contacted him for help, he explained. Immigration and Customs Enforcement (ICE) officers had come to the hotel where they worked at the time and were searching for the young women. Blanca had managed to hide, but Jazmin, who had come to the United States fleeing poverty and violence and seeking asylum as a minor, had been taken. At the request of the family, who was afraid to go near the hotel in fear that ICE officers would apprehend them too, we rushed to the hotel to pick up Blanca. *"Me duele mi corazón, tengo dolor en mi corazón* [My heart hurts, I have pain in my heart]," she repeated as she climbed into the passenger's seat of the pastor's Suburban. Blanca went on: "My head hurts. *Tengo miedo, no sé porque, tengo miedo* [I am afraid, I don't know why, I am afraid]." As we drove away from the hotel, Blanca explained what happened. Sitting in the back seat, I documented her account in my field notes:

> Two tall men, ICE officers, came looking for the two cousins. The men had pictures of Jazmin and Blanca, which they showed to the hotel manager. A coworker told Blanca to stay seated where she was and to not come out. Blanca works in the kitchen of the hotel. . . . Her cousin, Jazmin, who was apprehended by ICE, works in the laundry room. A coworker had alerted ICE of Jazmin's location in the laundry room. Blanca did not see the ICE officers take Jazmin; she just knew they took her away because the manager told her. She was very afraid and did not know what to do or whether she could call anyone. Blanca said the manager told her she was fine, to not worry and to keep working. Blanca finished her entire shift that day.

Even though Blanca knew that immigration enforcement was searching for her and knew that her cousin had been apprehended, she nevertheless completed her shift—embodying the theme of *aguantar,* a mode of survival and the internalization of legal violence.

Gendered Workplace Violence

For immigrant women, experiences of workplace violence are shaped by the intersections of ethnoracial background, class, immigration status, and gender. Undocumented workers endure precarious working conditions, which can be heavily gendered and have gendered consequences. Although mestizo Latina immigrants frequently face gendered workplace violence,[16] it was the Indigenous women I met who shared their stories in detail. When Victoria, Indigenous, arrived in Kansas from Missouri, for example, she endured a very difficult experience:

> I worked also in that restaurant, it is nearby. . . . They sell Italian food, all pasta. I worked there for some time when I first moved in with her [youngest daughter's] father. I was pregnant, and I had a miscarriage there because the manager did not let me take the trash out more often [in smaller increments rather than a heavy load at the end of the day], just at the end. Yes, the cooks were gone and everyone at night [was gone], so *a fuerza* [by force]. I have to pick it up and take that trash to the container. [It was] very heavy, it felt like rocks, and I picked it up. I *aguante* [endured] four months. I had the miscarriage for picking up heavy [loads of trash]. I felt it down here [pointing to her abdomen and legs].

Victoria used the term "aguantar" to describe how she survived in her workplace. She had limited options to find other work and had a child who lived in Mexico and depended on her sending regular remittances for her everyday needs.

Other pregnant Indigenous immigrant women told me how their employers refused to make accommodations in the workplace, risking the women's health and that of their unborn children. Nina, an Indigenous Maya Guatemalan woman, shared an experience similar to Victoria's. A few months into her pregnancy while working at a meat processing plant, Nina asked to change her position on the line to avoid heavy lifting. "I felt like I couldn't do it anymore," Nina recalled. The manager "said 'no, you want to work, you have to do your job.'" Nina's male coworkers also refused to help her. "Sometimes there are some men there, and I told them, 'Hey, could you help me put this over there?' Some don't say anything, and others say 'No, why me? It's your job.'"

Both the Pregnancy Discrimination Act and the Americans with Disabilities Act require employers to provide pregnant employees with reasonable accommodations and without negative ramifications. As Victoria and Nina demonstrated, however, undocumented pregnant workers (Indigenous in this case) were denied accommodations and were subjected to strenuous physical labor, which directly impacted their health and well-being. This is a clear example of gendered workplace violence, a form of legal violence. The women's immigration status and geographical location compounded their vulnerability, as they lacked worker protections and would struggle to find alternative jobs in Kansas. Additionally, since Indigenous immigrant women were often their household's main breadwinner or cobreadwinner, losing work could have catastrophic repercussions for their families both in the heartland and abroad. Denouncing workplace violations also may heighten deportation risk via employer retribution. As a result, immigrant women *aguantan* (endure) injurious working conditions, produced through the sociolegal context.

Immigrant women also face sexual violence in the workplace, a problem encountered across lines of gender, race, sexuality, class, and labor sector.[17] As Villegas has argued, widespread gendered workplace violence reflects the state's role in the reproduction of violence, as laws prove inadequate to halt such violence or, in the case of undocumented immigrants, perversely enable it.[18] When their immigration status intersects with degrading working conditions and systematic gendered workplace violence, immigrant women are especially vulnerable. Moreover, immigrant women are unlikely to report gender and sexual harassment in the workplace due to resource limitations, language barriers, power imbalances, and the fear of deportation.[19]

HOUSING

Laura, an Indigenous Tlapaneco Mexican mom of a three-year-old girl, described the struggle of living in Kansas *sin papeles*. When her daughter was just four months old, Laura's partner was apprehended and deported to Mexico. Shortly afterward Laura's father—living in her home village in southern Mexico—passed away. Mired in grief, Laura became a single parent and the sole provider for her child. She moved in with her brothers and some coworkers—also Indigenous and undocumented—but soon hoped to find a home that was more baby-friendly. Laura said, "Well, it is not that easy sometimes. It was very hard because I really wanted to get an apartment, and I couldn't." Despite having a full-time job and always paying her part of the bills on time, Laura struggled to find a local landlord who would accept her as a tenant. Likewise, Isabel, a mestiza Mexican woman, shared some of the difficulties of securing quality housing. She and her husband also struggled to secure housing for their family. Isabel said, "Making our life here has been difficult. It took time; we started from the bottom. We got here and spent two months sleeping on the floor. The kids would sleep on blankets."

Although Kansas does not directly forbid undocumented immigrants from renting—via housing ordinances, for example—landlords nevertheless systematically exclude undocumented immigrants from accessing quality housing.[20] One obstacle concerned the request for an SSN during the application process. SSNs are used to conduct background checks and to reveal whether a prospective tenant has a criminal record.[21] The lack of an SSN, however, immediately prevented immigrants from renting even if they had no criminal record. Undocumented and semilegal immigrants are denied access to SSNs.[22] While many immigrants have access to Individual Taxpayer Identification Numbers to pay income taxes, these numbers cannot always be used for criminal background checks required in housing applications.

A lack of credit history was another obstacle for securing rental accommodation. Jaime, an Indigenous Mixteco Mexican man, told me about his family's situation. He'd lived in the United States with his partner Saturnina for over a decade. They were employed full-time and had repaid all the loans provided by their Indigenous friends and family on time. But because they lacked an SSN and had difficulties building federally authorized credit,[23] they were ineligible to rent. "They [the landlord] make a lot of questions. Our boss made a letter. He said that we rented from him, and they asked if we paid on time." Jaime went on to say, "They wanted like a credit."

Immigrants navigated such housing exclusions by sharing information about where they could rent. This information, however, was primarily passed along via coethnic ties. For instance, Isabel and her husband Ernesto eventually found a place of their own through Ernesto's friend, who is also mestizo Mexican. After Ernesto visited his friend's house, Isabel recalled, "Two weeks later the same friend told him about some apartments, and he rented one." Similarly, Rita's family, mestizo Salvadoran, learned about housing options via Rita's uncle. Laura, with her daughter, eventually found a place to rent with her brother's help and was soon joined by her friend, another Indigenous Tlapaneco woman.

Deportability also left undocumented immigrants vulnerable to landlord abuse. This practice was commonly experienced regardless of ethnoracial background. Vicente, for example, shared his experience of renting an apartment when he first entered the United States:

I didn't have anywhere to arrive or a social [SSN], well, to get an apartment or nothing. I was left without money because I spent the money in transportation [on the journey to Kansas]. So, I arrived there with this guy. A very stingy and bad man, because even if you paid him he wanted to cheat to make the most [money] that he could. So, sometimes . . . There were times that he would charge the gas [bill]. And during the cold times he would cut off the gas.

The landlord used the threat of deportation as a control mechanism to scare Vicente into accepting poor living conditions and to overcharge for bills he had already paid. "And the man was abusive," Vicente said. He recalled the words the landlord would frequently yell at him when he protested the overcharging of bills or shutting off the gas even after he had already paid the bill: "'If you don't shut up, I will call *la migra!*'"

Similarly, Saturnina and Jaime were threatened with deportation if they did not pay an exorbitant cleaning fee. They lived with their daughter in a one-bedroom apartment, shared with another Mixteco Indigenous couple who also had children. The two families had been saving money and were hoping to shortly move out and rent separate places because room was tight. After they gave notice, the landlord sent the families a "cleaning fee" bill for over $1,000 and demanded they pay it before vacating the building. Saturnina told me that the apartment was in a dire condition when they had moved in, as it was the only place—for all the reasons discussed above—that would accept their application. The landlord threatened to give the couple "bad credit" if they didn't pay and even threatened to call immigration enforcement. "We had to borrow the money," Jamie said. Despite a sizable loan from coethnics, the two families were unable to pay the demanded amount. Jaime and Saturnina didn't know that without an SSN or an established line of credit the landlord's first threat was toothless, and they truly feared that the landlord would call immigration enforcement. "We are afraid," Saturnina confided, "because this is where we live. What if they come looking for us?"

Regardless of ethnoracial divides, deportability was co-opted by individual actors and used to exploit immigrants. As the cases of Vicente (mestizo) and Jaime and Saturnina (Indigenous) demonstrate, statutes that create and reinforce hierarchies of power through exclusionary policies reproduce legal violence within individual interactions. Landlords exploit those who live *sin papeles* and are under the constant threat of deportation. Yet due to their undocumented status, lack of protections, and limited housing options in Kansas, immigrants must endure (*aguantar*) these forms of legal violence.

The net effect of these exclusionary policies and practices, however, is that immigrants were pushed to live in unkempt buildings and overcrowded homes. Other scholars have found similarly that undocumented families tend to live in poor-quality housing and in less-advantaged neighborhoods, enduring holes in walls, mold, pests, exposed wires, and other hazards.[24] In Kansas, however, I find that immigrants across ethnoracial lines endure such living conditions because they are systematically excluded from quality housing via discriminatory renting practices tied to their immigration status. These practices push Indigenous and mestizo immigrants alike toward housing with deplorable building conditions. The immigrants I met lived in such circumstances by *default* and not by *choice*. Additionally, they lived under the constant threat of deportation if their landlord wished it, creating the conditions for interpersonal violence and abuse within the broader framework of legal violence.

DRIVING

Vicente, the mestizo Mexican man who experienced landlord abuse, told me that he used to walk twenty-two blocks to work each morning for the first year when he first arrived in the heartland. "I didn't have a car, and I used to go walking," he said. Carolina, an Indigenous Tlapaneco woman, also walked to work when she first arrived in Kansas, careful to avoid the possibility of apprehension if she drove. "I'm telling you," she said, "when you first arrive, you don't know how to move around or nothing, I used to walk [to work]. But then I had to learn to drive, I was *forced* to drive because it took over an hour [walking] just to get there." She went on to say, "It is so far. So, I am forced to drive, that is why I drive."

In Kansas, as in most places in the American heartland, driving was an everyday necessity.[25] Public transportation in rural areas was nonexistent, and in urban areas it was less than accommodating, operating only in certain locations and at limited times. For their daily activities—going to work or school, shopping, and attending medical appointments—most Kansans drove or relied on others for rides.

Undocumented immigrants were ineligible for a Kansas driver's license. However, because driving without a license was a misdemeanor, the act of driving made their presence "more illegal," placing undocumented immigrants at greater risk of apprehension and deportation.[26] Forbidding access to a driver's license thus effectively criminalized undocumented immigrants' daily activities. Indigenous and mestizo immigrants navigated this reality in ways that often depended on their gender and ethnoracial connections. Additionally, the racialization of illegality meant that mestizos and Indigenous immigrants faced varying levels of risk while driving.

Most of the women I met during this study, across ethnoracial lines, shared similar experiences of navigating mobility restrictions. They either avoided driving altogether or drove only in close proximity to their own neighborhoods. "Yes, I have my little car," Carolina declared. "But because of the problem [not having a driver's license], I do not want to go too far. I am afraid." Carolina only drove within her town's limit, and kept strictly to a route that connected her work, her child's school, and the grocery store. Liliana, a mestiza Mexican woman, echoed Carolina's fears of driving without a license. Liliana found it difficult to meet daily responsibilities without driving and thus limited her mobility to her immediate neighborhood. Liliana drove "just here, [not] to go to [out of the city] or something like that. I am scared, but here, I can go just around here."

Celestina, the mestiza Mexican woman who had the previous deportation experience, had never driven. "I have always taken the bus," she told me. "I don't have a license, and I get too nervous around the police, and then driving, I said, no, no." Renata, an Indigenous Tlapaneco Mexican woman, spoke similarly. "I do not drive," she said. "I do not want to because I do not have a license." When her brothers offered to teach her to drive, Renata refused. "I tell them 'no, I am afraid.'"

Some of the women too afraid to drive, particularly Indigenous women, relied on paid services for rides. *Raiteros* (drivers) were most often mestizo women with either semilegal status or citizenship or, in some instances, daring Indigenous undocumented men. Both groups who charged exorbitant amounts for this service.[27] This was especially true in rural areas. For instance, Flor, an Indigenous Maya Guatemalan, relied on Tania, a mestiza Mexican woman, for rides to a prenatal clinic for her routine checkups. The clinic was less than a mile from Flor's home, but given the prospect of a walk along the highway in 100-degree heat with only a few weeks left to her due date, she thought it was safer to get a ride. For this brief ride, Tania charged Flor $40.[28] Similarly, Sofia, an Indigenous Tlapaneco Mexican woman who lived in an urban area, relied on a mestiza coworker for rides to and from work. Sofia had tried using the public bus, which stopped outside her apartment, but the bus route did not allow her to drop off her child at the babysitter and still make it to work on time. The *raitera*'s weekly bill plus childcare costs frequently left Sofia struggling to afford her basic needs, including rent, bills, and food.

Unlike most of the undocumented women I spoke with, Rita, a mestiza Salvadoran, risked driving. She undertook a two-hour round trip almost every day traveling between work and her university classes. She had to drive, Rita explained, to balance her work and college schedules, because she could not afford to live near campus while also paying for classes and also because she would struggle to find a job near campus with no social network to overcome the burden of being undocumented. Rita was "always afraid" when she drove, she confessed. "I'm always looking out for police. If I see the police, I slow down, or I go a different way." The police had only stopped Rita once, for leaving campus at night without her headlights on. "When they stopped me, I explained, 'Oh, I forgot my license at home,' I told them I was here because of school." Despite Rita lacking a driver's license, she only received a verbal warning. Rita is a fluent English speaker, and her appearance, she believed, did not fit the Mexican or Hispanic racial stereotypes associated with illegality. "If you see me, I have light skin tone, so they [Anglo-Americans] don't consider me *too Latina*."

Similarly, Patricio, a mestizo Salvadoran young man, explained how his physical appearance shaped perceptions of his immigration status:

> When people first meet me, *they don't know I'm Hispanic*. They always think, 'Oh, you're white, you're something mixed with something.' But they don't say 'Oh, you're straight Hispanic, or you're straight Mexican.' . . . So, the appearance I have doesn't give it away immediately; my skin color is not that dark or anything.

Patricio's words illuminate the racialization of illegality, whereby darker skin tone, a certain accent, and Spanish names often become synonymous with undocumented status. Reflecting on the legacies of colonialism, social constructs related to indigeneity and distance from whiteness are marked as undocumented, leaving immigrants who exhibit those constructs at greater risk of discrimination and apprehension.[29]

While most undocumented women restricted their mobility and some avoided driving completely, almost all the undocumented men I met, across ethnoracial lines, reported driving to work every day. For some, this created fear and stress in their daily lives. Whenever Jaime, Indigenous, left the house for work, he worried about the possibility of being apprehended. Similarly, Patricio, mestizo, felt anxious when "going somewhere, driving somewhere," imagining an interaction with the police even if his appearance did not give away his immigration status. Javier, a mestizo Mexican man, was more ambivalent. "I am not afraid," he told me. "I have always been like this, since 1999. I don't have a license, I don't have anything, but I am not affected." As we spoke further, however, Javier admitted that "I guess sometimes I feel afraid when I drive, because at any point . . ." he said, taking a deep breath, "that's what worries me."

For Indigenous immigrants and mestizos who were perceived as "Mexican" or "Hispanic," driving posed a larger risk. Given Kansas demographics, nonwhite Latinos were visible targets for discrimination, reflecting colonial legacies in the racialization of illegality. When I discussed driving with Nina and Claudio, an Indigenous Maya Guatemalan couple, Nina shared some of their fears. "Yes, there was one [police officer] that grabbed people. Even if you are not doing anything, *they see that you are Hispanic,* and they grab you, because when *they see that you are not American right away,* they [police officers] go behind you, almost all of the Guatemalans, because they are [Guatemalan]; even the Mexicans, they [the police] stop them." Nina and Claudio felt at risk while driving because they thought the police *knew* they were Hispanic, therefore implying that they were undocumented, simply by looking at them, leaving them at risk of apprehension and possible deportation. Nina and Claudio's feelings were not unfounded.

One cold day while talking over tamales and *atole,* I spoke with Victoria and her brother Felipe, both Indigenous Tlapaneco. The police frequently stopped Felipe while driving, he said, for no reason other than looking *"too Hispanic."* A year after our conversation, late at night my telephone rang. It was Victoria. Felipe was detained in police custody. She was desperately trying to make bail and find an attorney before he was processed through ICE—a common practice when local policing agencies work with ICE under 287(g) agreements. Although Victoria searched for an attorney and secured money for bail, the bail came too late. By then, Felipe was already placed on an ICE detainer, and the attorney fee was too expensive for the family to cover. Felipe was later charged with driving under the influence. He spent several weeks in jail and was eventually sent to a detention center and later deported to Mexico.[30]

Some mestizo immigrants, who described themselves as fitting the racialized stereotypes of illegality, particularly those who were perceived as having "brown skin," also shared that they were in danger of racial profiling while driving. Ernesto reflected on one experience: "The police didn't even tell me the reason why they stopped me. Simply, *they saw me*, and they thought I didn't have a license. I feel like they were racist with me because there was no reason to stop me." Ernesto, however, unlike Felipe, was able to secure a lawyer and fight his charges, escaping imprisonment and deportation. "The judge wanted to put me in jail for six months," Ernesto said, "Because the judge said that I didn't have a license by choice, not because I can't have it." As Ernesto illustrates, undocumented immigrants in Kansas drive without a driver's license because they were precluded by law from having one, yet they were unable to conduct everyday activities without driving. "I spent six months without driving because I was afraid," Ernesto concluded. "But you know what? *La necesidad* [the necessity] made my fear go away."

CONCLUSION

The wider Kansas context—including its demographic composition, patchwork of state and local laws, and institutions—shaped immigrants' everyday experiences. Across ethnoracial lines and genders, immigrants referenced *aguantar* when sharing their survival strategies in the face of legal violence. Indigenous and mestizo immigrants all told me about experiences where *aguantar* proved necessary—occurring in the workplace, when they felt cornered between the denial of rights and lack of protections promoted through the law and exploited by employers; in their housing experiences, when they were denied opportunities to safe and quality housing and were abused by landlords; and in their mobility, when driving left them at risk of deportation, which was exacerbated by racial profiling and agreements between ICE and local policing agencies expanded under the 2017 presidential executive orders.

As colonial legacies transverse geographical spaces and are enhanced and further cemented in Kansas, Indigenous women faced multiple layers of control and oppression because of their gender, because of their indigeneity, because they lacked recognized immigration status, and, for many, because of their roles as mothers. Indigenous immigrant women in particular used *aguantar* as a survival tactic to fulfill the needs of their families, who lived in the United States and abroad. Within the immigration context, *aguantar* further reflected the role that colonial legacies play in reproducing vulnerable populations through the internalization of violence. The possibility of deportation at any imaginable moment was the most direct form of legal violence that undocumented immigrants and their loved ones could experience.[31] Deportability is a form of legal violence because it renders immigrants, their family members, and those who fit stereotypes associated with illegality subject to short- and long-term harm.[32] Importantly, the racialization of illegality—that is, connecting social constructs of race with perceptions of undocumented status— reproduced different surveillance and policing experiences between Indigenous and mestizos as well as those who were perceived as having brown skin tones, as we saw in immigrants' accounts of restricted mobility.

Immigrants' accounts showed that to maneuver around exclusion, they utilized their coethnic ties to gain pertinent information and access to resources. With such information, immigrants across ethnoracial categories ended up engaging in behaviors that were further criminalized under the law, such as buying documents for work and driving without a driver's license. While these behaviors made their presence "more illegal" and therefore more vulnerable to deportability,[33] immigrants were unable to conduct everyday activities, such as finding or going to work, securing housing, and driving, whether it was to pick up their children from daycare or going to the grocery store, without these strategies. Ethnoracial hierarchies further intersected in the case of Indigenous immigrants, who arrived in deprived economic circumstances and further encountered limited resources to overcome the struggles of legal exclusion, such as the exorbitant amounts charged for work documents and interethnic exploitation in transportation practices. Additionally, gender-segregated labor markets intersect with gendered social ties; women relied on other immigrant women to find work.[34]

This chapter has highlighted some of the commonalities affecting immigrants across ethnoracial lines and illuminated the institutional context for legal violence as it connects to systems of oppression operating through colonial legacies in the workplace, in housing, and in driving. Subsequent chapters highlight some of the differing paths that Indigenous and mestizo immigrants take as they make the heartland their home.

4

"NO VINE A APRENDER INGLÉS"

Language in the Community and at Home

JAIME, INDIGENOUS TLAPANECO, called on a Saturday afternoon. "I need your help really quick," he said, talking fast. "Look I'm at the store to ask about the car, and I don't know how to say it—I need to get some oil." When another, slightly confused, voice on the line asked, "Hello?," I translated Jaime's request. Back on the phone, Jamie thanked me, said he would call again if he needed more help, and hung up. These phone calls were common during my fieldwork. With some instances, such as this, the conversations were brief. Other instances—because most Kansas institutions lacked in-person interpretation and translation services for non-English speakers—involved extensive, complicated conversations with various actors ranging from health care professionals, attorneys, and caseworkers to teachers. English is not the only language useful for navigating life in Kansas, however, and both Indigenous and mestizo immigrants found creative ways to overcome linguistic challenges—whether these occurred at home, at work, in school, or elsewhere in the community.

In the same way that ethnoracial divides were established in the Americas to maintain power and social inequities, early linguistic hierarchies were entangled with race.[1] Under colonialism, language and race became conaturalized, as assimilative policies encouraged the acquisition of colonial languages while devaluing Indigenous speech—a process that continues today.[2] In this chapter, I investigate how Indigenous and mestizo immigrants in Kansas used language to navigate relationships, community institutions, and family life. In this chapter, I consider immigrants' *linguistic capital*—how immigrants use language to gain information, form or maintain family ties, navigate social institutions, and so forth. Importantly, besides English, knowledge of Spanish and Indigenous languages also unlocked resources and opportunities, highlighting immigrants' *linguistic wealth*. Indigenous and mestizo immigrants experience language barriers that create tensions in the community and at home; however, they also find creative ways to maneuver their realities.

LINGUISTIC CAPITAL AND LINGUISTIC WEALTH

Language legitimizes and justifies particular ideas and knowledge and reinforces power divides. For Bourdieu, "legitimate languages" are those "bound up within the state, both in its genesis and in its social uses,"[3] and thus language is institutionalized through the linguistic practices of the powerful. Only those who can understand and engage in such practices can participate in legitimate linguistic exchanges; those who cannot are excluded, reinforcing the dominant group's position in the social hierarchy. Other languages, along with their speakers, are thus devalued, stigmatized, marginalized, and left out of resources and decision-making processes.

This dynamic is perhaps most visible in regions where colonial languages are imposed and Indigenous languages are suppressed or erased, such as the imposition of Spanish and Portuguese in most of Latin America and English in the United States. Following Bourdieu's theorization, *linguistic capital* refers to language that can be utilized within a "linguistic market," and, as Silver has noted, "its value is embedded in the predispositions of those engaged in the exchange and the power relations."[4] In contrast, Yosso invites us to interrogate the knowledge, linguistic abilities, and communication means possessed by devalued social groups that are not typically valued as "linguistic capital."[5] When examining immigrants' experiences in a new country, scholars have paid special attention to immigrants' linguistic capital acquisition—the newly acquired language skills help with their integration into the new society. Most research on language acquisition has followed this perspective, showing how immigrants' acquisition of English increases job opportunities—including higher wages and educational attainment—while those who do not learn English fall behind on income and other mobility measures.[6] These understandings of linguistic capital conceal immigrants' other assets and resources. It is through *community cultural wealth*, Yosso argues, that communities of color accumulate the assets and resources required to overcome structural violence and oppression.[7] Significantly, this includes *linguistic wealth*—mobilized in ways that differ from an ability to navigate the dominant linguistic markets. Linguistic wealth encompasses the knowledge, traditions, and strategies passed between family and friends and across wider social networks, transmitted via *consejos* (advice), *cuentos* (stories), *dichos* (proverbs), music, and art. Linguistic wealth also encompasses certain speech characteristics, such as volume, pitch, rhythm and rhyme, and whistles, enabling communication with various audiences in different circumstances.[8] Applying Yosso's lens, immigrants I met utilized linguistic wealth in Kansas to navigate their daily transnational relationships and communities in the heartland.

Indigenous Linguistic Wealth

The Indigenous immigrants I met spoke the following languages as their mother tongue: Chuj, K'iche', Tlapaneco, and Mixteco. Although I spoke none of these languages, Indigenous immigrants openly discussed their languages with me and often spoke them in my presence while I observed their family interactions. Indigenous languages were used for important activities, including transnational parenting decisions, exchanging *consejos* between loved ones, and as a protection strategy when facing threats in public, reflecting Indigenous immigrants' linguistic wealth.

Victoria, for example, continued to talk on the telephone as she welcomed me into her home and gestured for me to wait in the dining room until she finished. She cradled the phone in her shoulder while she chopped onions and seemed visibly worried by her conversation. Every few minutes she caught my eye. Despite my repeated offers to leave, Victoria urged me to stay. Although I could not understand her Tlapaneco conversation, I recognized the word *escuela* (school), said in Spanish, and Sara, the name of her eldest daughter. After almost an hour later—which I spent with Victoria's three-year-old daughter, a US citizen, who was drawing in a coloring book and playing with dolls—Victoria finally sat down, put her hands on her forehead, and tried to hold back tears. It had been her sister on the telephone. Victoria's eldest daughter, Sara, was skipping school and—more worrying—was beginning to self-harm. With tears streaming down her face, Victoria explained the actions, decided with her sister, that she'd now undertake. First, she would call her mother, Sara's main caregiver, in Mexico. Victoria would then make an appointment with a counselor at Sara's school and send money to her mother and sister to cover their travel expenses as they accompanied Sara to the appointment, which was an hour away from their village.[9] The appointment with the counselor would have to be in Spanish, Victoria told me, because none of the school staff spoke Tlapaneco, so her sister would have to also attend to translate between school staff and Victoria's mother, whose Spanish was limited. And Victoria would also be present via the phone. Linguistic wealth was present in Victoria's use of multiple languages to support her daughter and make parenting decisions from afar.

I also witnessed Ofelia, an Indigenous Maya Guatemalan woman, activate her linguistic wealth while doing transnational parenting. When I dropped by to visit her, she urged me to sit in her small kitchen, beside a boarded-up window, while she continued to talk on the phone. As she spoke, in Chuj words I could not decipher, she waved an arm in agitated circles, her typical smile gone. Ofelia sighed when she hung up. The call was with her sister in Guatemala. Ofelia's teenage son, Alfonso, who is deaf, had been caught drinking again by a neighbor. Ofelia's family sent routine remittances for her son's necessities. However, wider knowledge of these payments, Ofelia confided, as well as Alfonso's deafness meant that local people often tried to get money from him and bullied him for being deaf. The bullying would lead to fights, and after Alfonso would fight, he drank. Because of his drinking, Alfonso's wife (who was also a teen) had recently left him. Ofelia decided to telephone other relatives to collectively address her son's well-being. First, anxious to prevent her son from living alone, Ofelia would talk to her mother-in-law and see if Alfonso could move in with her. Then Ofelia would ask her other son to check in on Alfonso and prevent further drinking. Before any of this, however, Ofelia would first convene a video call with her sisters to hear their *consejos* on what else she could do from afar. Ofelia was wary of asking too much of her elderly and ailing mother-in-law and also worried about her son's well-being.

Indigenous languages were strategically utilized in circumstances where immigrants felt unsafe or unwelcomed in the heartland. On one occasion I attended a child's birthday party hosted by Dolores, an Indigenous Mixteco Mexican mother. As I enjoyed *pastel de tres leches* (a

Mexican traditional cake) in a fully packed living room, Dolores's extended family talked together in Mixteco. Suddenly Dolores's young cousin pointed at me, and everyone laughed. I joined in, wondering what I had missed. He then explained, in Spanish, that they had been discussing a recent encounter that he and another cousin had experienced in a store. While shopping, they'd noticed a guard staring at them. Not knowing whether the guard was associated with *la migra,* the two cousins decided to forgo their items and leave the store immediately. The cousins were grateful that they were able to debate their decision in Mixteco so that other shoppers and the guards—assuming they did not speak Mixteco—were unlikely to understand them. These other shoppers had resembled me, they had told the birthday party, who had not understood any of the Mixteco conversation in the room— hence the pointing and laughing. We all laughed again.

On another occasion, Dolores, her husband and I were in a hospital emergency room while Dolores's youngest son received treatment. As a nurse checked the drowsy boy's temperature, Dolores's husband whispered to her in Mixteco, and their faces looked tense. I assumed they were discussing their child's health. Days later and unprompted, however, Dolores recalled that conversation at the hospital—explaining that her husband had wanted to know whether the hospital administrator had asked for Dolores's Social Security number at the check-in desk, which to the couple meant possible check of undocumented status. This was also shortly after Donald Trump announced an enhancement to the Public Charge Rule, a mandate that left immigrants inadmissible and limited the possibility to shift their status if accessing public benefits (which most immigrants are ineligible for) and after the 2017 executive orders that enhanced immigration enforcement in local communities. After the immigration policy changes, it was common to hear rumors among immigrants about the risk of apprehension in health care settings. Speaking in Mixteco allowed for private discussions and ensured their safety in places that felt unsafe. Indigenous immigrants thus utilized Indigenous linguistic wealth as a tool for managing family relationships from afar, sharing *consejos*, and navigating potential threats of immigration enforcement in public spaces.

Spanish Linguistic Wealth

Sitting in a fold-up chair in the middle of his living room, Teodoro, an Indigenous Mexican man, told me about his experience of learning Spanish. Nobody in his hometown in southern Mexico spoke Spanish, he said. "Where we are from almost no one speaks Spanish, only Mixteco." Almost half a million Mexicans speak Mixteco in various forms, of whom over 77 percent are also bilingual in Spanish.[10] But Teodoro never attended school and only learned basic Spanish after migrating to the United States for work. Once in the United States, Teodoro, with the help of Mixteco family ties, found employment as a restaurant cook. Most of his kitchen coworkers were Spanish speakers, and so Teodoro steadily improved his Spanish skills through these daily workplace interactions.

Like Teodoro, the majority of Indigenous immigrants had minimal or nonexistent Spanish-language skills prior to migration and instead learned the language once in the United States—typically through workplace activities and informal interactions with Spanish speakers. This process reflects the continuance of colonial legacies in important ways, both before and after migration. First, Indigenous immigrants associated their limited facility in Spanish with a lack of access to formal schooling in Mexico and Guatemala, where Indigenous groups have lagged behind their mestizo counterparts in educational attainment. Although there have been significant advances across Latin America, by no means are all schools bilingual, nor do all teachers respect Indigenous-based knowledge and languages.[11] Poverty and poor governmental oversight still prevent many Indigenous youths from accessing high-quality education. Schools are often located far from

Indigenous communities, are in physical disrepair, and are staffed by teachers who have limited educational attainment themselves.[12] Twenty-seven Indigenous immigrants told me that they had encountered significant barriers to education while growing up in Mexico and Guatemala. This was especially true for Indigenous women, who were even further disenfranchised by patriarchal gender norms. Carolina, an Indigenous Tlapaneco Mexican mom, explained to me that school simply was not an option for most girls in her community in Mexico.[13]

Second, the lack of Spanish-language proficiency prior to migration illustrated the entrenched divides between Indigenous and mestizos in their countries of origin. None of the mestizo immigrants I met reported speaking an Indigenous language when asked how many languages they understand and speak. Such language boundaries mirror colonial legacies and the conaturalization of race and language, with Indigenous groups positioned as inferior to European origins in the racial hierarchy.[14] While Indigenous groups were thus expected to learn Spanish to navigate social institutions and work, mestizos were not expected to learn Indigenous languages. Spanish (along with other colonial languages such as Portuguese and French in some countries) has remained the region's "legitimate language,"[15] and Indigenous languages such as Mixteco, Tlapaneco, Chuj, and K'iche' have continued to be delegitimized and stigmatized, despite Indigenous linguistic wealth and grassroots mobilizations geared toward language maintenance.

Knowledge of Spanish was useful for navigating life in the US heartland—something that became clear in the story of Saturnina and Jaime, an Indigenous Mixteco Mexican couple. As we sat together on their couch, the couple described their two very different experiences with pregnancy and childbirth—one that took place when they were recent arrivals in Kansas and could not speak Spanish or English and another, a decade later, when they were fluent in the Spanish language and the demographics in the state had also changed. Saturnina first became pregnant a year after the couple moved to Kansas at a time when they depended heavily on their coethnic Mixteco networks to find work and housing. Nobody else in their community of mostly new arrivals to Kansas, however, had ever been pregnant in the United States, and the couple did not know anyone who could translate between Mixteco, Spanish, and English fluently enough to navigate the health care system in such an important moment. "When one cannot speak Spanish, one suffers," Saturnina recalled. After learning she was pregnant, the couple reached out to their employer, the owner of a Chinese restaurant, for information on accessing medical care and the costs associated with childbirth. "Why are you going to have a child?," Jaime recalled their employer snapping. "It is a lot of money. More than $15,000," the employer had told the couple. Saturnina and Jaime worried that they might lose their child to state custody if they could not pay such fees and decided to give birth in Mexico instead. Saturnina went on to say that "We could not have our daughter here; we did not have any help." One month after their baby girl was born, with no job opportunities in their home village, Saturnina and Jaime returned to the United States. For ten years they had sent monthly remittances to Saturnina's mother, who cared for their child. "She was one month old," Jamie said as his gaze turned to the floor. "Since then, I have never seen her again."

Saturnina's second pregnancy occurred a decade later, again in Kansas. This time, however, after such a long spell working alongside immigrant Spanish speakers in the restaurant industry, both Saturnina and Jaime spoke fluent Spanish. The couple also became involved in a local church that held weekly services in Spanish. By then, too, the Latino population in Kansas had reached over 10 percent, and some of the state's main institutions such as health care and education had incorporated limited Spanish-language services. One of Saturnina's Mixteco friends, who was also a mom to US-citizen children born in Kansas, connected her with a bilingual Spanish- and English-speaking mestiza social worker. "They helped me," Saturnina recalled. "Now there is a person that helps at the hospital. Before, no—there was nobody." With the Latina social worker's support, and growing social ties to other Mixteco moms in the community, Saturnina gave birth to her second baby in a Kansas hospital. The social worker also guided Saturnina in finding resources to cover some of the hospital fees.

English Linguistic Capital

Overall, English language proficiency has remained low among Latinos in Kansas, with only 33 percent speaking English at home.[16] The majority of Kansan Latinos, over 60 percent, reported speaking English either less than well or not at all.[17] Of the mestizo immigrants I met, twenty-eight told me that they spoke English well or at least could understand and speak the language at a basic level. Among the Indigenous immigrants, however, only three said the same.

Although immigrants were well aware that English-language skills could lead to better wages and upward mobility, learning English was not always their first priority when migrating. As Alejandro, an Indigenous Maya Guatemalan man, put it, "I did not come to learn English." Rather, he said, he came to the United States to work and sustain his family back home. Yet in the midst of living and navigating life in Kansas, English became vital to this endeavor, particularly so in order to avoid dependence on the more exploitative aspects of intraethnic, third-party translation services. During my ethnographic fieldwork, I observed how mestizo and Indigenous immigrants had vastly different experiences of English-language acquisition—experiences that developed both through community-led language classes and informal learning settings.

Community-led English-language classes reflect an institutional reaction to a growing immigrant population in a particular region, underpinned by integration strategies that view proficiency in the language of a host country—English, in this case—as a major vehicle for immigrants' integration for accessing both social institutions and opportunities for economic mobility.[18] In Kansas, English-language classes were frequently offered in churches and community centers either free of charge or at low cost.[19]

During my fieldwork, I volunteered teaching English at a language program for immigrants that was hosted in a local church. Jaime, a mestizo Mexican man, had attended this English program for almost seven years. He spoke English fluently and was steadily improving his writing and reading skills. Jaime hardly never missed a class, attending twice a week. As a single father, he found the program's free childcare invaluable, allowing him an hour of focused learning while his daughter played with other children. Jaime's dream was to reach a level of English proficiency that would enable him to gain a formal English certification. "I could go more, to a more formal school. There you finish. They give you your diploma like 'English as a Second Language,' and there you can see what other programs they have, like the careers." To become a criminologist, Jaime told me one day. "That career has always called my attention. Since a few years back I knew about that career, but I never had the opportunity to go to school again. Well, it's more that English didn't let me. I only speak it; I didn't have instruction. And now every time I speak and write more, I feel as if the world is opening for me."

Vicente, another mestizo Mexican man, had taken English classes at an established language school of the kind Jaime hoped to one day attend. "I was working fewer hours, so I had time to go," Vicente recalled. "I went three times a week, three hours a day. I didn't graduate only because I didn't go the final week." Mestizo men such as Jaime and Vicente clearly benefited from attending English-language classes. However, none of the Indigenous immigrant men I met in Kansas ever mentioned participating in one—a fact I attribute to cumulative causes including the time constraints they faced while working extensive hours and most often multiple jobs and their lack of educational past experiences. Like Teodoro, many Indigenous men had never attended school in their home countries, making it challenging to attend any education settings, including volunteer-led community language classes.[20]

In women's accounts of community English-language classes, gendered expectations emerged as a highly prominent theme. As a volunteer teacher, I noticed that there were typically more men than women in the classroom. Among mestizo women, gendered expectations of intensive motherhood created strong barriers to attending language classes even when childcare was provided. Liliana, a mestiza Mexican woman, told me about her experience. When Liliana first arrived in the United States, she lived in San Antonio, Texas, where the large Spanish-speaking population made daily life possible without much knowledge of English. But in Kansas, she said, "everything is in English, everything in English." Like Jaime, Liliana was attracted by the free childcare available during English classes and enrolled. But Liliana struggled to balance learning with leaving her daughter at childcare. Liliana said, "I would leave her with those who cared for them, the childcare. As soon as I would go in the classroom, I would feel *como un aire* [a gut feeling], and I felt like I had to go—I had to go back because my baby was crying."

Other mestizas noted how the responsibilities of intensive motherhood, that is, the expectation that women are the main parent responsible for the well-being and care of their children, coupled with work outside the home, left them with very little time to attend English classes. I once asked Isabel, a mestiza Mexican woman, if she wanted to join the class where I taught. She asked, dryly, "*¿A qué horas?*" In English, this translates directly into "At what time?" Conversationally, however, the phrase implies that there are not enough hours in the day to attend. Other mestiza immigrant women told me that their childcare responsibilities and household upkeep should be prioritized ahead of any English-language classes.

Although no Indigenous men mentioned enrolling in an English program, a handful of Indigenous women—including mothers working outside the home—had attended classes in their local communities. These classes, however, were described as unhelpful and ineffective. Some Indigenous women went further and told me they had felt uncomfortable in the classroom. Sofia, an Indigenous Tlapaneco Mexican woman who had earned a high school diploma in Mexico, was among the Indigenous immigrants with the highest educational attainment from their home countries I met during my fieldwork. Yet when Sofia, eager to continue her education, attended her first English class, she felt uncomfortable and somewhat embarrassed. "There are a lot of Mexicans, and they look at you weird," she told me, implying that the other students were mestizos who were unwelcoming. Sofia never went back to the class after only one week. Renata, another Indigenous Tlapaneco Mexican woman, took the same class, in a different year, and completed the one-year-long course. However, despite attending class regularly, Renata felt as though her knowledge of English had barely improved. "I went to the church—they gave me a diploma and everything, but I didn't learn anything," she recalled. As a volunteer teacher, this remark did not surprise me. The language program where I taught, although important for the community and well intended, had no teaching requirements for instructors besides English-language proficiency, and there was little support for curriculum development. As Reierson and Celedón-Pattichis have observed, English instructors in community classes are frequently ill-prepared or lack the skills required to teach students with little or no previous formal education,[21] which was the case for most of the Indigenous immigrants I met in Kansas.

Besides formal instruction, immigrants obtained English-language proficiency through informal workplace interactions—similar to Indigenous immigrants' acquisition of Spanish. Jenny, a mestiza Mexican woman, arrived in the United States with no knowledge of English. Working in a fast-food restaurant, Jenny initially found it very difficult to communicate with her coworkers who were all English speakers.

Over time, however, daily life in the restaurant enabled Jenny to improve her English and make social connections with US citizens and other established residents. One coworker in particular stood out in Jenny's memory. "She would tell me, 'I'm going to teach you.' And I would say, 'I'm scared.' She taught me the dollars, she showed me the computer, she taught me a lot of things." Before long, their friendship extended beyond work. "She used to take me to the casino," Jenny recalled. "There she would tell me, 'Say this and this,' and I repeated what she would tell me. I learned [English]." As Jenny's English skills improved, she was promoted to a supervisor position and then to a managerial position—with a commensurate increase in wages. "*Yo le eché muchas ganas* [I worked very hard]," Jenny told me. "Every day I tried to be better, and better."

Alejandro, Indigenous Maya Guatemalan, was the only Indigenous immigrant who shared about learning English at work. Alejandro grew up speaking Chuj in a small village in Guatemala. After migration to the United States, he first improved his Spanish while working in a restaurant kitchen with Spanish-speaking coworkers. Alejandro's grasp of English came later, he explained, as he learned to decipher the written food-order tickets that the servers passed in through the hatch to the kitchen staff. "Only the boss speaks English, but all the tickets, because I read, all the tickets that get there, with that I learned English," he told me. "Now I can read the tickets, see what's in one [dish] or what's not in a [dish]. I can read that now. It is like two hundred dishes, all tickets, that come today, tomorrow, all the time." As Alejandro's confidence grew, he began to practice English with the English-speaking servers and hosts of the restaurant. In time his new skills led to a promotion. Alejandro no longer had to lift the heavy pans and deal with the kitchen heat; his job involved checking the tickets and making sure diners received exactly what they ordered. His skills and confidence helped beyond work too. With relatively few immigrants in Kansas, English came in useful while shopping for groceries and asking directions in public. "It is nice to learn English," Alejandro concluded. "Here there is nobody that speaks Spanish; you will not be able to buy things or ask." So, although his goal or intention was not necessarily to learn English, this skill opened up many opportunities including at work, proving English to be an important form of linguistic capital particularly in the heartland where Spanish was—although growing— limited in public spaces.

LANGUAGE BARRIERS AND TENSIONS

As the Kansas Latino population grew, some institutions and community organizations—located in areas with a larger share of the Latino community—responded with language services, as Jaime and Saturnina's experience with childbirth showed. According to Indigenous immigrants' accounts, however, bilingual services were not always accessible to them, and sometimes these services were denied. Dolores, who had invited me to many of her family's gatherings including many of her kids' birthday parties and Christmas, for instance, had been living in Kansas for over a decade. Her first language is Mixteco. She spoke Spanish fluently (having learned it in her US workplace), and she could understand basic English due to experiences as a student in the K–12 education system. However, when one of Dolores's sons was hospitalized for several days, she was denied interpretation services at the local hospital. On a separate occasion than the one described earlier when her husband whispered nervously about the Social Security number in Mixteco, Dolores had telephoned me, on the verge of tears, asking for help. She had been in the hospital for a couple of days, yet none of the medical staff would update her on her son's condition or explain their diagnosis. Instead, they would only communicate with Dolores's daughter, who was only in third grade and unable to grasp the complex medical terminology and had difficulties recounting the information back to her mom. Phone interpretation services were supposedly available at the hospital, but Dolores shared that these had not been offered beforehand. I met Dolores in the hospital and documented some of the interactions in my field notes:

> When I got to the hospital Dolores was sitting in a chair, two kids on one bed, one kid on a chair, and the others were on the ground playing with some toys. . . . They had been there since Thursday; it was Sunday. I said hello and handed the McDonald's I got for the family. Dolores had said in our phone conversation earlier that the kids had not eaten all day. Then I sat at the feet of one of the beds where the oldest kid was sitting. . . . Dolores told me that she thought the nurse was very rude and mean, that the nurse yelled at her sick child to eat and drink, and then when he didn't eat, she just took the food away when her other kids could eat it. She explained that yesterday the kids didn't eat until 11 p.m. when the dad brought them some rice from work [at a Chinese restaurant]. The dad took the kids home at night, and she stayed with the sick child at the hospital.

Later, Dolores shared that she was not given an interpreter and did not know whether they could leave the hospital or if they had to stay. She asked if I could help talk to the nurse or doctors while I was there. The following is from my field notes:

> After about two hours, the nurse came into the room. The nurse, looking straight at the sick three-year-old child, explained that she was leaving and that a new nurse was going to take over and went on to explain details of medicine schedules. I turned to Dolores and asked if she understood, and she said no. So, I repeated what the nurse said in Spanish. The nurse quickly turned and glared at me and with a rough tone asked me, "What did you just say to her?"

I worried that my presence could make things worse. Per Dolores's request, however, I explained that I was just there to help since the interpreter had not been to the room yet. Dolores and I were relieved that this nurse was finishing up her shift. After the new nurse arrived, we again requested an interpreter. A few hours later, Dolores called me sharing that she was finally given an interpreter through the phone and was able to understand the medical provider.

While, like Dolores, some immigrants were harshly discriminated against in places that had language services (such as hospitals), in other cases Indigenous immigrants shared that the existing language services were not very useful. Nina, for instance, an Indigenous Maya Guatemalan woman whose first language is K'iche', told me that she had difficulties understanding the Spanish-language telephone interpretation services used at her prenatal doctor appointments. As a result, she instead paid a mestiza immigrant woman (with no medical or interpretation training) to act as her interpreter during the appointments—a sum above $40 per visit and depending on appointment length, including waiting time (in addition to any costs associated with rides if those were also needed). Situations such as this could lead to exploitative relations across ethnoracial lines, with some community interpreters charging exorbitant amounts for such services, pushing some Indigenous women into debt.[22]

Other Indigenous immigrants shared that they felt uncomfortable interacting with Spanish-English bilinguals, who were often mestizo immigrants or US-born Latinos. Esperanza, an Indigenous Maya Guatemalan woman, told me that when she sought language assistance from a local Hispanic-serving nonprofit organization, she felt ignored by the Latino workers and received no help. Dolores shared similar feelings. When she sought help in a Hispanic-serving organization, she told me, that the organization's staff "do not help me because they do not want to" even though this organization, and others like it, was specifically created to serve the local Latino immigrant population.

One winter afternoon Victoria, the Tlapaneco mom of a teen who lived in Mexico and a three-year-old who lived in Kansas, invited me over to make tamales. Victoria's friend Josefina, an Indigenous Tlapaneco woman, was also present. When Victoria asked if I could help Josefina complete some documents, Josefina opened her purse and immediately offered to pay me $20. Victoria motioned at Josefina to put her purse down and explained that I was a student researcher and would not charge anything. I affirmed this, explained my study, and offered to translate without any expectation of Josefina's research participation. After cooking tamales together for a few hours, however, Josefina became interested in the project and offered to talk privately. She was tired of paying for translation help, she confided later. The Spanish-English mestizo bilinguals charged her large fees and often wasted her time by canceling at the last minute, just as she most needed their help. "They don't really want to help," she added.

Indigenous immigrants with limited Spanish and English literacy also struggled to read documents. "I cannot read; it is very hard to read," Esperanza admitted shyly. Similarly, Luz, also a Maya Guatemalan woman whose first language is Chuj, told me, "I cannot speak Spanish well. I cannot write; I cannot read." Eleven of the Indigenous immigrants I met in Kansas had very limited reading and writing ability in Spanish or English—reflecting wider patterns of literacy inequity across Latin America more broadly. Among Indigenous women, who were often removed from school at a young age as discussed in Chapter 1, illiteracy rates were especially high. As a result, Indigenous immigrants frequently depended on mestizo bilinguals to read documents and fill out forms. Nina, who could not read Spanish or English, also paid a mestiza woman from her church to translate documents that arrived in the mail and from her children's school, paying between $10 and $20 per document even for junk mail (in addition to paying for interpretation help at her medical appointments and sometimes for rides). Thus, Spanish and English illiteracy—rooted in colonial legacies of exclusionary education in Latin America and the United States—created further barriers to Indigenous immigrants' integration and left them vulnerable to exploitation by the established Hispanic community.

Mestizo immigrants who could not speak English also encountered challenges. Jenny recalled one of the most difficult times in her life several years earlier, when she could not yet understand English and her six-month-old baby fell sick and passed away. "My son died," Jenny said. "I didn't know how to speak English. So, the doctors well they would tell me what was happening. But, who knows? There was nobody to help me." After taking a deep breath, she went on. "The only thing I understood was that he was going to die, that he was going to die. So they told me to take him home. I had a huge heartache. I would wonder, 'Why is he dying? I don't know. I don't know what the doctors are telling me.' And then, well, he died. And I was angry." As Jenny's painful recollection indicates, limited language services can leave long-term scars. "Now I can talk about it without crying, without tears coming out," she told me. And sitting next to me in the chair she said, "Every time I talk about it, I become stronger. But I don't know. I sometimes still feel the pain. His birthday was the sixth, *el día de reyes* [Three Kings' Day]."

Immigrants' limited English and Spanish ability as well as strong accents can also lead to discrimination and racial profiling, particularly in already precarious circumstances. While Alejandro was being apprehended by immigration officers, with his wife looking on from the window, the officers asked him why he didn't speak English. In shock and panicking about possible deportation, Alejandro reflected, *"Yo no vine aquí a aprender inglés, vine a trabajar* [I did not come here to learn English, I came to work]," which he repeated to me during our conversation. Other Indigenous immigrants recounted moments of discrimination after they could not speak fluent English or Spanish, like the time Jazmin was held in detention when she was seeking asylum and encountered anti-Indigenous discrimination from both Anglo officers and Spanish-speaking detainees, discussed in Chapter 1.

While Indigenous immigrants faced discrimination from both Anglos and fellow Latinos, mestizos emphasized that heavily accented English or limited Spanish betrayed their undocumented status. Patricio, a mestizo Salvadoran young man, told me that although he did not fit the visual stereotypes associated with illegality, his accent made it clear that he was a foreigner and therefore potentially undocumented. Similarly, Vicente said, "They never thought I was Mexican until they heard me talk, then yes with this huge accent, of course." Rodolfo, also mestizo Mexican, said in reference to people discovering that he is Mexican, "I think once they hear me talking, they see my name in Spanish, and then hear my accent. Well, I don't have another option." Heavy accents as well as a lack of English skills connected to the racialization of illegality with Indigenous and mestizo immigrants' public language experiences, demonstrating how language and race are rooted in colonial powers.[23]

EN LA CASA: LANGUAGE AT HOME

Language was also a complex feature of immigrants' domestic lives in Kansas. According to classical assimilation studies, as successive generations are born in the United States, English typically becomes immigrant families' primary language, while the mother tongue is slowly forgotten.[24] Although bilingualism is common among second-generation immigrant children in the United States, third- and fourth-generation immigrants will likely only speak English.[25] Retention of the mother tongue is associated with an immigrant family's ties to the traditions, norms, identities of their home countries and to their ethnic communities. Among US immigrants, Spanish speakers are more likely than other migrants to retain their language,[26] as are immigrants who live in ethnic enclaves.[27]

Scholarship exploring Indigenous immigrants' language retention in the United States reveals its ties to enduring legacies of colonialism. Indigenous parents aim to support their children's educational achievement by instilling Spanish and English proficiency,[28] while at the same time supporting cultural and linguistic knowledge based on Indigenous roots.[29] Indigenous youths nevertheless continue to face anti-Indigenous discrimination in the diaspora even when they live in Latino-majority contexts such as California.[30] In the heartland, Indigenous and mestizo families formed bilingual and multilingual homes, shifting family roles and creating new challenges in intimate spaces.

Multilingual Homes: Indigenous Families

Dolores's daughter Nicky, a US citizen, was nine years old when we first met. As the only girl and the second oldest of six siblings, Nicky followed strict gender expectations at home while also meeting her school responsibilities. Nicky loved school. The first day we met, she proudly announced her goal for the year ahead: a perfect school attendance record. She had almost won this prestigious title the previous year. But her younger siblings had fallen sick, so she had missed a few days to help her mom talk with the doctors, she said. When Nicky returned home from school each afternoon, she helped Dolores with childcare of her younger siblings, completed household chores such as folding laundry, and diligently completed her homework at the dining room table, where most times when I visited she sat with an open notebook and a pencil at hand. Yet Nicky's brother, two years older, had no such expectations placed upon him. While Nicky never complained about this discrepancy during my visits with Dolores, she often glared at her brother—who would be lying on the couch playing with Dolores's cell phone—whenever she was asked to perform a domestic task.

Nicky and her brothers grew up in a multilingual home. Her parents and resident uncles spoke to each other in Mixteco. The children spoke to each other in English, which they learned at school. The adults spoke to the children in Spanish and, in some instances, Mixteco. Nicky was fluent in Spanish and English and, according to Dolores, understood Mixteco, although she did not speak it. "My children speak Spanish or English," Dolores once declared. "They don't know [Mixteco]. They don't want to. They don't like it; 'it sounds very ugly' [the kids tell Dolores]." Nicky, sitting behind Dolores on the couch, rolled her eyes and shrugged her shoulders. When I was there and Nicky was talking with her mom, she would first say a phrase in English and then promptly repeat it in Spanish as if she were interpreting for herself. This communication style was common between children and parents in the other Indigenous families I spent time with.

As with society's "legitimate languages,"[31] colonial languages also shape power relations within multigenerational families. All of the Indigenous immigrants I met in Kansas had US-born children who had attended K–12 public schools. Although most of these children could understand their parents' Indigenous languages, none could speak them fluently. Like Nicky, Indigenous children often spoke in English, Spanish, or Spanglish to their parents, while the parents responded in Spanish. These parents had mixed feelings about teaching their Indigenous mother tongue to their children. Nina and her husband, for example, communicated with each other in K'iche, a Maya language. I once asked Nina if she spoke K'iche with her children. "No, they don't understand," she said. "But the [oldest] girl understands. Whenever we talk, 'I know what you are saying,' she says." Nina went on to share that although her daughter was interested in learning K'iche', her oldest son was not. "They understand, it is just they don't want to talk. And the boy also, the oldest, he understands everything, but to talk he doesn't want to. He says, 'No, I don't want to. I don't want to say how you talk. I don't want to learn.' But they understand." Nina wanted her children to learn K'iche' so they could one day travel to Guatemala and meet their grandparents, who only speak K'iche'. The couple were apprehensive, however, about teaching their children K'iche' while living in the heartland. Nina went on:

> This is what the teacher said. "Your son understands English well, well, well, well," she said. Like there at school they asked, "How do you speak at home with the kids?" And I tell them "in Spanish." "You don't speak K'iche' with them?" "No," I told them; [when they are] a little older they

will learn. Since now they are little, maybe they forget English and Spanish. So then let them grow a bit more; they will learn.

Another Indigenous Maya Guatemalan woman, Catia, told me that she only wanted her children to learn English and Spanish, recalling the difficulties she had encountered when she first arrived in the United States speaking only K'iche, her first language. Like the case of Saturnina and Jaime presented earlier, Catia too had difficulties navigating the health care system without Spanish or English.

These Indigenous immigrant mothers' stories resonate with social forces in their home countries too, where sometimes Indigenous parents believe that teaching their children Spanish is more useful than their mother tongues for navigating society.[32] Indigenous children in Latin America also face discrimination from other schoolchildren teachers, and various mestizo social actors and across various social institutions. Indigenous origins and languages are devalued, and thus a strategy is to learn Spanish in order to pass as mestizo, facilitating the navigation of social institutions.[33] The loss of Indigenous languages within the family thus further reflects challenges in the maintenance of Indigenous cultures, knowledge, and worldviews due to the imposition of colonial legacies and legitimate languages.[34] It is also possible that because the Indigenous immigrant diaspora in Kansas was small and relatively new, these dynamics heightened barriers toward generational language maintenance. These language dynamics certainly are different in places such as California, where Indigenous immigrant communities have a longer history and a larger population which has enabled Indigenous languages to be maintained across generations.[35]

Bilingual Homes: Mestizo Families

The mestizo immigrants I met in Kansas lived in bilingual homes, where Spanish and English were both spoken. Quantitative studies have found that domestic language choice shapes family social interactions and the quality of family relationships.[36] The family of Isabel and Ernesto highlight this point. Their children—Selena, age fourteen, and Ivan, age eight—were both born in Mexico. But after several years living the heartland and attending public schools, both children rapidly learned English. Ernesto and Isabel spoke only Spanish at home, while Selena spoke both English and Spanish and Ivan understood Spanish but only spoke in English. This situation created a great deal of household miscommunication and a rearrangement of family roles. In tears, Isabel shared her feelings:

> It reached the point that the boy [Ivan] stopped talking, so it was very sad for me, because he comes from school: "How did it go?" He doesn't tell me absolutely nothing, because . . . because he knows that I don't understand him. So, it is very traumatizing for me. Another thing is the homework. I can't help him because I really don't know. I use the translator on the phone; it doesn't translate well. So, it is very traumatizing for me, because I feel that like as a mom at school, they need me, and I can't [help]. So, for me that has been very hard and for the kids as well.

The miscommunication between Isabel and Ivan struck at Isabel's identity as a mother, since she was unable to fulfill traditional gendered expectations of intensive motherhood. Given Selena's fluency in English and Spanish, she became a mediator between her younger brother and her parents. And like Nicky, on some occasions Selena also missed school to help translate between Isabel and Ivan's doctors. This was especially the case the day Ivan fell off the monkey bars at school and broke his arm. Isabel shared that one day the school called. She could barely understand what happened, so she first picked up Selena at her school. They drove to Ivan's school, where Selena helped with talking to the school staff and learned of the monkey bars incident. They then rushed to the hospital, where Selena again served as an interpreter, talking to the medical staff on behalf of her mom and little brother. Selena also took on some of the roles that her mom would normally do, such as helping her little brother with homework and bossing him around to do various household chores.

Paloma, a bilingual mestiza Mexican woman, also had children who could not or would not speak Spanish. In her case, the entire family spoke mainly in English at home. Talking about her eldest child, she shared, "Yes, I tried a bit. He understands everything that you tell him in Spanish, but he can't pronounce the words. Now I am trying to help him." Her youngest child, however, refused to learn Spanish. "Flatly told me that 'No Spanish,'" Paloma said. She went on to explain why she did not teach her children Spanish. "I also didn't want to force them because like I told you, I ended up so confused that I didn't want to do the same." Just like the Indigenous moms felt about Indigenous languages, Paloma also worried about confusing her children if she pushed them to learn Spanish at home.

The dynamics of communication at home reflect the legitimacy and, conversely, the devaluation of languages in society—reproducing colonial legacies. Although Indigenous and mestizo immigrants both had a supply of linguistic wealth that could be passed within the family, colonial legacies maintained English and Spanish as the norm. These mechanisms pierced the intimate spaces of the family, sometimes changing familial roles and shifting communication. Children and youths enacted their agency through domestic language choice and communication strategies.[37]

CONCLUSION

Colonial legacies shape linguistic capital throughout history and have maintained the dominance of colonial languages—such as English and Spanish—while denigrating Indigenous languages. However, following Yosso's conceptualization of cultural wealth,[38] language can transmit wealth across generations and family members. Linguistic wealth shows how immigrants used language strategically to navigate their lives and intimate relationships across borders and in the heartland. As the cases of Carolina, Saturnina and Jaime, and Dolores's families showed, Indigenous languages were used to make parenting decisions from afar, share *consejos*, and manage potential threats in public. Indigenous languages were also conduits of important information to navigate life for those newly arrived in Kansas. Yet Spanish and English remained the languages used to connect to the more established Latino community and also navigate important resources and institutions such as medical care, work, and education.

As the Latino immigrant population continued to increase in Kansas, social institutions began to provide more services in Spanish, and new Hispanic-serving institutions established themselves in the area. The Spanish language thus also acts as linguistic wealth, providing newly arrived immigrants with the ability to access resources and services and navigate daily life. Yet as the accounts of Indigenous immigrants demonstrated, not all Latino immigrants spoke Spanish as their first language. This puts them at an ongoing disadvantage in this particular linguistic market.

English-language acquisition provided immigrants with direct access to organizations and resources and the ability to avoid third-party mediators and the risk of exploitation. Intersections of race and gender, rooted in the legacies of colonialism, were present in English-language acquisition among both mestizos and Indigenous immigrants. Among mestizos, it was men who reported using community language classes to improve their English-language skills. Intensive expectations of motherhood often derailed mestiza women from engaging in English-language education. In contrast, none of the Indigenous men reported attending English-language classes mainly due to work and time constraints. While some Indigenous women tried joining English-language classes, they reported discrimination and feeling unwelcomed in the class, thus reflecting long histories of Indigenous exclusion from education in their home countries that carried over to the Kansas diaspora. Although most immigrants did not migrate to the United States with the goal of learning English, proficiency in English was an extremely useful tool for not only social mobility but also communication with family members and gatekeepers who provided access to multiple resources such as schools, health care, and everyday spaces such as grocery stores. As with Spanish, immigrants improved their English-language skills at work, as it provided opportunities for social mobility across ethnoracial backgrounds.

Language interpretation services can provide a bridge to institutions, yet these services can create tension if they amplify the colonial legacies inherent within Latin American immigrants' social relations. By upholding colonial languages' socially encoded legitimacy, institutions that aimed to provide services to Latin American immigrants may not be capable of delivering these in Indigenous languages.[39]

When social institutions failed to provide formal interpretation services and when gatekeepers—such as the nurse in Dolores's case—denied services, a common enough occurrence in rural Kansas but one that also occurred in urban areas including in health care settings, government offices, and schools—Indigenous immigrants told me that they paid mestizo bilinguals for Spanish-English interpretation. This dependence could then lead to exploitative relationships between mestizo and Indigenous immigrants, with translation costs ranging from $10 to $20 for a one-page document—such as a medical form, a letter from a school, and legal papers but also including junk mail—to much higher amounts for interpreting at in-person appointments. Indigenous women in particular talked about these costs and exploitative dynamics. Following typical gender roles, they tended to be responsible for childcare and had more frequent interactions with social institutions, such as medical facilities and schools. Language hierarchies also shaped family dynamics. As parents' accounts demonstrated, legitimate languages in society—English and Spanish in this case—continued to be used over Indigenous languages even within the family. In some instances this caused tension, particularly when parents were unable to communicate with their children and family roles were reconfigured.

5

"TAL VEZ UN DÍA
ME PUEDO ARREGLAR"

Hopes and Worries

AFTER FINISHING a delicious meal of *mole*, a Mexican deli-
cacy, and almost at the end of our conversation, Celestina sat
back, setting her fork on the empty plate. "I wish that one day
the laws could change," she told me. "Our children were born
here. They could *arreglar* [fix] the parents, even if they have
deported them." Taking a deep breath she reflected, "But oh
well, that is how life is for immigrants." Wishing to one day
be able to change their immigration status was a hope that
most undocumented immigrants I met shared, even those
who, like Celestina, a mestizo Mexican woman, had suffered
a deportation in the past. For those who, like Celestina, were
parents, the idea that their children could one day help them
to *arreglarse*, fix their status, was a common belief among both
Indigenous and mestizo immigrants—although unachiev-
able for most under existing immigration policies. Yet the
shift of immigration status did occur for some, mainly mestizos, while others—all the Indigenous immigrants I met and

a few mestizos—remained stuck undocumented. The shifts in status shaped immigrants' family dynamics and roles by creating new mixed-status families, that is, families that have a variety of immigration statuses in the same family ranging from undocumented to semilegal to citizens; by impacting intimate relationships and family roles; or due to rising new worries and concerns. Importantly, immigrants' legal consciousness, that is, their understandings and interpretations of the law[1] and diverse access to resources, led to distinct experiences for immigrants and their loved ones across ethnoracial lines.

SHIFTING IMMIGRATION STATUS

On a coffee shop patio, Carlos and I discussed how his immigration status had changed over time. Carlos is a mestizo Honduran man and had lived in the heartland for fourteen years. During this period, he had held a tourist visa, had been undocumented, had applied for Deferred Action for Childhood Arrival (DACA), had received legal permanent residency, and would shortly become a naturalized citizen. His undocumented period—which began after he overstayed a tourist visa—lasted eleven years. As we sipped our iced mochas, Carlos told me how tense he had felt as the only undocumented person in his immediate family and how this had come to a head in a conversation with his mom, who had a visa at the time. "I told my mom, it was a day I was really mad, and I kind of blamed her. 'I don't know why you brought me here. Like, you know, we might have everything that we want and all that stuff, yet I can't do what I want to do, or a basic thing, and that is to get a higher education.'" Thinking about life in the United States and being undocumented, he shared his feelings with his mother. "You have freedom and all that stuff, yet I can't do anything. It is your fault that I am living in this golden cage, yet I can't fly."

Carlos pointed out the paradox of having a better life than he had in Honduras while also facing the difficulties of undocumented life. "I felt like a bird trapped in a cage, like it is very comfortable. I have every-thing I want except for what I want to do with my life, and that was, you know, to drive without being afraid of being detained and getting my family in trouble." Carlos's mention of "the golden cage" referenced the eponymous corrido by Los Tigres del Norte that became an anthem of undocumented life in the United States. On the one hand, the United States offered a level of material stability unmatched in Honduras. On the other hand, living in the United States came with the constant threat of deportation and the negative repercussions this could have for Carlos and his family.

In 2012, Carlos qualified for DACA.[2] "I was like in tears. I was like, oh my God, I can't believe this is actually happening." Although Carlos was relieved to obtain DACA status, he was also frustrated by DACA's liminality and how its temporary protections tended to exacerbate the ambivalence of his legal position. "I was happy and pissed off at the same time," Carlos recalled. "They just kind of put a band-aid on us."

While under DACA status, Carlos met Jim, a white Anglo US citizen. They first encountered one another in social media when Jim replied to Carlos's questions about a university program. Soon Carlos and Jim began dating. They eventually moved in together and later married. Carlos explained, "We got married, and we went to [a lawyer] to get all of our documents set up, and he [Jim] was the reason why I was able to fix my documentation." This process, Carlos noted, was made a lot easier because he had originally entered the United States on a tourist visa. Carlos recalled, "It wasn't really hard because I came with a visa, so I had a legal entry. So, you know, it was a really quick step. If I had not had a legal entry even though I would have had Deferred Action, I would still have to go to Honduras because I had, like, you know, an unlawful entry to the US. So, that helped us a lot." Without that lawful entry, as Carlos pointed out, his shift to legal permanent resident status would have been a lot more complicated, almost impossible. Carlos's immigrant status shift coincided with important legislative changes, including the legalization of same-sex marriage,[3] which allowed immigration laws to recognize Carlos and Jim's marriage and allow for spousal sponsorship. Prior to this ruling, LGBTQ+ couples were excluded from this legalization pathway.

Rodolfo, a mestizo Mexican man, also changed his status through marriage. Several years earlier, he had fallen in love and wanted to propose to his girlfriend, Alicia, a Mexican American woman. The couple had lived together for two years, sharing bills and even buying a car together. At the time, however, Rodolfo's immigration status depended on a work visa, which was drawing to a close. "I was transparent with her," Rodolfo remembered. "Since we started dating, before we even moved in together, I mentioned to her the process [of the visa]." He elaborated on that period of his life, when his immigration status was at risk of being revoked at any time. "It was stressful, both financially and emotionally. I had a lot of money saved for the ring," he remembered. "When I asked permission to her parents if I could ask her to marry me, I told them. I was very honest. I told them, 'Look, I have all the intentions to marry your daughter, but I want you to know that I am here with a work visa, and I am in the process of renewing it, but there is a possibility that it will not be renewed. If she agrees to marry me, we might have to have an earlier wedding so I can stay here.'" Weeks after the proposal, Rodolfo's work visa was not renewed. He and Alicia had a small courthouse wedding. "It was almost like a secret. The only ones that knew were her parents, my parents, and our siblings," he told me.

Like Carlos and Rodolfo, immigrants in emerging and newer destinations were more likely to marry citizens, compared to immigrants living in traditional destinations with a larger Latino population.[4] Further, immigrants' interpretation of the law—their legal consciousness—shaped their decisions about who to date and when and why to begin romantic relationships.[5] For Carlos, his relationship allowed for a complete shift in his status to gain the security he always searched and lacked with undocumented and DACA status. For Rodolfo, the expiration of his visa pushed for a quicker wedding, which although already in motion changed the couple's romantic and family plans.

Among the immigrants I met in Kansas, however, it was only mestizos who reported such romantic ties to citizens even when these romances did not end up in marriages or help shift their status. For example, as we sat in the corner of a fast-food restaurant eating french fries and drinking a coke, Justino, a mestizo Honduran young man who had obtained DACA status as a teen, reflected on a complicated five-year-long relationship with a Mexican American woman.

The young couple had two daughters, both US citizens, and lived together, although they struggled to keep their relationship afloat. Justino said, "Honestly, a lot of stuff has happened. I think that a woman deserves everything, you know? Everything, everything, everything. And as household head, I work to support the family." Justino paused and sat back into his chair. "It hurts, you know? I don't know what she wants. I don't know what her intensions are." Later he continued, "I mean, imagine she has . . . the opportunity to help me, you know? She is a citizen, and she could help me with my situation. And she, in these five years, she hasn't said anything. Even after all the work, all that I do. I mean, she could." As Justino told me, their relationship was not doing great; they struggled to communicate and work together. But he was hurt that his partner and the mother of his two daughters had not offered to help fix his status through marriage, especially since they were already living together as a family. Justino clarified that he would never ask her to do this, "People tell me 'aprovecha [to take advantage].' I think it is not about that; it is about the relationship, how it is going. I am not that type [of person]." Thus, while not all romances with citizens ended up in a shift of status, such as Justino's case, the possibility to do so affected couples' relationship.

The Indigenous immigrants I met had formed romantic relationships with fellow Indigenous immigrants, and all of these romantic partners were similarly undocumented. Thus, segregated romantic relationship formation further reflected legacies of colonialism, as these reified the ethnoracial hierarchies that divided Indigenous and mestizo groups in the diaspora.

Including Carlos and Justino, however, seven of the mestizo immigrants I met were able to shift from undocumented to DACA status. Elena, for instance, had lived in the heartland since she was a child, mostly undocumented. She obtained DACA status months after its announcement in 2012. Elena told me that "DACA opened a new world. [Before DACA] I was here, but I couldn't be." Elena felt that she "had never been able to be exactly part of a real world" until her status changed to DACA. However, DACA remained a temporary protection. Semilegal statuses such as DACA exacerbated liminality because they retained the instability of being undocumented while offering only limited protections in comparison to citizenship.[6] Although the DACA-mented mestizo immigrants I met, such as Elena, gained basic protections for activities such as working and driving, this status provided no long-term stability and left their loved ones undocumented.

Valentina and Ximena, mestiza Mexican sisters, talked to me about their DACA experience. Both grew up in the heartland undocumented until shifting their status to DACA. Valentina said, "It was a big hype of something that could happen, that we could work and get driver's licenses and things like that." The sisters borrowed money from their parents to contract a lawyer and pay for their DACA applications, which were approved. Valentina reflected that "My parents were willing to put in that much amount of money so we could have an opportunity. They did that. I mean, once we actually got it, it was kind of a relief, you know?" Similarly, Ximena, on a different day, talked about her experience with DACA. "Yeah, so it's definitely opened a lot of opportunities for me." She continued, saying "I'm glad that I can make my parents proud in some way because I know that they're struggling too." However, after Donald Trump had won his first presidential election, rumors of DACA's termination were swirling among Valentina and Ximena's peers and in social media. In tears and shaking, Valentina told me:

> For us, DACA expires. It expires in November. I don't know if I'll be able to renew it after that. So, just kind of thinking, like, at the end of this year I'll probably be jobless. I won't be able to help my mom and dad like I did before. I don't know what they're going to do with all the information that they have for us. What's going to happen to everyone? It's just kind of scary thinking about it.

STUCK UNDOCUMENTED

While most of the mestizos I met in Kansas were able to eventually shift their immigration status, nine of their fellow mestizos along with all of the Indigenous immigrants remained "stuck" in their undocumented situation. Magdalena and Teodoro, an Indigenous Mixteco couple, met at work in Kansas, but their hometowns in Mexico are only a few miles apart. They have lived undocumented in Kansas for well over a decade, and their three children—a six-year-old boy, a three-year-old girl, and a one-year-old boy—are all US citizens. As we sat on folding chairs with a telenovela playing in the background in their bare living room, Teodoro talked about the future. "Sometimes I miss Mexico a lot, and I feel unwell," he said. "But maybe when the kids get older, they can help us." Like most Indigenous parents I met, Teodoro and Magdalena hoped that their US-born children could one day sponsor their US status through the family visa program. Despite the mythology of so-called anchor babies, however, immigration policies made the regularization of immigration status via their children almost impossible.[7] For this process to work, citizen children must be at least twenty-one years old and capable of financially supporting their parents. Importantly, if the parents entered the country unauthorized or if were previously deported, they could be facing a reentry ban ranging from three to ten years to even permanent, and it would be almost impossible to adjust their status. And if a parent ever had a removal order or any contact with the criminal legal system, the chances would be even slimmer. If the petition were to be approved, the parents would be first granted a family-based visa and then eventually could apply for legal permanent residency and then eventually apply for naturalization after at least five years with legal permanent resident status.[8] It would thus be decades before most new parents could potentially become citizens, and only then if they had entered and been in the United States continuously with a visa or a semilegal status, highlighting the complexities of family legalization processes.

Although the chances of children successfully sponsoring their parents are slim to none, especially for those who entered the United States unauthorized and lived undocumented, almost none of the Indigenous parents I met were aware of exactly how slim. On the contrary, speculations about this possibility were common. For instance, Catia, an Indigenous Mayan Guatemalan woman, said, "A lady told me that she got her papers, and she has a ten-year-old daughter that applied and she got her papers." Catia was unsure whether this information was true, however. "I would also like to do that, but what if I lose and they deport me?" Other Indigenous parents were similarly ambivalent about the opportunity to be sponsored by their children, yet it remained a hope for the distant future. Laura, an Indigenous Tlapaneco Mexican single mom, shared the same aspiration. Not long before we met, her partner had been deported. Laura hoped that if she kept "doing the right thing" and avoided being apprehended, she could one day gain permanent residency through her daughter and be able to visit her partner in Mexico. Like Laura, many parents told me how they altered their behavior to "do the right thing" or to "stay out of trouble," which often meant avoiding spending time in public spaces as much as possible. Catia also avoided doing "bad things" to avoid deportation and to preserve the possibility of shifting her status. These "bad things" included driving, spending time in public spaces such as stores and parks, and avoiding raising concerns at work. These active strategies in reaction to the law intensify Indigenous women's isolation, limit their mobility, and hinder their ability to seek help when they most need it.

The nine mestizos I met who remained undocumented also had slim chances of changing their immigration status. Liliana, for instance, arrived in the United States unauthorized, following her husband, a construction worker who had been working in the United States for years. Lilliana's husband eventually overstayed his visa and became undocumented, and they also had a daughter born in the United States. Although Liliana was active in the local immigrant community and had built friendships with Latino citizens through Spanish-language religious services and Mexican grocery stores, her undocumented entrance would complicate the future possibility of a family sponsorship once her daughter turns twenty-one.

None of the Indigenous immigrants I spoke to reported having any temporary or semilegal status. One twenty-three-year-old Indigenous Mixteco man, Paco, arrived in the United States as a minor and was eligible for DACA but decided not to apply. Paco was the only Indigenous migrant I met who had graduated from a US high school and attended some college. Despite his DACA eligibility, Paco didn't have the funds or social connections necessary to submit the application, and he also worried about the repercussions of the government having his information if DACA would be terminated. Paco worked as a restaurant cook and saved most of his wages, hoping to one day return to Mexico. "I am not very sure what I want to do," he said, "because I don't have papers, but my dream is to first do my things there, in Mexico." Applying for DACA, he said, would force him to stay in school, whereas his main goal was to ensure the economic stability of his future life in Mexico: "I mean, I don't have it guaranteed to be here. So, my plan is just that."

At least four of the Indigenous immigrants I met could have applied for a U visa, which offers temporary relief for immigrants who suffered a violent crime in the United States. None, however, sought this regularization path.[9] Felipe, for example, an Indigenous Tlapaneco Mexican man, had lived and worked in Kansas for over eight years when he experienced a violent incident at the hands of a coworker. When I was visiting his sister, Victoria, I noticed a car ridden with bullet holes parked in front of their apartment. I came in, and without my asking, Victoria promptly called Felipe to come out of his room to tell me what happened. Felipe and his coworker, a US citizen, had gotten into an argument a couple of nights prior at a local bar. After the argument, Felipe and his Tlapaneco friends drove away from the bar to avoid any potential contact with the police, but the coworker followed. At the stop light, the coworker fired a gun at their car, hitting the passenger side multiple times. Miraculously, nobody was hurt. As Felipe and his friends gathered themselves, a police car appeared. The police took their contact information and left. Days later Felipe found out through his friends from work that the police had apprehended the coworker using surveillance footage from a stop light, and the coworker was charged with attempted murder. Soon after, Felipe received a letter asking him to be a witness in the trial. Victoria insisted that he seek legal guidance, because she had heard about the U visa. However, Felipe doubted that any lawyer would actually help him rather than simply take his money. A few days later his suspicions increased when he tried to make an appointment with a lawyer, recommended by a family friend, and found out that there was a $100 fee for the initial consultation. The lawyer promised to call Felipe back after the consultation but never did.[10] Being undocumented, Felipe knew that his time in the United States was likely limited, and he preferred to save as much hard-earned money as possible rather than potentially lose it all in an uncertain immigration process. Furthermore, he did not feel comfortable testifying in court, as he was worried that Immigration and Customs Enforcement (ICE) could apprehend him there. Felipe was more worried about encountering ICE at the court or near the court building than he was about encountering the coworker who had shot at him. Only a few days after our first conversation, Felipe had already sent his car to the body shop for the bullet holes to be fixed and paid for out of his own pocket. A bullet-ridden car could catch the attention of police when he drove to work, he told me, so it was better to fix the damage quickly.

MIXED-STATUS FAMILIES

Most immigrants I met had families with a variety of immigration statuses, including citizenship, undocumented, DACA, and other semilegal statuses. In the United States, approximately 16.7 million people live with at least one undocumented family member in the same household, and Kansas has one of the highest rates of naturalized citizens living with undocumented relatives.[11] Heartland states are home to a growing number of mixed-status families, where different individual statuses—and thus the distribution of associated rights—profoundly shape power dynamics between couples, parents, children, and other family members.[12] Importantly, this affects families' access to resources and their social mobility.[13]

Undocumented Parents

Almost all the Indigenous immigrants I met in Kansas were parents to at least one US citizen. Among the mestizo immigrants, nineteen were parents to citizens or DACAmented youths. Importantly, the exclusions faced by undocumented parents—regarding work, housing, health care, and driving—trickled down to their children, even when these children were citizens.[14] Vicente, a mestizo Mexican man, explained these difficulties and frustrations. "My children are US citizens," he said, indignantly. "Why don't they have the right to live in a house? Why do they have to live in an apartment if I can pay for a house? It is because I don't have papers that my children can't live in a house. And they are citizens; they deserve to live in a house. It is because I don't have papers. That is the only reason." Laura Enriquez has termed this kind of intrafamilial effect "multigenerational punishment,"[15] in which undocumented and semilegal parents' status impacts their citizen children's well-being and potential for upward mobility.

While some parents acknowledged the limitations their children faced due to the parents' undocumented status, most Indigenous parents also emphasized the many opportunities that US citizenship afforded their children. In these instances, Indigenous parents compared their children's situation—born in the United States and raised in Kansas—to their own often impoverished childhoods abroad. Dolores, for example, an Indigenous Mixteco Mexican mom of six US citizens, repeatedly told me that she often reminded her children of their relative privilege. "They have a school here, they have clothes, they have shoes. We didn't even have shoes when I was growing up." Dolores grew up in extreme poverty in Mexico, reflecting the lingering colonial dispossession of Indigenous groups in Latin America. Although her family also faced economic challenges in Kansas, Dolores frequently reminded her children that "Being poor here is not the same as being poor there."

Elisa, an Indigenous Tlapaneco mom, echoed this sentiment. "The benefits that the children receive are a great advantage, because sometimes there in Mexico, well, we don't have the same benefits that they have here." She said to me "Health insurance, especially this, yes. Also being able to have childcare. They help you pay part of this, and you pay the other part; in Mexico you must pay for everything. My daughter receives childcare and WIC." Elisa was the only immigrant who described receiving financial support to pay for childcare. However, some of the less financially stable families also described utilizing Women, Infant, and Children (WIC) benefits for their US-born children. In such instances, however, mothers always emphasized that these benefits were for their children and not for their personal use. Dolores, for instance, mentioned that her children qualified for a government-subsidized cell phone but that she only used that phone to make her children's health care appointments.[16] Indigenous moms, who were more likely to use these resources for their children, would mention in informal conversations with me that they did not want the government to think they were personally using the benefits. Furthermore, moms worried that using subsidized programs, even those that citizen children qualified for, could one day affect their chances of shifting their immigration status.

Undocumented mothers who were more financially stable and mestizas such as Celestina refused to use these services altogether even when their children qualified for the programs. Celestina said, "We don't ask them for help. We don't ask the government for money. There are some places they can say you can apply for food stamps, but no. Thanks to God my husband has a job. I don't want one day for them [the government] to say that they [government] are sustaining me." She clarified as we enjoyed the delicious meal she had prepared. "My daughters have their health insurance because it is their right." Both are US citizens, she said, "But I never ask for anything. For what, so they will ask for it later?"

Immigrant mothers' fears and worries that the government would ask undocumented parents to repay subsidized aid for their citizen children were also discussed in the waiting area when I volunteered at a health clinic. This topic was also common in the news during my fieldwork due to the Trump administration's changes to the Public Charge Rule, first proposed in mid-2018, that would eventually become a rule change by 2019.[17] The 2019 Public Charge Rule changes expanded the definition of who is considered a "public charge" under immigration processes, redefining eligibility for legal permanent residency and other visas. However, given misinformation and disinformation, immigrants I met were confused about what this would mean for them and their children. As a result, many, such as Celestina, opted to avoid any government-funded benefit if possible.

Undocumented parents in mixed-status families across ethnoracial lines were worried about the possibility of being deported, and what would happen to their children. Gerardo and Elena, a mestizo couple with mixed statuses when we first met—Gerardo was undocumented, Elena had DACA status, and both were parents to US citizen children—discussed their fears of possible deportation. Elena remembered a conversation they had a few days earlier. "I told him, because it is very real, it can happen at any time. I told him, 'Look, if one day they arrest you and deport you, well, I can move to my mom's house, sell the cars, keep working. And no matter what, I promise that I will bring you back." Later in the conversation, Gerardo reflected, "We are a big family. My children are big. Do they think that if I get deported or my wife that we would leave my children here? We think about it." Like Elena and Gerardo, undocumented and semilegal parents across ethnoracial backgrounds considered the ramifications of the possibility of apprehension and deportation, and for some this was an actual reality, which they could mediate according to the resources they had.

Sitting on her pistachio-green couch in her living room, Carolina, an Indigenous Tlapaneco Mexican woman, told me the story of her husband Miguel's detention and ultimately how it impacted their son, Mateo, a US citizen. Talking nervously and in a soft voice, Carolina said, "He [Miguel] was punished, and now I don't know when they will send him to Mexico. Next month it will be a year, and I don't know anymore; he must be in Louisiana now. Since he went inside I have not seen him." A year prior, Carolina's husband was detained while driving and eventually charged with driving under the influence. This made it almost impossible for Carolina to bail him out of jail before he was moved into immigrant detention. Carolina was most worried about her son, Mateo. "My son cries and cries. He wants to go see him, but I can't take him," she confided.

Fidgeting with her hands, Carolina explained that it was difficult to find a way to get Mateo to see her husband safely without putting herself at risk of detention, since she also was undocumented. She recounted the conversation she had with a lawyer who was helping with Miguel's case:

> I told her, "I want to go visit my husband, what is the address?" And she told me "I can find the address and I can tell you where he is, but you can't go because you don't have papers." She told me "Your son can go because he was born here, but you need someone who was born here to take your son."

Carolina then reached out to a local pastor to ask him to take Mateo to visit his dad in the detention center. "But he never reached back, and then when the time came [Miguel] was moved, and now . . . They took him to Louisiana, and now I don't know when they will take him out to Mexico." A common practice by ICE has involved moving immigrants to isolated areas where detention centers are located, which makes it even more difficult for mixed-status families to stay in contact. Carolina went on to talk about the challenges of even trying to call Miguel:

> I don't have enough money to pay, because one time he called me, and I had to pay to receive the phone call. I don't have enough money anymore. He sometimes buys a phone card or they give him a phone card and he calls, for three minutes or four minutes, and that is all to talk with my son because I don't have enough money. I am paying for my son's school [in Mexico], and I am paying here [in Kansas], and how am I going to have enough money? I don't have enough for anything.

Carolina struggled to keep her family financially afloat while also dealing with the emotional toll that Mateo faced from the detainment and eventual removal of his father.

Mestizo families also experienced detention and deportation in some cases. However, for the most part they were able to mediate this suffering through their networks by accessing resources to reunify their families as was the case for Celestina, whose deportation through a workplace raid was detailed in Chapter 3. Celestina had a six-month-old daughter in the United States and could not stand to leave her baby behind. "So, I came back," she told me. "I walked back all night, but I came back on a Wednesday." Celestina remembered, "I had a keychain with her picture, and that is all. I was afraid to walk through the mountains, but I asked for my daughter to give me the strength." Celestina, with the financial support of her husband who remained in the United States, was able to come back to the heartland after just one week. This separation was nevertheless traumatizing, Celestina recalled. "I came back dirty and ugly, and my daughter . . . I wanted her to hug me, and no. She thought I was not her mom. I cried because my daughter didn't recognize me."

Given the ethnoracial segregation of immigrants' networks and their varying access to resources, Indigenous and mestizo families had different tools to manage apprehensions and deportations. When deported, not everyone was able to come back, and when apprehended, not everyone was able to get their loved ones out prior to deportation. Erica, a mestiza Honduran woman with Temporary Protected Status, and her husband José, a mestizo Mexican man, had a blended family of four—including Erica's oldest son, who had DACA, and three young US citizen children. José was in the process of getting his legal permanent resident status, but for most of his time in the heartland he had lived undocumented. Erica recounted a frightening phone conversation with her husband when he was apprehended by ICE during a work trip. "My husband said, 'You know what, Erica, immigration arrested me.' I told him, 'Don't be playing, don't be joking.' 'Seriously, immigration got me.'" She then said, "I didn't know English or who could help me." Erica mobilized all the resources she could think of to compile the $6,500 for the bond to bail him out. "I had a van. I pawned it with a woman, and she gave me $1,000. Then my brother had no money, but he gave me $500. A friend let me borrow $300, then my husband's friend lends us $1,000, and another lends us $500." Borrowing from friends and family, she eventually raised the $6,500. "They apprehended him over the weekend, so I had to have the $6,500 by Monday. It is a lot of money." José was apprehended with his coworker, who had two US citizen children. Together Erica and the coworker's citizen children drove thirteen hours to the ICE office to pay the bond. Erica explained that she was very lucky that the sons of the coworker were US citizens, since they had driver's licenses to make the trip, and they also spoke English fluently.

While the apprehensions and deportations of Indigenous and mestizo immigrants may take place in different contexts, their families' ability or lack thereof to mobilize resources in response to these apprehensions is significant, as reflected by the experiences of many mestizo and Indigenous migrants described above.

Mixed-Status Youths

While parents' undocumented status can negatively impact their children's lives, their children's citizenship and semilegal statuses can bring a family new advantages—as well as new responsibilities for these youths. In Kansas this was most visible in mestizo families, possibly due to their children's older ages. Indigenous parents' citizen children were below the age of thirteen, while many of the citizen and DACAmented children of mestizo parents were in their late teens and early twenties. Reinalda, a mestizo Ecuadorian woman, had an eighteen-year-old DACAmented daughter, Olivia, and an eleven-year-old US citizen son, Abel. Once Olivia turned eighteen and received DACA, although this status is not permanent, it alleviated Reinalda's worries about the risks that she and her husband faced while driving. Chatting inside a church, Reinalda shared about her relief. "The girl has her license, so obviously when we travel, we pray and trust in God, and we are very careful in case that . . ." As she took a deep breath, she went on. "Because when one doesn't have a driver's license, you drive more carefully, because you never know if something is going to happen or if the police will pull you over. But we go prepared that in case something happens, we can be driving and say you drive, and she drives. She is our lifesaver." As in Reinalda's family, shifting status for the youths meant added family responsibilities and changing family roles. Reinalda continued. "I have always told her, for instance, when I go somewhere, if the police ever grab me, God willing nothing will happen, but there are a lot of people that they take. I tell her, 'Look, if something happens to me, don't worry, don't cry, just go and take care of your brother.'"

Like Reinalda's daughter, youths with citizenship or semilegal status had to be prepared in case their undocumented parents were deported. Unsurprisingly, youths who had a chance to shift their status through DACA continued to worry about the possibility of their parents' deportation. I chatted with León, a mestizo Mexican, in his two-bedroom apartment that he shared with a college friend. He was studying fashion design in the local community college. León said,

> Once I got my DACA, it relieved so much weight off my shoulders, but I still worried about my mom. My mom is still my main focus, and I still feel we were able to take weight off our shoulders, but she wasn't. It's harder to see. I feel like now it's more like if something happens, they're taking my mom away. When we were little, it was like they're going to take us all away, so we'll just end up in Mexico, which was . . . We don't want to be deported, but we'll be as a family. Now it's kind of like I have my family in the United States, my own education, my career and everything, but then I have my mom too. If she gets taken away, I'm gonna divide in two. That is what still scares me at the moment.

In tears and catching his breath, León continued. "If they took my mom away it would just be a big hit to me." Similarly, Ximena, one of the mestizo Mexican DACA sisters, reflected on her parents' lack of protection, also in tears as she shared:

> But you kind of forget that your parents are not okay. It's kind of on the back of your mind, just thinking, like, I'm okay but my mom and dad might

not be. I don't know. It's kind of hard because you can't really do anything about it. So you just kind of think about it and feel sad. You kind of have to remind yourself that you're not in the best situation either, but if anything was to happen, you're probably the support that your parents need.

As these cases demonstrate, a shift to semilegal status does not always provide an easy solution to mixed-status families' complex circumstances. Besides worrying about their parents' potential deportation, youths with liminal status often took on new family responsibilities and new worries about having to carry on without their parents in case they were to be deported.

Additionally, undocumented youths also had to deal with the possibility of being apprehended and deported and separated from their families. This was the experience for Hugo, a young mestizo Mexican man who arrived in the United States at age two with his parents. He had lived in the heartland almost his entire life and was deported around age twenty-two. Talking in a dark living room with sports playing on the large TV, he recounted what happened: "I got in trouble right after I turned eighteen," Hugo told me as he turned away from me. "I got caught with some marijuana. Eventually I got in trouble again and was handed over that time to immigration. I was released. I fought the case, I want to say about two years, but eventually because of the marijuana possession, I want to say it was an aggravated felony under immigration law, and so I was deported." Taking a deep breath, Hugo concluded, "I was just young and dumb. . . . I was deported." With charges being retroactive in immigration law, although Hugo had already served time in the criminal legal system for the marijuana possession as a minor, he was still deported on the same charge and as an adult even years after the initial conviction.

Hugo arrived in Mexico with little memory or ties to family or place. "I was with cousins I had never met, so I just felt like a stranger. So, it was really tough to get adjusted. I never really adjusted. I always felt out of place. People, from my accent they could tell I wasn't from there," he recounted. After eight months and feeling homesick, Hugo returned to the United States with some money he saved from working at a call center in Mexico City, a big labor market for deportees, and with support from his family in the United States. He undertook the treacherous unauthorized journey across the desert, and even years after returning he had nightmares about the journey, having to walk through the desert in the dark and being afraid of being caught by Border Patrol.

Further attesting to how immigration law is internalized by immigrants themselves, although Hugo tried to distance himself from the "bad immigrant" stereotype, he nevertheless blamed himself for his deportation:

> I would get really down sometimes and then angry with myself because I knew a lot of the things that I got in trouble for were just dumb things. It's not like I was out robbing people, stuff like that. It was just petty things. You're in high school, you're out drinking with friends, and it's stuff that happens. And then just to get deported over it, you're just mad at yourself because it changes your entire life.

Sibling Relationships

The diverse set of rights and protections associated with immigration status created inequities and sometimes tensions between siblings. Hugo's siblings in the Rodriguez family ranged in ages and statuses: the oldest sister and Hugo were undocumented, Olga had DACA status, and two younger siblings, Lily and Simón, were born in the United States and had citizenship. I met Olga in her Frida Kahlo–inspired bachelorette apartment. She invited me to sit on a sofa decorated with Día de los Muertos–themed pillows, told Lily, her youngest sister, to bring us two glasses of water and then asked her to leave us alone for our conversation. "We're all very different," Olga began. "We all get along in our ways, yeah. And of course, she's like the baby," pointing at

Lily, who had disappeared into Olga's room. Olga had very high hopes and expectations for Lily, given Lily's full citizenship rights that Olga, undocumented in the United States from age three and now holding DACA status, had never had. "I do get frustrated with that," Olga confessed, referring to her siblings' citizenship status, "Cause that's the citizen here and we do talk about this with him all the time, and he gets mad at us," referring to his younger brother, Simón. "And even with her [Lily] I talk to her and I'm really honest with her when it comes to things like this. And I always tell her 'Hey, just so you know, you're a citizen here, you can do what you want to do if you want to do it.'" Olga reflected on the difficulties she had experienced doing basic things that her citizen siblings did not have to worry about. "For me especially, it takes, like, to get this apartment, it took like fifty steps where like a normal person it took like two steps, you know. With her [Lily] it's just like two seconds, you know, two steps like, here's an apartment." Olga went on to explain:

> So, I get very frustrated with my twenty-two-year-old [brother, Simón] because he's not very motivated to do anything. Like, he is very motivated to live with my mom and dad, and I'm like "[Simón], when are you going to go back to school?" Like, "What are you thinking about?" Like, "What are you going to do with your life?" He's very comfortable with his life. And I'm just like "You have all these tools in front of you that you can use; you're a citizen. You could get grants, and you can apply for scholarships and loans, and like all these things that could help you. Like, in school and not even in school, like in so many ways." So many opportunities and they're just like throwing it away.

Olga compared Simón's opportunities to the struggles she faced to try to finish school:

> I can't really apply for financial aid because, you know, I was illegal, and they wouldn't accept my financials thing. So, I always had to work a whole bunch of crazy hours just to make sure that school was paid for. So, it's

always just kinda, like, frustrating. Darn, why does my life have to be like this? And he has it just like, whatever. You know? I'm working, I'm fine, I have a house and food and all that.

Later in the interview, Olga also recollected the difficulties when her brother Hugo was deported. It was a big hit for the entire family, she remembered. But because Hugo's deportation caused too much discomfort, she preferred to not go too much into detail during our conversation.

In a separate conversation, Hugo echoed Olga's thoughts about their brother Simón. "I try to motivate my brother because. He's a citizen, and I don't know if he's motivated to do anything with it more now. He just works. He wanted to be a police officer, but I feel like he could work a little more." Hugo admitted that "If I had the opportunity, if I was a citizen, I would take advantage of it. I wouldn't waste my time. So yeah, I hope, I try to push him, but he's kind of a quiet guy." Reflecting on his citizen siblings, Hugo confided, "I'm happy that they don't have to live the life that I'm stuck with."

I did not get a chance to meet Simón, so we do not know his side of this story or how he felt about his siblings' lack of citizenship or his brother's deportation. The Rodriguez siblings, however, show us that legal consciousness also creeps into sibling relationships. It is true that citizens have access to greater economic and educational opportunities than undocumented immigrants, and it is also true that citizens do not face the legal exclusions around work and housing, for example, that undocumented migrants encounter. The perception of Simón's choice as a purely individual decision, however, also obscured structural inequities of immigration law that left members of mixed-status families at the margins of society, even impacting those who are citizens.

As noted, all of the Indigenous immigrants I met in Kansas as well as all of their siblings and adult family members were undocumented. As a result, legal consciousness manifested differently in Indigenous sibling relationships. They relied heavily on each other to orchestrate complex migration processes and navigate daily life in the United States. Sibling relationships were especially important because most Indigenous immigrants did not have parents in the United States—unlike several of the mestizo migrants who had arrived as children and youths.[18]

Sofia arrived in Kansas with the help of her older brother and sister, who were already living and working in the heartland. When she and I met to talk, Sofia lived with her brother, her brother's coworker, and the coworker's one-year-old son, a US citizen. Sofia's sister also lived nearby and frequently visited. "Sometimes in the evenings I visit my sister, since she is also alone," Sofia told me. "That way he [the baby] can play and go out. Sometimes my sister helps me with childcare; we help each other." Like Sofia, Carolina also lived with her brother. "We live together, but he is almost never here," she said. "Sometimes he helps me a little bit [to pay the bills] because I don't have enough. He works in the [factory], so he is almost never here."

Indigenous sibling relationships were also very important in navigating brushes with immigration enforcement, even when financial resources were too limited. When Felipe survived the car shooting discussed earlier, his older sister Victoria encouraged him to meet an attorney and pursue a U visa. On another serious occasion she again came to his aid, reaching out to her social network when Felipe was apprehended in the middle of the night while driving. However, Victoria's Indigenous Tlapaneco and undocumented social network had few economic resources to spare. Unable to pay bail, Felipe was quickly placed on an ICE detainer and weeks later was sent to an ICE facility while Victoria continued to search for help. Eventually Victoria found a lawyer with the help of a fellow Tlapaneco friend. It transpired that the ICE bond was set at $25,000—an exceptionally high amount that the family and their wider network simply could not afford. Although her efforts could not free Felipe, Victoria still helped to mediate his eventual deportation by coordinating with their family in Mexico and by sending money to her family in preparation for his arrival.

CONCLUSION

Immigrants' accounts reveal how immigration law was interpreted and internalized through their legal consciousness. This was seen in their hopes for shifting their status, in their experiences of being "stuck" undocumented, and in the expectations placed on family relationships. Through this internalized legal consciousness, immigration policies shaped the daily behaviors of immigrants and relationships with their loved ones. Thus, the internalization of illegality altered immigrants' sense of self and their relationships with relatives and friends, shaping romantic decisions, parenting practices, and sibling dynamics.

Although Indigenous and mestizos alike hoped to one day be able to shift their status, the potential for changing their immigration status was very limited, given legislation that denied a path to citizenship to anyone who entered the country without authorization or lived undocumented in the United States for more than a few months. However, as seen in Chapter 1, given the ongoing colonial legacies that shape immigrants' journeys to and forms of entry into the United States, these mechanisms were further cemented the longer migrants stayed in the United States. Only immigrants who entered with a visa then had an (admittedly slim) chance at legalization. As we saw in previous chapters, visa requirements are rooted in colonial hierarchies of economic status, prestige, class position, and educational achievement. Thus, immigrants excluded from bank accounts, pushed out of schools, and denied access to their birth documentation or with long-established networks of undocumented migration were cast as ineligible to enter the country "legally" in the first place. As such from the moment migrants arrived, they began their lives in the United States on an unequal footing. These divides were then further cemented with time living in the heartland, when immigrants started romantic relationships and created families.

Most immigrants I met in Kansas were members of a mixed-status family. One family member's undocumented status directly and indirectly affected the wider family, even when other family members were citizens or had marginal protections. This uneven distribution of rights and protections created tension between mixed-status siblings and placed new responsibilities on citizen and DACAmented youths. Undocumented parents and youths faced the reality of possible detention and deportation, which had direct impacts on their loved ones' well-being.[19] Indigenous and mestizo parents and family members had access to different sets of resources with which to manage the ramifications of deportability.

Shifting one's immigration status brought protections and rights to immigrants and their families even if the new status was temporary and liminal. However, despite the enormous relief and security it provided, immigration status alone was not the sole marker of social mobility (or lack thereof) among immigrants living in the heartland. As Chapter 6 will show, Indigenous and mestizo immigrants and their families alike must *seguir adelante* (move on, get ahead) within a growing anti-immigrant context, where immigration status—and its associated legal consciousness—profoundly affected how immigrants internalized their relative mobility or stagnation.

6

"VOY A SALIR ADELANTE"

Strategies to Get Ahead

AS WE SAT in her dining room table, toward the end of the conversation Erica, a mestiza woman, reflected on her life. She had fled gender violence in Honduras and endured a dangerous journey while pregnant, and now, years later, we sat in a spacious house, which she and her husband, a mestizo Mexican man, owned. Taking a deep breath, she looked out the window and said, *"Diosito me ha dado chance de salir adelante, y sacarlos adelante* [God has given me the chance to get ahead and to get my children ahead]."

On a very different day, Justina, an Indigenous Maya Guatemalan woman, and I sunk into an old couch in the trailer that she and her husband rented. Reflecting on her experiences of attempting and failing to get asylum for her and her oldest son, who was only a toddler when we first met, she revealed that she nevertheless would do what she could to get ahead in her new life in the heartland. She told me when concluding our chat, *"Pero a ver cómo voy a salir adelante.* [We will see how I can get ahead]."

When reflecting on their past and thinking about their hopes and dreams, the mestizo and Indigenous immigrants I met in the heartland frequently used the phrase *salir adelante* (to get ahead). In examining how immigrants *salen adelante*, this chapter critically considers how they navigate, resist, and overcome barriers in their formal education and employment, the two social institutions that immigration scholars consider vital to integration and that immigrants themselves see as key for improving their lives and getting ahead in the heartland. First, I examine immigrants' educational journeys, exploring their learning aspirations and the obstacles they encountered. Ethnoracial divides were immediately apparent here. While many mestizo immigrants discussed their experiences of the K–12 school system and US colleges, only one of the Indigenous immigrants I met had graduated from a US high school. The other Indigenous immigrants, including those who arrived in the United States as youths, had left education relatively early in favor of employment.[1] Second, I delve into immigrants' work trajectories. While in Chapter 3 I examined the barriers immigrants encountered when finding work and the violence that they experienced at work, in this chapter we learn from immigrants' work trajectories and their strategies for *salir adelante* through work, despite past obstacles or abuses. Across both social institutions, mestizo and Indigenous immigrants' accounts of *luchar para salir adelante* (striving to get ahead) reveal the ongoing presence of colonial legacies as ethnoracial background intersect with gender, immigration status, and socioeconomic background to shape their internalization of success and failure.

EDUCATIONAL JOURNEYS

In the United States, Latina/o/x college students typically come from lower-income families, are the first in their families to attend college, and have a lower rate of degree completion than other demographic groups.[2] Increasingly, however, Latino immigrants have arrived in the United States already in possession of a college degree.[3] While undocumented and semilegal students graduate from US high schools at comparable rates to their US citizen counterparts, they have a much lower rate of college enrollment.[4] They encounter financial barriers, the stigma of being undocumented, and having to cope with their own deportability as well as the deportability of their family members.[5] Importantly, place does matter in regard to access higher education while undocumented due to state-level immigration policies, among other institutional barriers. In Kansas, undocumented and DACA-mented students who graduate from a Kansas high school were eligible for in-state tuition during the period of the study. However, there were no opportunities for state-sponsored financial aid, and there were no policies that expanded access to state occupational licenses for undocumented immigrants after graduation.[6] Furthermore, ethnoracial background intersected in immigrants' educational journeys. Indigenous scholars have called attention to the anti-Indigenous discrimination that Indigenous immigrant students encounter from their peers and teachers in the school system in the United States.[7] And I find that most Indigenous youths were pulled and pushed out of formal educational opportunities while living in the heartland.

Pulled and Pushed Out of School

Almost all the Indigenous immigrants I met in Kansas had been pulled out or pushed out of the US education system due to competing financial pressures and, for women, parenting expectations. Nevertheless, Esperanza, an Indigenous Maya Guatemalan young woman, viewed both school and work as avenues to *salir adelante*. "I am an adult now," she told me, although she was just twenty years old. "I don't have any diplomas or certificates, because I did not study." Esperanza had no educational opportunities in Guatemala and had focused on work after moving to the United States and attempting to seek asylum. "I would like to go somewhere where adults can study or where they teach English," she continued. "I wanted to learn English; maybe I can." Looking down at her baby girl, who laid gently asleep in a circle of fluffy pillows and soft blankets, Esperanza said, "Here I am alone with her [the baby], and sometimes, I think, how am I going to go to school? I have to work." Although Esperanza hoped to one day attend school, the responsibilities of being a young new mom to provide financial support for her daughter came first. She also faced added barriers. "I don't even have a car," she confided, adding to the challenges of navigating work and the possibility of school. Nevertheless, she looked back at me and firmly stated, *"Pero voy a salir adelante."*

While like Esperanza some Indigenous immigrants hoped to one day go back to school, others set multigenerational goals for their kids to achieve an education in Kansas, something that Alejandro, Maya Guatemalan, could not realize himself. "Here, they [children] have more opportunities. I mean, they can study, learn a lot. There [in Guatemala] you don't learn a lot; it is different. Here there is an opportunity for them. That is why *voy a luchar* [I will strive]." Talking about his kids' future, Alejandro went on: "They can decide what they want to be: a lawyer or a professional." Echoing Alejandro, Dolores, a Mixteco Mexican woman, shared her hopes for her children: "They can have a good job if they study and have a better future than what we had. They can enjoy life."

Most of the twenty-one Indigenous immigrants I met in Kansas arrived in the United States between the ages of thirteen and seventeen and did so without their parents. The primary migratory motivation for all Indigenous youths was economic—to help support their families back home and their newly formed families in the heartland. As we learned in Chapter 3, most Indigenous immigrants found jobs promptly after arriving instead of enrolling in the formal K–12 education system.[8]

However, three of the Indigenous immigrants I met—Dolores, Facunda, and Paco—had varying experiences in K–12 public schools in the heartland. Their stories demonstrate the complexities of educational attainment for Indigenous undocumented youths who migrate without their parents to the heartland.[9]

Dolores came to the United States at age thirteen with her much older husband. Prior to her life in Kansas, Dolores had received just a few years of formal schooling in her isolated Mixteco community in Mexico. By the time we met when Dolores was twenty-six years old, her living room wall was decorated with family pictures of her six children, a painting of the Virgin of Guadalupe, and a blanket with detailed embroidery of the Last Supper. Another picture, next to the front door, showed Dolores with a big smile holding a sign that read "[Kansas] High School." At age eighteen, with the help of a bilingual social worker whom she met during her first pregnancy, Dolores enrolled in a Kansas public high school and studied there for two years, learning basic English. She talked about this period as the "best time" of her life. Dolores had hoped to graduate from her high school and continue her education. However, she was pushed out of school: "The teachers talked, and the principal decided it was impossible," she recounted. "When one doesn't have papers, they can do whatever they want." She said that "If they would have given me the opportunity, I would have finished."

Four months short of finishing high school and a few weeks before her twenty-first birthday, Dolores was told that she had to leave school and that if she wanted to complete her degree "I would have to do it here, at home," she said. "But I don't know how to use the computer, and we don't even have internet." Dolores was aging out of K–12 as her twenty-first birthday approached. However, in her family in Mexico and in the heartland, no one had attended high school, let alone a US public school. Thus, she would be on her own trying to navigate online classes from home.[10] She would have to do this in addition to her mothering duties and with scare resources—lacking a computer and the internet—since she and her husband struggled to make ends meet. Finishing school, Dolores concluded, would be impossible. Nevertheless, she remembered this period of her life and was glad of what she gained while at school: some English skills and friendships. "But with English *he salido adelante*," she told me.

Facunda had a very different experience with the K–12 system. Originally from a Maya community in Guatemala, Facunda arrived in the United States at age sixteen as an unaccompanied minor. She was apprehended at the border and later released into her father's care, after which she enrolled in high school. Many undocumented youths who had entered the United States as unaccompanied minors seeking asylum told me that they had heard that enrolling in school instead of getting a job would improve their chances of asylum approval. Following this rumor, Facunda had enrolled in a public school shortly after she arrived. However, things did not go smoothly. "I went to school four months or five months I think, then I left school. I didn't want to go. I told my dad, 'I don't want to go.'" Facunda went on to share her main reason for leaving school: "I don't understand, because all they speak is English, and *no puedo* [I can't]." K'iche' is Facunda's first langugage, and she arrived in the United States with limited Spanish and no knowledge of English. Additionally, she had received no formal education in Guatemala. Facunda's goal in the United States was to get a job and send remittances back to Guatemala to support her eldest child, whom she had left in her mother's care. In her efforts to *salir adelante*, a job was therefore more important than attending school. However, lacking language skills and adequate teaching, Facunda was deterred from pursuing an education that might have advanced her longer-term job and earning prospects.

Dolores and Facunda were both young moms when they enrolled in high school, and these gendered mothering roles also competed with their educational experiences. Dolores's son lived with her in Kansas during her time at school. While she had help from relatives when she attended school, she had to fulfill childcare responsibilities before and after classes. Facunda's daughter lived in Guatemala, and upholding her daughter's financial well-being involved mothering care work from afar, mainly sending remittances.[11] Thus, for these two Indigenous women, their mothering roles further affected their school experiences, as school competed with both parental responsibilities and financial opportunities. Dolores and Facunda spoke limited Spanish and no English upon arrival to the heartland. Places such as the heartland did not always have appropriate English-language instruction for non-English speakers. Indigenous students also may have encountered anti-Indigenous discrimination at school.[12] While neither Dolores, Facunda, or Paco, whose story is shared below, reported experiencing anti-Indigenous discrimination, this is another potentially camouflaged structural "push" factor to bear in mind.

Paco, an Indigenous Mixteco Mexican young man, was the only Indigenous immigrant I met in Kansas who had graduated from a US high school. He migrated alone, arriving with an uncle in hopes of working and saving money for his family back home. "I turned fourteen, and then, well, I owed my uncle [who] paid the money for me [to come to the United States]. So, I was looking for a job or something, no? But nobody wanted to give me work because they said to work . . . They said that I was a minor." Despite his young age, Paco eventually convinced his uncle to help him find a job in a restaurant kitchen washing dishes. At work is where Paco found the information and resources to enroll in school. He explained, "I met a guy, a coworker. He came and started in the high school. He called me. He said if I wanted to study, he said, 'If you can come here, we can help you, I just started.' And I said, 'sounds good.'" With the help of his coworker, Paco enrolled in a local high school and continued to work in the restaurant after school and on the weekends. In the following months, he switched schools three times. He had to move whenever he could find a job, which occurred either because he needed to avoid immigration enforcement or to secure higher wages. Paco completed his schoolwork and tried to never miss class, and, unlike his coworker, eventually graduated. He recalled,

> Sometimes I am very shy, a little at first. I stayed very quiet when I was there [in school], but my teacher would try to talk with me. She would give me candy. And it was fun. I started to talk more, and later . . . Sometimes yes, I felt embarrassed, but later I got used to them [English-speaking classmates]. That is when I started talking. Some [students] spoke Spanish, so I talk more. Later I felt that I did not speak very well in English, but I was not shy anymore. That is when I started meeting more friends, I mean, the ones that spoke English.

Paco enjoyed school, and after graduating from high school he soon enrolled in a local community college, earning a scholarship to fund his education. However, he encountered obstacles in his path:

> I had bad luck. I liked it a lot [college]. You have to right away pay a lot of attention to the teachers. That's it, I liked it a lot. I had my first semester, and I passed. And I was going to start the next semester, but I had bad luck. They stole my car, and then I couldn't travel to work and to school [college], so I had to stop going.

Losing his car was tragic, as it prevented Paco from being able to drive between class and work. This accumulated to another unlucky event. Paco told me that at the time he was couch surfing, living part-time with his uncle and part-time with friends. Paco's funding letter for the second semester was sent to his uncle's house, and he received it after the acceptance deadline had passed. The series of events that Paco attributed to "bad luck" are reflective of the cumulative barriers that undocumented youths who grow up in the United States without parents encountered, many of whom are Indigenous.[13]

As we learned in Chapter 5, Paco was the only Indigenous immigrant I met who qualified for DACA but did not apply. He was too mistrustful of what the government would do with his information.

Paco's undocumented status and potential deportability fueled his ambivalence about formal education, especially given the Trump administration's anti-immigration measures at the time that heightened immigrants' worries of a future in the United States. Paco's immediate focus was to work—trying to save as much money as possible to support a future return to Mexico, whenever that would be.

Navigating School Barriers

Eighteen mestizo immigrants I met had arrived in the United States between the ages of two and seventeen, traveling with their parents and siblings. Immigrant youths raised in the United States from an early age are considered to belong to the 1.5 generation: growing up partly in the United States and partly in their home country.[14] Ximena, a mestiza Mexican woman who arrived in the United States at age seven, shared her experience of the US public school system. "I was in second grade in Mexico, but they were like 'Oh, if you can't speak English, you have to go back to first grade.'" Getting moved to a lower grade level due to lack of English proficiency was common for non-English-speaking students. Ximena had high expectations of obtaining a college degree:

> Like [in] junior high and high school, they would ask me, like, 'What do you wanna major in when you go to college?" And all these influences of like it's the normal thing to do. My mom and dad both have bachelor's degrees in chemical engineering, so they're both educated people. They know the value of an education and that getting that is very important. So, they've always stressed that above anything else.

Like Ximena, many undocumented mestizo youths described educational achievement as something their parents expected, encouraged, and supported. Emilia, a mestiza from Chile who migrated at age five with her parents, told me, "I feel like it was an expectation in my household, at least from my mom. My mom was like 'You're going to college.'" Emilia grew up in a mixed-status family, and her own status had shifted between undocumented and semilegal. When we met, she was already in college with ambitions to become a political leader. Rita, a mestizo Salvadoran college student, echoed Ximena and Emilia. "Since I was little, that has always been our goal," Rita said of achieving a college degree. "Our parents would tell us that everything they do is for us; you can pay us with your studies. I love going to classes and all of that, but we do it to pay back our parents, [for] all that they have done. They have sacrificed too much; it has been difficult." As Rita illustrated, educational attainment—and a college degree in particular—was a multigenerational aspiration for mestizo immigrants, just as it is for Indigenous immigrants. In the mestizo case, however, educational attainment acquired an additional layer of meaning, framed as a child's way of "repaying" their parents' sacrifice of undocumented migration.

Many undocumented and semilegal mestizo youths, however, had limited resources for navigating the US higher education system—exacerbated by the fact that many were first-generation college students whose parents had never attended university in either the United States or their country of origin. Carlos, a mestizo Honduran man who grew up mostly as the only undocumented person in a mixed-status family, explained his situation:

> I was the first one of my entire family. They didn't have no sense of how to apply or anything like that; I had no idea. Because my counselors, you get to high school and all these counselors are like trained and professional, but whenever they get to a population of people that are different from white society, they didn't know how to handle my situation. They told me, there is nothing else that you can do. They told me, you might have to look into job opportunities and stuff like that. What am I going to do? There was a point in my senior year that I was like, why should I graduate? What is the point?

Like Carlos, many undocumented high school students struggled to find information about the college process. As a result, undocumented youths could become discouraged from pursuing a higher education. Although Kansas high school graduates qualified for in-state college tuition, in the absence of other forms of financial aid, college could be prohibitively expensive for undocumented students. Given the risks of disclosing their undocumented status, many students also felt anxious and worried if they discussed their situation with teachers or counselors who could potentially help. "There are no [scholarships] for me," Rita explained. "I remember, one day I went to [the Spanish teacher] and cried. I cried and I cried, and I told her everything. I told her my fear: That I don't have papers. I was afraid. I don't know why I was afraid, I didn't feel comfortable there, so I talked to her and shared my situation, that I couldn't apply for scholarships."

When undocumented students could not find resources through their schools, they sought information from their peers instead. Carlos recalled, "I came across [a local immigrant rights organization], and a lot of members of the organization had gone through that same scenario and they were like, 'Okay, this is what you gotta do.'" Likewise, Olga, a mestiza Mexican woman who arrived in the heartland as a toddler and eventually became eligible for DACA, was able to build a very supportive peer network. After high school and before DACA, she began working at a restaurant and had no intention of continuing her education:

> I graduated, and I just worked for three or four years, maybe. I just kind of dedicated myself to working. And then I think it was actually our friend that, like, shoved me and said, "No, you're going to school. You're going back to school whether you want or not. You got to go back to school. You can do better than just work. You need to go back." So, she was the one, like, dragged me over to community college, signed up, enrolling there, thanks to her. She helped me enroll and helped me get my classes and all that.

Olga continued:

So, I started going there and getting involved and taking school a lot more seriously. I just graduated from there last year, I believe. It was a long road, yeah. It was like three, four school years, so yeah. But I had to work still, because at that time I wasn't living with my parents anymore, so I had to work two jobs and still go to school.

In returning to education with her friend's encouragement and assistance, Olga also obtained DACA status, which helped her gain scholarships, internship opportunities, and more stable employment. By the time of our conversation, Olga was enrolled at a larger university and was studying to become a K–12 teacher. What she lacked from her family—in terms of resources and assistance—she had found through her friends. However, immigration policies in the heartland could prevent her from obtaining a teaching license after graduation. And the Trump administration's DACA reforms loomed large during our conversation. All of Olga's efforts for a future career as a teacher were in limbo.

While familial expectations and social networks were crucial in shaping immigrants' educational aspirations, not all immigrants pursuing an education had this support. For example, Amanda, a mestiza Mexican woman, arrived in the United States at age seventeen. She dreamed of achieving a college degree, but gendered family pressures became a challenge, she told me:

In 2003 I graduated from high school. I took the credits that I needed to have my high school degree. When I got here my mom sent me my brother. . . . So, it was very difficult to study, work, and take care of my brother. So, well, I had to pause again my school when I had everything ready to go to the university and start again from zero. In 2011 I started going to college, and now I have forty-five of sixty-four credits. Sometimes I've had bad streaks, so I have had to stop studying.

Amanda persevered to *salir adelante* with her education, at her own pace. "Sometimes I leave one year, sometimes I leave one semester," she said, "but I don't give up. I keep going. Sometimes I tell myself,

'No, that was too much.' But when I look at how much I have left, I say, 'No, well, I am almost there. It is nothing, just a bit of patience.'" Amanda clarified that she did not have much support from her family to continue her studies. "Even though I have a lot of family here it is not the same support. Studying is not indispensable for them." It is also possible that because none of her family members had attended school in the United States or had college degrees they simply did not know how to provide the resources she needed. The pull of responsibilities, including caring for her brother (and the resulting financial burdens), slowed Amanda's progress in school. Nevertheless, she never gave up. She hoped to finish her associate's degree in the coming year after our interview and to eventually go on to a larger university and pursue either a finance degree or an education degree.

Education is a significant marker for immigrants' integration and overall social mobility. More importantly, however, Indigenous and mestizo immigrants alike viewed education to *salir adelante* in the heartland. According to Yosso,[15] aspirational capital is "the ability to maintain hopes and dreams for the future, even in the face of real and perceived barriers." For all immigrants I met, education was thus a very real form of aspirational capital, created amid the uncertainty and pessimism of hostile anti-immigrant realities. Nevertheless, Indigenous and mestizos' educational trajectories differed in important ways, reflecting cumulative and structural forms of oppression rooted in colonial legacies. Indigenous immigrants reported being pushed and pulled out of school—both in the United States and in their home countries. Early motherhood among Indigenous women created additional gendered barriers to educational attainment. While undocumented and semilegal mestizo youths also faced educational barriers, enrolling in K–12 schools helped most of them to at least finish high school, with several going on to attend college. Unlike Indigenous youths, most mestizo youths had the support of their parents while growing up in Kansas. In immigrants' attempts to *salir adelante* through education, important intersections of immigration status, ethnoracial background, gender, and access to resources determined their strategies to success.

WORK TRAJECTORIES

While Indigenous and mestizo immigrants had markedly different experiences with formal education, every undocumented immigrant I met in the heartland pursued *salir adelante* through work. In the classical assimilation framework, occupational mobility is equated with immigrants' social incorporation and upward socioeconomic mobility.[16] As time in the destination country increases, new skills, education, and language proficiency are acquired, leading to positive correlations between human capital (i.e., one's newly gained skills such as education or on the job training), income, and occupational status.[17] By contrast, another important theory in immigration studies, segmented assimilation theory, holds that newly arrived immigrants accrue occupational mobility according to existing stratification systems and an immigrant's social location—determined by their immigration status, class, ethnicity and race, nationality, educational level, gender, etc.[18] Simultaneously, the social context upon arrival dictates which labor markets and occupations are available to new immigrants.[19] While Chapter 3 revealed structural barriers to immigrants' employment and the exploitative violence that undocumented workers faced, turning our attention to how immigrants *salen adelante* through work reveals parallel insights into immigrants' agency, social mobility, and forms of resistance to the violence they encountered in the workplace. Importantly, Indigenous and mestizo immigrants experiences reveal complexities to existing immigration theories of integration, shedding light on both the importance of the existing segregated ethnoracial labor market and the skills acquired by immigrants with time living in the United States. However, colonial legacies remain visible, as existing divides between groups are further cemented through immigrants' work trajectories.

Segmented labor markets create job hierarchies, with low-wage jobs stigmatized as low status and viewed as "bad jobs."[20] Those who can leave a "bad job" for a better job will do so. Nonetheless, some immigrants—although described as having "low skills" and "low educational attainment"—are categorized as "good workers" to fill such "bad jobs," reflecting the job hierarchy's racialization, which equates job prestige with requisite educational attainment and, through this, to de facto racial categories—and to gendered expectations. As a result, certain groups are deemed better positioned for low-wage labor. These racialization and gender mechanisms, however, simultaneously ignore and naturalize the social divides that exclude racialized groups from educational opportunities—as seen above—while devaluing their skills. Additionally, perceptions of who fits a "good worker" ideal among new immigrants reflect the illegalization of immigrant labor, as these perceptions reify the limited protections in the workplace that immigration policies produce.[21] In my conversations with immigrants in Kansas, it became clear that while all the immigrants experienced some form of work mobility, the type of mobility differed significantly between mestizos and Indigenous immigrants.

Occupational Mobility

On an early evening in a busy coffee shop, I chatted with Jaime about his life in Kansas. Jaime, a mestizo Mexican undocumented single father, had lived in Kansas since he was eighteen years old. Via his social connections to other mestizo Mexicans, his first job was in a fast-food restaurant kitchen. After only a couple of years, an unexpected opportunity emerged. "A gentleman offered me work in construction." Jaime had since worked in several construction positions, eventually gaining informal training for a specialized role. "And that is how I got into the various jobs until I achieved a profession," he shared proudly. At the time of our coffee together, Jaime worked installing air-conditioning units in houses and office buildings. "The work that I have now is a bit risky," he said. "Working with blades is a bit . . . You have to be careful; they can fly out." Jaime had gained the informal training for this role through his family ties and after gaining experience in the construction sector. "My brother started in this job, and I have only been there for two years. I learned by observing." Jaime clarified, "Because nobody, in any job, teaches you nothing. Nothing. Nobody explains to you anything. One has to find the way alone. Like in life." Jaime's specialized position meant that he gained significantly better wages than at his first job at the fast-food restaurant years prior and better than the construction odd jobs he took on as he began his journey to his profession.

Jaime explained that the lack of help or guidance at work and in life in the heartland reflected the values of the United States more broadly: "Here, everyone fights to earn one dollar. They do whatever it takes even if it is to take others down to get ahead, to move up." He concluded, "That is how this country works." Although Jaime felt strongly that he did not have a lot of guidance or help to gain his new skills at work, nevertheless working alongside his brother allowed him to gain occupational mobility and better wages.[22] Yet he attributed his occupational mobility to his own hard work.

Vicente, another mestizo Mexican man, offered a similar reflection on his work trajectory. "Thank God I did not suffer too much," he said, "of course, working hard." Vicente shared similar feelings as Jaime regarding working hard with little expectation to receive help from others: "I have always worked very hard, and I never expect nothing from anybody. I was taught since I was a kid that you must work to have things that you want. That is what I was taught. . . . This country is really great because it gives good opportunities, but you have to work for it."

Vicente arrived in Kansas at age seventeen. His first job, obtained with a mestizo friend's help, involved operating large landscaping machinery on the edge of the highway. In this job Vicente's boss abused him frequently, scolding and taunting him, leaving him in life-threatening situations with the dangerous machinery, and stealing his wages. Over time, however, Vicente expanded his skills and social connections. Significantly, he married Jenny, a mestiza Mexican woman who had shifted her status from undocumented to legal permanent residency by the time they married. Eventually after working on the edge of the highway for several years, Vicente learned how to fix the landscaping machinery. These informal mechanical skills enabled him to find a job with better pay and fewer hours—a move that provided the time to improve his English skills. "I went to school, instead of working so hard," he said. "After I learned a little English, I got a better job." By the time of our conversation, Vicente had also obtained legal permanent residency status through his wife and had become a licensed mechanic in a specialized position at a larger company.

Mestiza women who gained better-paying jobs through occupational mobility also attributed their mobility to hard work. Although it often came along a shift in status too. Amanda, the mestiza Mexican woman who had persevered to slowly gain a college degree, began her working life in the United States at a fast-food restaurant. By the time of our conversation, however, she was employed as a tax preparer and had a second job working with immigrant families at a nonprofit organization. "I work to have what I have," she told me. "Nobody gave it to me. Like I tell you, my family is not very united; *todos se rascan con sus propias uñas* [everyone makes it on their own]." Nevertheless, Amanda had access to various resources to achieve her career goals. First, she was one of the mestizos who was able to shift her status from overstayed visa to legal permanent residency status. With a large family in Texas and Kansas, she also used family ties to find work. "I worked with my family members," Amanda said. She recounted how she ended up working as a teaching assistant and later at a nonprofit organization. "My cousins were going to school there. So, when the teacher's assistant left, the coordinator spoke Spanish—he was Cuban—and he knew us very well because they are twins. So, they asked them if they had a family member, a friend, or someone who wanted to work there [at the school]. So, I did all the process, all the interviews." This job then opened other work opportunities, she explained: "Then I worked there for four years, and the principal got an email that [an organization] was looking for a bilingual person to work with immigrant families. So, I saw the opportunity and I thought, 'Why not?' They paid three times more than what I was doing as a teacher's assistant, so I accepted."

Just as we saw with changes to immigration status in Chapter 5, workplace mobility can also be nonlinear and bidirectional. Sometimes—whether pushed through immigration enforcement policies, sociopolitical changes, or individual action—cherished opportunities were taken away. Elena's case is especially illustrative. Elena, a mestiza Mexican woman who had lived in the heartland since she was very young, being part of the 1.5 generation. Growing up in Kansas, she became fluent in English and graduated from high school. A couple of years prior to our conversation, she obtained DACA status after seeing an announcement on a Spanish-language news channel. Prior to obtaining DACA, Elena told me that she'd been a housewife. "From school I never went to work," she said. "I [stayed] at my house until I was given the opportunity to obtain DACA in 2012 and I started working."

Sitting on her couch beside her husband, Gerardo, also a mestizo Mexican immigrant, Elena explained her situation further. When she had been undocumented, she was anxious about having a job. As the mother of five children, all US citizens, she feared the possibility of being apprehended in the workplace and, even worse, deported. Once she obtained DACA, however, her life and the rest of her family members' lives completely changed. "I am a freelance interpreter," she told me, sitting up straight and with a widening smile, about her multiple gigs and jobs. "I work part-time for [a nonprofit]. It is a job in a shelter for women that have suffered domestic violence. Yes, overnight. And then everything else that comes up. Sometimes someone needs a translated letter, a notary stamp for a letter. I have license to wed." As Gerardo made clear during our conversation, even though he worked full-time in construction, Elena's income helped sustain the family, "Because if it was only one paycheck, well, things would be more complicated," Gerardo reflected.

The last time I saw Elena, however, occurred when we ran into each other at a pro-immigrant rally a few months after Trump took office in 2017. She told me that her DACA status had expired, and she was worried about renewing her application in case immigration enforcement used her data against her. Consequently, she could lose her multiple licenses and jobs, increasing her family's financial uncertainty.

Indigenous immigrants frequently arrived in the United States with the expectation of equality in the labor force. As Teodoro, a Mixteco Mexican man, put it, "They used to say that you come here and earn more. To be the same." Indigenous immigrants quickly discovered, however, that the possibilities for mobility and equality were limited. Indigenous immigrants changed jobs frequently, yet their mobility was strategic and lateral—to avoid immigration surveillance and E-Verify programs, to escape discrimination or exploitative working experiences, or to find better wages. Each new job, however, tended to be of the same type regardless of how many years an Indigenous immigrant had worked in the United States. "Without papers, I can't have a good job that pays good," Jaime, a Mixteco Mexican man, explained. "Only those that pay cheap, like here [his job in a restaurant kitchen]." Jaime's Mixteco Mexican partner Saturnina added, "We go looking for a job that would pay more." However, their undocumented status created barriers to finding higher wages, the couple confessed. Jaime and Saturnina had lived in Kansas for over a decade, working multiple jobs throughout the years, but had always worked in restaurant kitchens for similar pay.

Similarly, Teodoro had lived in Kansas for twelve years. Since arriving at age sixteen, he had worked continuously as a restaurant cook. Periodically switching jobs to avoid E-Verify situations, he always worked long hours in restaurants—averaging twelve to thirteen hours per day during his early years in Kansas and describing a forty-hour workweek as "part-time" when we talked. At that time he was earning $9 per hour. Teodoro's horizontal moves within the restaurant industry also reflect the fact that most immigrants relied on their social networks to find employment opportunities, which were typically segregated by ethnoracial backgrounds, gender, and immigration status and thus stratified in terms of the occupational mobility they afforded.

Both Indigenous and mestizo immigrants experienced occupational mobility, yet these mobilities differed in both kind and degree. Even when immigrants experienced upward occupational mobility, both immigrant groups reported experiences of precarity and exploitation at work (see Chapter 3). Indigenous immigrants remained in the same occupations over time, pointing to lateral occupational mobility, while mestizo immigrants reported greater vertical moves into occupations that were less physically demanding and better paid and require specialist skills. Despite these inequities and obstacles, however, every immigrant I spoke with had pursued occupational mobility to *salir adelante* and improve their relative position in the United States.

Resistance and Gendered Mobility at Work

At a more granular level, gendered power relations also influenced immigrant women's experiences of *salir adelante*. Latina women's labor continues to be broadly devalued. In the United States, Latinas earned fifty-five cents for every dollar a white man earned in 2020, a wage gap that has remained almost constant since 1989.[23] Despite this wage gap, however, immigrant women relied on their social networks to increase their wages and gain better-paying occupations.

Paloma, a mestiza Mexican woman who once worked as a farm-worker in Florida, noticed that her wages were lower than those of her male coworkers. "There was no equality," she recalled. "The pay was always a bit less for women than for men." This motivated her to move out of agriculture. With the help of her family, Paloma and her husband, also a Mexican mestizo immigrant, found work at a Kansas food-processing plant, where wages, she said, were more "equal" to those of men.

For Indigenous women, however, gender discrimination intersected with anti-Indigenous discrimination, compounding work immobility.[24] Victoria, for example, an Indigenous Tlapaneco woman, worked in a restaurant kitchen. As described in Chapter 3, she faced discrimination and difficulties at work. She worked for three years as a dishwasher and for the last five years as a cook. The promotion from dishwasher to cook came with a higher wage, but the move would have come earlier, Victoria explained, if she hadn't been a woman. "Since I was the only woman and all men were cooking, they did not take me into consideration." She said that her coworkers and manager assumed that "I couldn't do it." She went into more detail:

> I told the manager "When are you going to give me a raise?" She [the manager] said, "But what do you want a raise for if you are washing dishes?" "No, if you give a raise I move to the kitchen," I told her. "Ah, okay, I will take you one day and let's see if you can throw the plates up."

Victoria had to prove to the manager that she could reach the top of the stand where dishes were placed before they were sent to the front of the restaurant (without accommodations). However, Victoria already had ample experience with this during the evening shift, which the manager did not attend. Victoria explained, "When she wasn't working. I [also] worked the evenings. I would go inside [the kitchen] to help the cooks in the evening. So, when they moved me to the morning shift, they kept on putting me to wash dishes. It was when I told her that I want my raise."

Once Victoria reached the position of cook, it also involved carrying a large flour-filled bowl that, by her estimate, weighed ninety pounds. Women did not stick around to work in the kitchen, Victoria told me. "They [women] feel it is hard, that is very hard for them to pick it up. And I do it. That is all I do. Every morning I make the dough for the cake. That is what they feel is hard, I think." Victoria's manager held both gendered and racialized assumptions that Victoria—stereotyped as better suited for low-status labor as an Indigenous woman—could not perform a cook's duties because of her physical stature. Short stature is often tied to stereotypes surrounding Latin American indigeneity and tied to specific types of jobs—in Victoria's case, dishwashing. This in turn kept Victoria from securing a better-paid position until she confronted the manager.[25]

In her eight years at the restaurant, Victoria had only missed two periods of work—once when her daughter was born and a second time when her first husband passed away. A few months after our conversation, however, Victoria called to tell me that she had quit her job after discovering that her male coworkers had been receiving periodic raises and were all paid more than she was, even those who had been hired after her. With the help of an Indigenous woman, Victoria found a new job at a restaurant almost immediately. Although she initially earned less than before, she soon received a small raise and felt that upward mobility might finally be possible. About a year later in 2019, Victoria excitedly called me to tell me that she had been taking English classes at a night school and that her boss had offered to make her a manager.

During our conversation, however, Victoria confessed that while she was excited to take the new position as manager, she worried that her male coworkers would be offended by her promotion as a woman. After weeks of consideration and with the encouragement of her family, Victoria accepted the managerial role. Of the thirty-five Indigenous immigrants I met in Kansas, only Victoria had managed to attain a management-level position. Nevertheless, her story reflects both the burden of colonial, anti-Indigenous, and gendered discrimination and the importance of human capital—especially language skills and social connections—for *salir adelante.*

Occupational mobility for women also involved a switch from paid employment to working inside the home as stay-at-home mothers. Several mestizas I met had experienced this, reflecting the intersections of gender, their family's income, and race. Although all the immigrant women I met, Indigenous and mestiza alike, were responsible for most of the housework and their children's care, mestizas invoked the intensive motherhood ideal to explain a decrease in their working hours or their decision to step out of the labor force altogether. Intensive motherhood ideal reflects women's main responsibilities centered on the everyday and minute aspects of care for their children, often competing with work responsibilities.[26] After Paloma moved from Florida to work at the Kansas food-processing plant, for instance, following years of hard work she eventually was promoted to manager—a move accompanied by her bilingual proficiency and a change in her immigration status. Despite her pride in becoming a manager, with its corresponding salary boost, Paloma ultimately found that her considerable work responsibilities conflicted with her expectations of intensive motherhood:

> I was too focused on my work, I entered at 6 a.m. and left at 7 or 8 p.m. Honestly, I was never home. All the time I was at work. It got to the point that I was always tired. I didn't want anything; I just wanted to be lying down. I never saw work as a bad thing—until this day I feel very proud of what I am. I always reached the numbers that they asked for. But suddenly I felt that I was, like, losing a lot. Like, I felt that I was losing a lot of time with my children.

Although Paloma's husband supported her by taking care of some of the housework and childrearing such as cooking and feeding the children when she was not home, she eventually quit her management position to find a job with more flexible hours:

That time I told my mom that I wanted to stay at home and that I was going to clean the church. She told me "Are you sure? Are you going to leave your job after so many years? Why would you leave everything?" I didn't know how to explain it, to be honest. I think it was more because my children were growing up. I can't explain it. It is something very odd, especially when your children are growing up and you feel a lot of things that I had never felt.

As with Paloma's case, intensive motherhood expectations—which characterize women as responsible for their children's care—create tension and conflict when women are unable to fulfill this role due to competing work responsibilities. In Paloma's case, these tensions clearly affected her mental well-being. However, by no means could all the mestiza women I met afford to become full-time stay-at-home mothers, nor did they all have an opportunity to work flexible hours. These decisions depended on their family's financial standing—typically linked to their immigration status and to whether they had a partner with a stable job in Kansas.

Unlike mestizas, all the Indigenous women I met in Kansas worked outside the home, and those who were not employed at the time of our conversations were actively looking for work. Indigenous women also expressed intensive mothering ideals. Most took on the full responsibilities of childcare and household duties, juggling work and family. Yet Indigenous women also relied on their partners, friends, and family for help because they simply could not do it all; they could not be at work and with their children at once (although in some industries such as crop agriculture women often bring their children to work). Camila is an Indigenous Tlapaneco Mexican woman and the mom of Bruno, who was a toddler when we met. As we sat on Camila's couch, Bruno dug through my purse in search of something interesting—possibly candy or toys—and tugged at my long necklace while Camila explained her daily routine:

I wake up, make my coffee, and then I play with him [Bruno]. Sometimes I also take care of his cousin, and I play with them. I feed them. Then at two I get ready to go to work. I start at three and I get out at ten. And at ten I come back, I pick him up at his aunt's, and I come [home]. I cook, if I didn't cook earlier. I come to cook, and we eat and we go to sleep.

Camila's partner, Rodrigo, also worked full-time and had multiple jobs, yet the family's childcare duties fell largely on Camila. She and her sister-in-law, also Tlapaneco, tried their best to coordinate their shifts and provide childcare for each other. In other instances, working Indigenous women paid fellow Indigenous women for childcare services. Quetzali, an Indigenous Maya Guatemalan woman, paid her neighbor about $60 a week to watch her baby while she was at work. As in other aspects of life, immigrant women who strived to *salir adelante* in their working lives relied on social ties with fellow immigrants in similar social positions, from similar ethnoracial backgrounds, and with similar immigration statuses.

CONCLUSION

Indigenous and mestizo immigrants' experiences demonstrate that *salir adelante* required a proactive approach to overcoming the challenges of a hostile anti-immigrant environment as experienced in the heartland. All the immigrants I met viewed education and work as means to *salir adelante* and strived to find ways to survive and thrive amid uncertainty. The diverse experiences of Indigenous and mestizo immigrants in the education system and the labor force reflect the deep constrictions of colonialism, forcing immigrants to *salir adelante* through these institutions in creative ways.

Education is a space for the integration of new immigrant children and youths into their new societies, as it is here where children and youths learn about US cultural norms and language, among other skills beyond academics. As the experiences of all undocumented and semilegal immigrants demonstrate, however, institutional barriers continued to thwart immigrants' educational opportunities, despite undoubted positive intentions among many school administrators and staff. These included a lack of information for navigating the US educational system, immigrants' lack of language proficiency in English or Spanish, a dearth of support from some administrators and staff, and limited financial opportunities to pay for higher education.[27] Although most of the immigrants I met in Kansas aspired to obtain at least a high school education, the possibility of significant educational achievement— especially a college degree—was limited to the 1.5 generation of mestizos who, for the most part, had their parents' support in the heartland. Indigenous immigrants were both pushed from and pulled out of the US education system, and Indigenous women faced not only race and socioeconomic barriers but also gendered mothering obligations that also impacted their educational trajectories.

Although almost all undocumented and semilegal immigrants are often racialized as "good workers" for low-renumerated and physically grueling labor, Indigenous and mestizo immigrants experienced vastly different work trajectories. Mestizos—even those who remained totally undocumented or lacked much formal education—frequently gained vertical work mobility into better-paying and less physically demanding jobs. They achieved these moves via their social ties to friends, family, and coworkers, and some were aided by the shift in their immigration status or language acquisition. By contrast, while Indigenous immigrants frequently switched jobs with the aid of their social connections, these were lateral moves into similar positions that paid an equivalent wage. Importantly, immigrants across ethnoracial lines internalized the difficulties they had endured in the labor force as well as the mobility they had gained, whether vertical or lateral, as "hard work," cementing both individualism values and the isolation experienced when trying to *salir adelante* in the heartland as new immigrants. While all immigrants used their employment to *salir adelante* as much as possible, these differing labor experiences demonstrated the significance of ethnoracial divides within immigrants' immediate networks and point to the segmentation of the US labor market more broadly.[28]

Gender played a significant role in immigrants' working lives, with both Indigenous and mestiza women utilizing their networks to leave jobs that paid women less than men for equivalent work. Among Indigenous women, however, the intersections of race, gender, immigration status, and class appeared cumulative—with Indigenous women not only racialized as "good workers" but also gendered as "docile workers" for menial positions and pay, all mechanisms that are rooted in colonial views of the Indigenous "other." Nevertheless, Indigenous women actively found ways to stand up for themselves and to search for new work opportunities. Finally, for many mestiza women, work mobility could also involve leaving the paid labor force to focus exclusively on work inside the home. Although both Indigenous and mestiza women expressed intensive mothering ideals, Indigenous women could not afford to leave the laborforce, while several mestizas had the ability and the relative financial security to stay at home. When Indigenous women took time off from work to give birth, for example, they returned to work relatively quickly. Overall, this chapter showed that while Indigenous and mestizo immigrants have varying educational and work trajectories, they all nevertheless navigate the heartland's hostilities on their own terms to ultimately *salir adelante*.

CONCLUSION

LATIN AMERICAN IMMIGRANTS in the United States are homogenized into one group via terms such as "Latinidad," "Hispanic," "Latina/o," and "Latinx/e." These terms certainly reflect a collective identity and provide a forum for political representation.[1] However, Indigenous and mestizo immigrants' accounts in this book have demonstrated that Latin American immigrants experience US immigration policies and their enforcement in different ways, especially in white-majority spaces such as the heartland. Colonial legacies across transnational spaces that have endured maintain immigrants' uneven access to resources, networks, opportunities, and the possibility of a life free from violence. The racialization mechanisms shaping Latin American societies also cannot be easily discarded when immigrants leave their home countries. Deeply engrained racial ideologies, hierarchies, and practices accompany immigrants on their long journeys into the diaspora. Upon arrival in the United States, immigrants then encounter a new system of race and racism—one that is intertwined within the US immigration system. As they navigate their complex transnational lives, both Indigenous and mestizo immigrants must thus find ways to negotiate these multiple constraining contexts.[2] Furthermore, race and racialization mechanisms constantly intersect with gender and immigration status, creating a diverse array of life trajectories for Indigenous and mestizo immigrants and their families.

In this book, I have observed how colonial legacies are maintained through neoliberal policies in Mexico and Guatemala—the principal countries of origin among the migrants I met in Kansas—as well as in the United States.[3] I find that although migration, regardless of ethnoracial background, is primarily motivated by economic aspirations and fleeing violence, mestizo and Indigenous migrants' journeys begin in very different circumstances—shaped by anti-Indigenous discrimination, ongoing gender violence, and the mounting socioeconomic differences between these groups across Mexico and Guatemala. While Indigenous groups and mestizos in Latin America both experience varying degrees of violence—perpetuated via corrupt governments' transnational policies and patriarchal states—Indigenous groups face additional layers of violence and instability resulting from the enduring structures of colonialism encoded within anti-Indigenous politics, all prior to migration. Studying migration through a colonial legacies lens therefore enables the decentering of immigrants' positionality even before their journeys begin. In turn, these existing colonial structures of oppression interact with contemporary immigration policies, shaping the nature of immigrants' journeys northward, their forms of entry into the United States, and their experiences once living in the heartland.

Once immigrants arrived in Kansas, they relied heavily on their social ties. These ties, however, were divided along ethnoracial lines, gender, and immigration status. Indigenous immigrants thus relied on fellow Indigenous friends and family, who, at least in the case of

Kansas, were all undocumented—limiting their networks to peers who also lacked the protections of citizenship. Mestizos, on the other hand, frequently leaned on social ties with other mestizos who were more established in the United States, often possessing citizenship or semilegal status, thus widening mestizos' access to a variety of rights and protections. Where relationships between Indigenous and mestizo immigrants occurred, these were largely economic transactions and mediated by the Spanish language. For Indigenous immigrants, especially women, such transactional ties often proved exploitative. Importantly too, both Indigenous and mestizo immigrants arrived in Kansas seeking *un lugar tranquilo*, a calm and tranquil place to live. In the heartland, however, they instead encountered a hostile anti-immigrant environment, which worsened as Trump-era ideologies and restrictive federal immigration policies trickled down to the state and local levels, resulting in forms of state violence that generated a state of chronic fear.

My fieldwork in Kansas, conducted between 2016 and 2019, coincided with an especially significant period in US immigration legislation, Donald Trump's first administration. During this period over one thousand immigration-related policies and rules were enacted, profoundly altering the US immigration bureaucracy. This rapidly changing legislative context, combined with increased local immigration enforcement and growing anti-immigrant rhetoric in the public, considerably heightened immigrants' fear of deportation and family separation. These fears occurred across ethnoracial lines and remained during the period of my study. However, compared to Indigenous migrants, mestizos had a wider net of resources for handling this fear and evading possible deportation. The production of fear, I have shown, is a result of state and legal violence, because it is through the creation of fear that governance, citizenship, and everyday life are controlled. Anti-immigrant policies relied on criminalizing tropes, deeming certain immigrants "dangerous" to the American well-being, thus generating fears of the racialized "illegal" immigrant for the public. And the harsh hypersurveillance and enhanced enforcement policies that produce fear among immigrants impacted their everyday lives, family dynamics, and sense of success and failure as well as their hopes and dreams for their future. Furthermore, while hostile political environments might theoretically create spaces of solidarity across ethnoracial divides,[4] immigrants' lives in Kansas revealed a more complicated picture. Paradoxically, the heartland's anti-immigrant sentiments reinforced ethnoracial hierarchies between Indigenous and mestizo immigrants, reproducing spaces of exploitation and reducing instances of potential solidarity to moments of transactional exchanges.

Although Kansas—and, more broadly, the US heartland—is rarely considered as home to Latino immigrants, this book has outlined contemporary migration flows to the region. Latino immigrants' heartland experiences thus contribute to our academic understanding of ethnoracial and gendered relationships in places with new and growing immigrant populations. Existing research on the relationships between new immigrants and established residents has shown the complexity of immigrants' integration and how this is affected by the social and political dynamics of local contexts.[5] Boundaries and social relations between new arrivals and established residents are mediated by existing racial, class, and gender hierarchies; government policies; institutional access; and the type of opportunities for social interaction that are available.[6] Likewise, social boundaries are created between new and established immigrants.[7] As a result, focusing on the racial, gender, and immigration status boundaries *within* immigrant communities, especially in a place with a small but growing Latino immigrant population, affords a more nuanced understanding of Latinidad and integration as well as how *mestizaje* and *indigenismo*—tools of colonial powers and its enduring legacies—function in the diaspora.

Despite the challenge of building a new life in an unfamiliar and frequently hostile environment, most undocumented Indigenous and mestizo immigrants hoped to eventually gain legal protection from deportation and a path to citizenship. However, the intricacies of colonial legacies, codified in US immigration policies, limited avenues for shifting status to only a small proportion of immigrants—excluding, for example, all the Indigenous immigrants I met. As a result, immigrants' perceptions of success, and the means to *salir adelante* (get ahead) were concentrated on two main pathways: education and employment. Crucially, the intersections of race, gender, and immigration status shaped migrants' internalization of success and failure, providing valuable scholarly insights into the workings of state and legal violence as well as structural oppression. While all immigrants used education and employment to *salir adelante*, Indigenous and mestizo migrants had vastly different experiences in these spaces, further cementing racial divides among Latinos in the heartland.

LATINIDAD, RACIALIZATION, AND ILLEGALITY

Illegality in the Heartland offers a significant contribution to our understandings of Latinidad, racialization, and illegality in the United States. Indigenous scholars have called attention to the importance of examining colonial pasts, presents, and futures in order to understand Indigenous daily life and the structures, institutions, and agents that shape it.[8] In this book, I presented Indigenous and mestizo immigrants' accounts alongside one another not to place their narratives in opposition but instead to demonstrate how differing experiences of migration and integration unfolded during a period of heightened, anti-immigrant hostility. Furthermore, the analysis of Indigenous and mestizo experiences allows for an in-depth examination of Latinidad and its multifaceted meanings, relationships, and identities within specific sociopolitical and geographical contexts.

Latin American scholarship examining colorism and racialization mechanisms suggests that whiteness and perceived whiteness generate socioeconomic, educational, and health benefits compared to those who lack such perceived attributes.[9] Likewise, Latin American scholars have noted how whiteness and its proximity shifts according to the intersecting axis of stratification, along with the sociopolitical contexts. Despite grassroot mobilizations, Indigenous groups continue to face significant disadvantages compared to mestizo groups.[10] In most Latin American nations, including Mexico and Guatemala, *mestizaje* and *indigenismo* continue to maintain the privileged status of European descent and whiteness. Because these mechanisms are assumed to be left behind after migration, *Illegality in the Heartland* seeks to address the past and present transnational structures of colonialism through an intersectional examination of race and racialization in the Latin American diaspora. Indeed, studies centering on the racialization of illegality demonstrate that perceived Mexican and Hispanic origins are connected to presumptions of illegality, rendering those stereotyped as such—especially Indigenous immigrants—prone to heightened immigration surveillance and apprehension.[11] In turn, mestizaje is tied to whiteness and perceived whiteness and thus serves as an important tool of survival within racialized societies,[12] enabling some to "pass" as citizens or appear "not illegal" within a highly hostile anti-immigrant political context.[13] At the same time, perceived whiteness—and its ties to citizenship—can render those who do not fit such categorizations as "more illegal" or more likely to be targeted as "illegal" (regardless of what the actual immigration status may be). Within the immigrant diaspora in the heartland, protections associated with whiteness map onto colonial constructs of *mestizaje* and *indigenismo*, exacerbating divides between Indigenous and mestizo migrants.

Just as Indigenous and mestizo immigrant networks were shaped by racial divides, intersections of class, gender, and immigration status also influenced immigrants' diverse trajectories. By attending to the fabric of immigrants' everyday lives in Kansas, *Illegality in the Heartland* shows, for example, that while all immigrant women experienced gender-specific instances of exploitation, Indigenous women faced cumulative discrimination and exploitation with the intersections of indigeneity, gender, and immigration status[14] and lacked the social ties, work opportunities, economic security, or immigration status that enabled many mestiza women to get ahead. These mechanisms were most visible in women's accounts of the migrant journey, experiences of detention and deportation of loved ones, their language and educational trajectories, and their time in the paid laborforce. Of course, Indigenous men too encountered the inescapable threat of racialized illegality, since their indigeneity and gender aligned with stereotypes of "illegality" the most, making them prone to apprehensions and deportation, stereotypes, and discrimination.[15]

This book also highlights how language shapes immigrants' experiences in the diaspora. While existing immigration scholarship has maintained the view that learning the host country's language is key to immigrant success,[16] I present a more complex picture of language use within Indigenous and mestizo families. These findings push us to reconsider Bourdieu's classic view of linguistic capital and instead uncover the value of "devalued" languages.[17] Following Yosso's conceptualization of community cultural wealth,[18] I document how Spanish and Indigenous languages represent resources for survival and success among Indigenous and mestizo families in Kansas—making these languages reflective of *linguistic wealth*. Although knowledge of English is extremely useful for accessing the heartland's social institutions—including schools, health care, and public spaces such as grocery stores—Indigenous languages and Spanish prove continually useful for navigating perceived threats in public spaces, gaining pertinent information about work and housing, navigating health care episodes, and achieving occupational mobility. These languages too can form bridges between parallel Indigenous and mestizo immigrant networks. Linguistic practices are particularly complex in bilingual and multilingual families. Most Indigenous families with immigrant parents and

US-born children spoke a mixture of Indigenous languages, Spanish, and English. Mestizos, on the other hand, relied on Spanish and English. Sometimes this created tensions within the family—for example, when children refused to speak Indigenous languages with their parents or when parents could not understand their children's spoken English. Parental attempts to maintain Spanish and Indigenous languages—and as a result transmit community cultural wealth to their children— were nevertheless present among both immigrant groups.

Illegality in the Heartland foregrounds the role of place. As Kansas has evolved as a destination, antimigrant hostility has been reinforced through federal- and state-level anti-immigrant rhetoric and associated policies. Furthermore, immigrants' experiences in the heartland proved to show the ever-changing heartland landscape following shifts in its demographics, institutions, and sociolegal contexts. Within this context, however, colonial legacies are present, shaping both legal realms of enforcement and informal rules that make undocumented immigrants lives more or less difficult.

This book also extends our sociolegal understanding of immigration policies' consequences for immigrants and their families. The criminalization of immigration via policy measures has made it very difficult for immigrants to shift their immigration status. While both Indigenous and mestizo immigrants hoped for eventual protection from deportation and a path to naturalization, the reality is that very few had this option. This book demonstrates how such narrow legalization pathways reproduce colonial structures that deepen existing divides. Immigrants' interpretation of the law and their immigration status—that is, their legal consciousness—shaped intimate aspects of their lives, including interpersonal family relations and their hopes and dreams. Scholars suggest that when some family members have access to legal protections while others do not, family ties can become fragmented[19] and even toxic.[20] My study contributes to scholarship on mixed-status families by showing that while one family member's access to immigration protection can bring valuable resources to the household, this can be a daunting responsibility. Differences in social location, perceived opportunities, and protections and rights can also produce new anxieties within mixed-status families, especially between siblings.[21] *Illegality in the Heartland* thus contributes to growing scholarship on how discriminatory laws and policies are internalized and the intimate family dynamics that result.

IMPLICATIONS

Extensive research by academics and advocacy groups has demonstrated the need for both federal- and local-level immigration reform. Although immigration policies are constantly changing, as this book illustrates, substantive progress in immigration reform has been slow. Importantly, quick fixes to immigration policy may create more harm than good, so making well-thought-out policy changes backed by social science evidence is crucial. My ethnographic immersion in the lives of immigrants in Kansas clarified four areas in which policy reform seems crucial. First, I call for a move toward the decriminalization of immigration that reconsiders illegal entry and illegal reentry penalties, expedited removal practices, and mandatory detention. Far from decreasing migration flows, these penalties directly harm immigrants and their loved ones. Second, I call for an end to racialization and the racial profiling practices that presume the criminality of Latino immigrants, particularly Mexicans and Central Americans of Indigenous descent. Third, I call for a reconsideration of gender-based violence within immigration and asylum processes. And fourth, I echo scholars, advocates, and activists in calling for a path to citizenship for all undocumented immigrants living in the United States, including the cessation of entry and reentry bars.

While federal immigration policies are pressing and important, federal policymaking is messy and slow. As a result, I also propose several changes to state- and local-level immigration policies that would help immigrants live a life without fear and make greater contributions to their communities. These include an end to 287(g) agreements (i.e., agreements between local policing agencies and federal immigration enforcement), granting driver's and professional licenses, and granting access to state-subsidized health insurance. Importantly, the role of place also matters in the implications of this book. I shed light on important steps that localities, institutions, and communities in the heartland can take to address immigration in their communities. Finally, it is imperative to acknowledge the role of Latin American nations and governments in shaping contemporary migration flows. I join the call to end government corruption and violence in Latin America and to establish functional and just democracies in the region.

Federal-Level Policies

My research with immigrants in Kansas reinforces a key insight of earlier scholarship—that the criminalization of immigration has severe negative consequences for immigrants, their families, and their broader communities. Signatories of the Universal Declaration of Human Rights have agreed that migration is a human right (Articles 13, 14). Yet existing immigration policies in the United States, at the nation's borders and in the interior, penalize immigration infractions through criminal, punitive measures.[22] Since 1929, unauthorized entrance to the United States, or "illegal entry," has been considered a misdemeanor, punishable with up to six months' incarceration and a fine.[23] Likewise, unauthorized entrance after a deportation, or "illegal reentry," carries a felony charge and is punishable with up to twenty years in prison.[24] Expedited removal accelerates individual illegal entry and reentry cases, streamlining pleas and sentencing and bypassing adequate representation and due process protections.[25] Expedited removal allows for the deportation of migrants without their cases being heard by a judge—imposing mandatory detention while denying hearings, appeals, and judicial review processes.[26] Illegal entry and reentry charges are thus "the most prosecuted crimes in federal courts," comprising 59 percent of all cases in magistrate and district courts in 2019.[27] In the past decade, illegal entry and reentry were among the immigrant charges that most frequently led to deportation.[28]

In 2017, the Trump administration strengthened penalties for illegal entry and reentry via several executive orders.[29] As Eagly noted, because the US attorney general leads the Department of Justice, the presidential administration "has direct authority over how criminal immigration proceeds in practice."[30] The executive orders of 2017 prioritized the criminal punishment of immigration infractions occurring at the US border and inside the country, and the secretary of homeland security authorized the Department of Homeland Security to refer border immigration offenses for criminal prosecution.[31] In 2018 a year after these policy changes occurred, the number of immigrants charged with illegal entry increased by 85 percent, and reentry charges increased by 38 percent.[32] Attorney General Jeff Sessions set illegal entry and reentry as top priorities for deportation, pursuing a "zero tolerance" policy that separated parents and children as they entered the United States seeking asylum. Five years after organizers and advocates stopped this policy, over a thousand children had yet to be reunited with their families.[33]

The penalties of illegal entry and reentry are long-lasting because convicted migrants are subsequently ineligible to apply for a US visa or adjustment of status without facing a multiyear bar (sometimes up to ten years)—even after marrying a US citizen or after living in the United States for decades. Illegal entry and reentry convictions thus make it impossible for immigrants to shift their status at a later date, confining them to undocumented status and exposing them to both the criminal legal system *and* the perpetual possibility of deportation.

In reality, criminalizing policies do not decrease or deter migration.[34] Instead, these policies put migrants in dangerous and life-threatening situations, as we observed in immigrants' accounts of their journeys to the United States. Following the lead of past scholars and immigration advocates, I thus also urge for the decriminalization of border crossings.[35] Decriminalizing US entry would help to end family separations, decrease the incarceration of Latin American immigrants, and reorientate magistrates' and federal judges' focus away from immigration offenses.[36]

Decriminalizing immigration also implies an end to expedited removal and mandatory detention. The first Trump administration expanded expedited removal at immigration officers' discretion through a memorandum written by Department of Homeland Security director John Kelly.[37] This created significant challenges for potential asylum seekers, who are often wrongfully deported via expedited removal without having a chance to present their case before a judge.[38] In *Al Otro Lado v. Mayorkas*, a federal judge ruled in favor of thirteen asylum seekers who were turned back from the US border by Customs and Border Protection officers because ports were "at capacity." This ruling argued that turning back asylum seekers defies constitutional and international laws and sets a precedent for the revocation of expedited removal—finding that capacity constraints cannot override asylum seekers' right to plead their case.[39]

Mandatory detention involves the detention of any noncitizen who has committed certain criminal actions, including crimes of "moral turpitude" or "aggravated felonies."[40] This permits the detention (and deportation) of a migrant regardless of when a conviction occurred or whether a sentence was already served—as in the case of Hugo, whose story we read in Chapter 5. Congress has the authority to decide which offenses are considered aggravated felonies for migrants. As a result, when a new offense is added to this category, persons who have already been charged and served their punishment in the criminal legal system are at risk of further incarceration and deportation.[41] Additionally, mandatory detention involves the detention of migrants awaiting immigration court hearings, including for asylum seekers—as in the cases of Jazmin and Esperanza, the asylum seekers whose stories are present throughout the book. As the American Civil Liberties Union argued, mandatory detention violates due process by removing the possibility of a predetention trial.[42] Ending mandatory detention would also be another mechanism for ending traumatic family separations during immigration proceedings.

Latino migrants are disproportionately impacted by the criminalization of immigration. Between 2003 and 2020 more than five million immigrants were deported from the United States, over 90 percent of whom were Mexican or Central American, most of them men.[43] The high numbers of Latinos targeted by immigration enforcement, immigration policies, institutionalized practices, and the stigmatization of social status collectively lead to the creation of associations between race and immigration status—in particular, tying Latinos and, more specifically, Indigenous Latinos to perceptions of illegality.[44] Policies that promote the apprehension of immigrants who are *suspected* of lacking immigration status or *suspected* of terrorist affiliation, such as those enacted by Trump's 2017 executive orders, reinforce racial profiling and justify legal violence toward immigrants.[45] US courts have explicitly and implicitly legalized immigration officers' use of physical appearance, language ability, and perceived race or ethnicity to apprehend people suspected of being undocumented, and these traits have been specifically tied to Mexican and Central American migrants.[46] Therefore, the criminalization of immigration coupled with the apprehension of Latin American migrants simultaneously reproduces the racialization of illegality.

In the United States, the Fourth Amendment is often used to protect citizens from racial profiling. Additionally, two federal statutes— 34 U.S.C. § 12601 and Title VI of the Civil Rights Act of 1964—can be utilized to hold local policing departments accountable. While racial profiling is a familiar practice in the criminal legal system, its practice is at least socially and supposedly legally condemned. "A hunch or in-articulable suspicion" cannot be utilized as a reason to stop, search, or apprehend a person within the criminal legal system.[47] Within the im-migration system, however, the racial profiling of Latinos as a means of targeting undocumented migrants is widely utilized and condoned. Immigration enforcement should thus incorporate anti–racial-profiling policies that define racial profiling, ban pretextual stops, avoid overpo-licing, and eliminate improper bias.

One way to end racial profiling and the practices that promote the ra-cialization of illegality would be through the abolishment of 287(g) pro-grams. Section 287(g) of the Immigration and Nationality Act enables and funds local policing agencies to undertake immigration enforce-ment. Once local policing agencies enter a memorandum of agree-ment with Immigration and Customs Enforcement, police officers can apprehend, detain, and process undocumented immigrants.[48] Given the racialization of illegality, however, Latino neighborhoods are the most acutely affected by these localized practices.[49] The involvement of local policing agencies in federal immigration enforcement thereby increases immigrants' fear of deportation, which in turn leads to so-cial isolation and disengagement from social institutions—as we saw in previous chapters.[50] Importantly, given the racialization of illegality, local policing of immigrants treats Indigenous and mestizo migrants differently, with Indigenous migrants and those characterized as "ille-gal" at higher risk of detention and deportation.[51]

From the accounts of immigrant women I met during this study, gender violence must be taken into consideration during immigration proceedings including the asylum process. Contrary to banning asy-lum claims due to violence under the first Trump administration, asy-lum proceedings must account for gender-based violence as grounds to grant asylum. Many women are fleeing gender-based violence in their countries of origin, only to encounter more violence on their journeys and finding no support or protection upon reaching the United States.[52]

Importantly, the requirement of documentation to "back up" asylum seeker's testimonies of violence is unhelpful. Ample research has demonstrated that immigrant women who flee gender-based violence lack protective government mechanisms in their countries of origin even if these countries have policies that supposedly protect women against violence.[53] Additionally, the discretion that Border Patrol officers and asylum officers have to decide whether an immigrants' claims to asylum are "credible" are often racialized and gendered, pushing many Indigenous, Mexican, and Central American women away from asylum protections.[54] Likewise, an extension to the cap on asylum relief is extremely needed.

By listening closely to the hopes and dreams of Indigenous and mestizo immigrants in Kansas, it is clear that a path to naturalization, a way to *arreglar los papeles* (fix the immigration status), would address many of the difficulties that immigrant families encounter in their daily lives. As scholars and activists suggest, a path to citizenship would alleviate undocumented migrants' ongoing fear of deportation and ease the multiple forms of exploitation and violence they face. Although a new policy to enable citizenship would be ideal, there are many ways in which the existing immigration system could be adjusted in this spirit. One method could involve enhancing the family-sponsored visa system, in conjunction with an end to entry and reentry bars. Currently, family-based petitions are limited to nuclear family ties, involving age restrictions alongside income and education requirements. All national allocations are capped too, despite some countries not using their annual quota.[55] Raising allocation caps and redefining the family ties that count toward family sponsorship would open a path to legalization for many. As the experiences of undocumented mestizo migrants show, however, entry and reentry bars currently prevent immigrants from activating family ties in pursuit of citizenship. The Illegal Immigration Reform and Immigrant Responsibility Act of 1996 requires immigrants who entered the United States without authorization to apply for a status change in their home countries. As López has argued, this leaves undocumented immigrants in a catch-22, since they are then barred from reentry into the United States for up to ten years.[56] Discontinuing entry and reentry bans would ameliorate this situation and help migrants apply for US citizenship via existing family reunification mechanisms and avoid long-term family separation.

Although Deferred Action for Childhood Arrival (DACA)—which provides deportation relief and limited rights to certain undocumented immigrants—is a commendable intervention, this status is only temporary and lacks a path to citizenship. Furthermore, under Trump's first administration DACA was entangled in a myriad of court battles, leaving DACAmented immigrants in limbo. As the experiences of Indigenous migrants in Kansas further underscore, many undocumented migrants have no ties to US citizens or residents. A large proportion of undocumented migrants also do not fit the eligibility requirements for temporary statuses such as DACA, which means that other paths to more secure immigration status are needed. Employment-based paths to citizenship are associated with those who possess "high skills," while workers with "low skills" are deemed seasonal or temporary. Given the many essential jobs that undocumented immigrants hold in the United States and their role in maintaining the country's economy during past and current crises, a path to naturalization could emerge from immigrants' many contributions to the labor force—in agriculture, manufacturing, food service, construction, waste management, care work, and cleaning and maintenance, among other sectors.[57]

State and Local Policies

While comprehensive immigration reform at the federal level may seem utopian in such politically divided times, there are other policies and institutional actions that can be implemented at the state and local level to support immigrants' well-being. First, local communities can demand an end to 287(g) programs and similar agreements that enable and encourage the local policing of immigrants. These agreements are signed by local policing leaders who are publicly elected. In 2020, 148 jurisdictions across the United States had 287(g) agreements with federal immigration enforcement.[58]

Second, providing driver's licenses and professional licensures (for technicians, teachers, medical professionals, attorneys, barbers, etc.) to undocumented and semilegal immigrants would simultaneously benefit these immigrants and the communities where they live. Providing access to educational licensures will help ease the many labor shortages that communities face, such as in education and medical fields. As noted in the accounts of Indigenous and mestizo immigrants alike, public transportation in the heartland is either limited or nonexistent, and driving poses a risk to apprehension and possible deportation. Access to driver's licenses would allow immigrants to conduct everyday activities with peace of mind and continue contributing to the many aspects of their communities, including going to work, picking up children from school, attending medical appointments, shopping for groceries, and visiting friends and family. Additionally, providing access to driver's licenses would generate wider economic benefits.

Third, because federal public health and immigration policies have excluded undocumented and semilegal immigrants from accessing federally funded benefits,[59] most undocumented and semilegal immigrants lack health insurance. Since most immigrants are active in the labor force, however, their income taxes subsidize the state and federal benefits received by their citizen peers. If states allowed undocumented and semilegal immigrants to access subsidized health insurance, this would significantly benefit immigrants' health and well-being and the overall health and well-being of the wider community.

Finally, reforming certain institutional practices would make life in the heartland and the United States more welcoming for undocumented migrants. Adequate language-interpretation services, for instance—in courtrooms, immigrant detention centers, schools, and health care offices—are vital for immigrants' survival. Crucially, interpretation services geared toward Latina/o/x immigrants should be able to accommodate Indigenous languages as well as Spanish.[60] Many Indigenous-led grassroots organizations already provide such services, which future language-service initiatives ought to consider. Likewise, in order to provide the best avenue possible for educational success, schools and other educational institutions must accommodate the needs of Indigenous and mestizo migrants with limited educational backgrounds. This would involve language program initiatives and appropriate adult education options with support for women to be able to accommodate for gendered responsibilities of parenting and care work. Housing and poverty alleviation programs should also reconsider requirements that make undocumented immigrants ineligible for their services. Additionally, support to immigrant-led and immigrant-owned organizations and businesses is vital. These organizations and businesses can provide important services and resources to our broader communities, allowing for immigrant integration and bringing new cultural wealth to the heartland and the country. Finally, community organizations should implement staff training and accountability mechanisms to mitigate discrimination and rights violations against undocumented immigrants. Institutional reforms should also include confidentiality policies to ensure that migrants are protected from the localized enforcement of federal immigration policies.

LATIN AMERICAN NATIONS AND ACCOUNTABILITY

Besides the many potential improvements that could be implemented at federal, state, and local levels, US immigration policy alone cannot ameliorate the suffering and inequities that Indigenous and mestizo immigrants experience. To truly address the legacies of colonial oppression, Latin American nations themselves must take accountability for the circumstances that make thousands of people leave their homes each year. Of course, national indebtedness and global wealth inequality can only be addressed at the international scale.[61] Individual countries too, however, must act on the endemic corruption that reproduces social hierarchies, growing inequality gaps, extreme violence, and impunity. According to the Center for Economics and Peace, peace in a nation requires, among other factors, an equitable distribution of resources, low levels of corruption, media transparency, a functional government, and trust in community members.[62] These factors could also deter emigration. Mexico and Central American countries face some of the highest levels of violence, including gender-based violence, in the world. While all groups in society are affected by increases in violence, Indigenous groups and people living in poverty have historically faced its harshest consequences. Additionally, while men are more likely to experience violent crimes, women tend to experience lifetime violence and extreme torturous forms of violence with little protection from local policing agencies or the state.[63] *Feminicidios* continue to be on the rise across the region, and even when policies are in place to supposedly "protect" women, these are in fact lagging protections and often reproduce violence toward women.[64] Latin American nations thus must address racialized, gendered, and sexualized systems of exclusion and violence that are perpetuated by the law and exacerbated by poverty and corruption.

In addition, women continue to lag behind in financial stability, work opportunities, and educational attainment and face worse health outcomes across the region. In 2020, about 28.6 percent of women, compared to 10 percent of men in the region, did not have their own incomes, rates that were higher among Central American women.[65] Women have continued to have the main responsibility for housework and care work for their families and other forms of labor that are not renumerated.[66] And women have historically been more likely to live in poverty across the region, rates that have always been highest among

Indigenous women, as discussed in Chapter 1. The increased feminization of poverty combined with gendered violence and lack of government support pushes women to migrate. Latin American nations must address gender-based inequities and gender-based violence, working alongside women political leaders and organizers to lessen these gaps. Importantly, bridges between Indigenous women, Afro-descendants, and mestizas must be built to generate transformative feminist change.

Indigenous groups across Latin America have continued to face discrimination, marginalization, and exploitation.[67] The social divides generated by colonial legacies are aggravated by globalization and neoliberal projects. While purportedly promoting socioeconomic development, these changes have actually impoverished Indigenous groups and ruptured social institutions through violence and militarization, causing further displacement and migration. Across Latin America, Indigenous groups have fought for constitutional recognition, self-determination, political representation, land rights, and cultural rights. Since the late 1980s as a result of such Indigenous-led movements, countries all across Latin America have incorporated "multiculturalist" policies and laws. However, the majority of these multiculturalist policies have maintained an Eurocentric assimilation lens, further reified by neoliberalism, and have failed to improve Indigenous groups' well-being. While Indigenous social movements have continued to demand change throughout the region, they continue to face barriers—often codified in enduring colonial hierarchies of power. For such inequities to be alleviated, Indigenous knowledge and people must be fully incorporated within national systems of power, including possibilities for self-sovereignty. Indigenous people across Latin America continue to lack basic human rights, including water, housing, food, health care, education, and political representation. Additionally, Indigenous women face multiple and cumulative layers of violence and discrimination. Latin American nations should also recognize the valuable contributions of their Indigenous citizens who live abroad.

Indigenous migrants develop transnational ties across countries, and via remittances and the deployment of social and cultural capital, they contribute to the development of their extended families and original communities.[68] Indigenous immigrants, one might even suggest, have stepped in to provide for their communities where national governments have failed to do so.

A FUTURE FOR IMMIGRANTS IN THE HEARTLAND

Communities across the heartland have had many leaders, organizations, and community members who have been actively—sometimes quietly and at other times loudly—working with and for immigrant rights in the region. Immigrant leaders and allies have created spaces to bring services to immigrants and to uphold immigrant cultural richness and contributions to their communities. Sometimes strategies have been welcomed and highlighted in local communities, and at other times actions have tried to fly under the radar in order to maintain the minimum protections that were available. Yet as the accounts of immigrants in this book reveal, the work must continue.

We need to push back from rhetoric that vilifies and criminalizes Latino immigrants and their families. For instance, working with educational and literacy organizations such as libraries, programs to educate the community on how to decipher disinformation and misinformation from social media and the internet would help us understand and disentangle such harmful discourse. Learning about disinformation and misinformation can help our communities better understand the roots of the criminalization of immigration and identify the differences between immigration trends and crime rates, which decades of empirical research have been proven have no correlation.[69] Universities should be encouraged to partner with local community organizations and literacy programs to activate such educational programming. These strategies can help communities increase awareness of the true root causes of social ailments in their communities with the realization that immigrants are most often not to blame and find collaborative solutions.

Another strategy is by creating spaces for interactions and intimate connections between immigrants and nonimmigrants in the community. For example, opportunities for children and youths from diverse backgrounds to work together to create music, poetry, murals, and other arts-based projects can teach both youths and adults about the basics of collaboration and respect and help them learn from each other through cooperation. Social groups where activities such as sports, crafting, and language learning can happen are other spaces to bring adult members of the community together. Soccer and basketball teams, for instance, are spaces for community members to spend time together in cooperation, allowing immigrants and nonimmigrants to create social ties.[70] Cultural celebrations that highlight immigrants' backgrounds, traditions, and contributions to their communities are also useful for building alliances between immigrant and nonimmigrant groups and bringing important cultural wealth to the heartland, such as the Mexican Fiestas that are celebrated in the heartland and in other US regions. Unions and tenants' rights organizations are also important spaces where workers can come together for a common goal whether in the workplace or in housing. Spaces where all people from the community are welcome must be safe from judgment, discrimination, and immigration enforcement. Following the lead of grassroots organizations, community leaders and youths can take our heartland communities to a space of *tranquilidad* that immigrants I met sought in the heartland and that nonimmigrants can cherish.

Latino communities in the heartland also have a key role to play, including multigenerational immigrant communities. For the most part, during my ethnographic observations the few Hispanic-serving organizations in Kansas were led and staffed by mestizos, many of whom had access to citizenship or other forms of semilegal statuses. As Indigenous immigrants' accounts showed, Indigenous immigrants often felt unwelcomed and in some cases felt discriminated against in these spaces. Whether or not these mechanisms occurred intentionally, Latino communities and Latino-leading and Latino-serving organizations must not only embrace indigeneity but also work closely with Indigenous immigrants and Indigenous community leaders. Many of the Indigenous families I met lacked institutional support from Anglo and Latino institutions and instead faced exploitative conditions from both groups. Support for Indigenous-owned businesses and Indigenous-owned/led organizations as well as leadership and inclusion in decision-making spaces must occur by breaking the colonial legacies that divide our Latina/o/x communities.

The accounts of the Indigenous and mestizo immigrants I met in Kansas demonstrate the consequences of the racialization and gendering of illegality and how long-established colonial hierarchies of race and gender shape the opportunities and outcomes of Indigenous and mestizo immigrants across international borders. In the heartland, anti-immigration policies and sentiments were reproduced in local communities. However, new alliances and spaces for solidarity were also emerging. Cities as well as small towns across Kansas have acknowledged the benefits of a growing Latino immigrant population, especially in areas where the population is in decline.[71] In places such as Kansas, the white-majority population is declining and in the process of retirement, and thus the growing Latino immigrant population helps fuel the state's economy and has contributed to a large share of the state's labor force growth in the past two decades.

During my time in Kansas, I observed many protests and rallies organized by both immigrant allies and immigrant leaders against the policing, incarceration, and deportation of immigrants during the first Trump administration. The rallies I observed included people of all ages, genders, sexual identities, racial groups, and immigration statuses. Immigrant allies and immigrants together marched on sidewalks and dirt roads in the heartland chanting "Hey, hey, ho, ho, Deportation's got to go!" and holding signs that read, for example, "Stop separating families," "Sin Miedo," "Undocumented and Unafraid," "Here to Stay," and "Immigrants Welcome." While some of the rallies were large—especially those organized in the aftermath of the initial executive orders of 2017, some were smaller and quieter, most often going unnoticed by the larger media but always calling for solidarity and support for immigrants throughout Kansas communities.

Alongside grassroots organizing, new organizations also have emerged, providing immigrant families with vital resources for fighting housing discrimination, wage theft, and unjust apprehensions. These organizations, alongside the well-established Hispanic-serving organizations, have been vital in regard to supporting immigrant integration and contributing to immigrant communities. Naturalized immigrants and second-generation immigrants as well as community allies have also entered local political arenas, such as school boards and city councils, to ensure representation of immigrant communities. These efforts are complemented with allies and advocates' work in health clinics, schools, churches, and nonprofit organizations, creating and nurturing safe spaces for immigrant communities to flourish in the heartland.

Appendix

Lessons Learned from a Mexicana Scholar

"YO QUIERO SER COMO TU" (I want to be like you), a little girl told me when I came to her house to interview her mom, an Indigenous Tlapaneco woman. *"Y que soy?"* (And what am I), I asked her, puzzled, since this was our first time meeting. *"Tu eres la que ayuda a la gente"* (You are the one that helps people), she responded confidently. A strong wave of guilt hit my stomach immediately after hearing these very generous words. How could *I* be helping anyone? I am just doing research, I thought. The little girl's words followed me throughout the rest of my graduate program and into the years to come as I began a career as a tenure-track professor. However, her words also point to the complex mechanisms that emerge when conducting research with populations that have been historically and systemically harmed as well as the importance of compassionate and caring research practices and the power of sociological research to guide and create social change.

DOING RESEARCH WITH HARMED POPULATIONS

Conducting research with groups or communities who face struggles every day, have been systemically silenced and harmed, and have been violated by state and legal powers, brings certain challenges and responsibilities that I was not prepared for when I began my journey as a researcher. In academia these groups are called "vulnerable populations" because they are vulnerable to researcher exploitation, including the extraction of knowledge and resources that are then utilized to benefit the researcher's interests (or the institution more broadly) and not the study population or group. My intension when I began this research project—which was my dissertation—was to capture the direct and indirect consequences of immigration policies on the lives of immigrant families with the hope that through their stories and testimonies solutions to their circumstances could emerge. After becoming involved in the lives of the immigrants I met during my research project, however, it was clear that immigrants were living in a constant and circling crisis due to the structural and sociolegal circumstances that were detailed throughout the book. Given this context, although my research purpose remained—to bring transformative change to the lived experiences of immigrant families—I had to adjust both my research practices and my research expectations.

I recruited immigrants to participate in the study by becoming immersed in the spaces where I thought potential participants would be. I visited churches and talked to priests and pastors about my research project and the purpose of my research, I presented to congregations to seek potential volunteers to interview. I visited Hispanic-serving nonprofits as well as grassroots organizations and met with the leaders of these groups. From there I was invited to their routine meetings and events (in churches, the doors were always open for their religious gatherings, but I was also invited to Bible study and smaller get-togethers). I also frequented Latino-owned grocery stores and public spaces, such as parks, where I could interact with other immigrants. In these spaces I presented myself as a Mexicana student researcher, explained my research project, and, when possible, invited potential participants to an interview scheduled for a later date (not during the event where I was recruiting).

These recruitment strategies worked to some extent, but as time progressed and as the sociopolitical environment became more hostile, immigrants became more distrustful. As a result, the connections and relationships I formed with key informants, that is, community members who immigrants already trusted, were especially important. I am especially grateful to two pastors, a community health worker, and a social worker who connected me directly to the first immigrant women that I interviewed. The key informants were people in the community whom immigrants already trusted, so getting introduced through them allowed immigrants to trust me too. From there a series of snowball sampling developed. Immigrants who participated in interviews gave their friends and family members my contact information and sometimes even introduced me to potential interviewees in person. To participate, immigrants had to be a member of a mixed-status family (that is, families with a variety of immigration statuses in the same family) and be over the age of eighteen and under age sixty-five.

Once immigrants agreed to participate in the study, I scheduled interviews in a location of their choosing. This was important, because as the fears of immigrants increased, I too was worried of the potential of interacting with Immigration and Customs Enforcement (ICE) and policing agents during interviews. So, most interviews took place in immigrants' homes, but sometimes we met in public places such as parks, coffee shops, fast-food restaurants, and churches. Many times, the immigrants did not show up to the scheduled interview. This was most often either because they forgot or because something last minute came up. For instance, sometimes immigrants would get called in to work, a child would be sick, or they would be running late due to rideshares. Sometimes immigrants would give me a heads-up that they could not make it, but many times they did not. I always tried to reschedule the interviews, but after a third failed attempt, I would give up, realizing that maybe the person just did not want to talk to me.

When I met with Indigenous immigrants, I was constantly aware of the strong ethnoracial divides present within our interactions. Growing up partly in Mexico, anti-Indigenous discrimination embedded within *mestizaje, indigenismo,* and *blanqueamiento* ideologies were present in every aspect of society including my family life and my identity. My dad was born in Spain, so my physical appearance of light skin, light-color eyes, and brown hair reflects the centuries of colonial oppression that I tried to highlight in this book. My *abuelito* on my mother's side, however, was a poet who wrote in Spanish and Nahuatl (an Indigenous language). As a mestiza, it was thus not surprising to me that some Indigenous families I met were wary of my true intentions even after being introduced to me through one of their close friends or family members. To build trust, I had open conversations about my background, how I came to the United States, and my research and discussed immigrants' needs and their hopes. Most often, I also had more than one encounter before conducting an interview. The first encounter was to introduce myself and get to know the immigrants, and the second encounter was to conduct the formal interview. Once trust was established, Indigenous families I met were welcoming and generous. They shared delicious food with me on many occasions, taught me basic phrases in Indigenous languages, and invited me to many of their family celebrations. Building trust with mestizo families took less time—given my positionality—and they too welcomed me into their homes and family life.

Most interviews lasted about an hour, but a couple of interviews lasted only half an hour and a few almost three hours. I recorded most of the interviews unless participants asked me not to do so. The seven participants who declined recording were Indigenous and declined recording in fear of immigration enforcement. In those cases, I took detailed notes trying to catch as much of direct quotes as possible. All the recorded interviews were transcribed. I conducted most interviews in Spanish, although a few of the second-generation immigrants preferred to speak in English.

For the ethnographic aspect of the study, I also had to consider the broader anti-immigrant climate and create strategies to build trust and maintain safety. I conducted participant observations in both public and private spaces where immigrants interacted. This included large gatherings in public spaces such as cultural events, religious gatherings, and pro-immigrant rights rallies and protests as well as smaller gatherings and get-togethers including in women's support groups, immigrant rights groups, English-language classes, and Bible study groups. I tried to not disrupt the flow of the event or activity. This was easy in large gatherings, where my presence was most often ignored. However, my presence was felt in the smaller gatherings, such as the women's group I observed for several months. I only conducted observations in the more private small gatherings after obtaining consent from the organizers, and I always shared the purpose of my presence and research during observations. My continuous presence eventually became normalized, allowing me to observe key interactions between immigrants. I was also invited into intimate spaces within immigrant families, including kindergarten graduations, *quinceañeras*, Christmas celebrations, *tamales* cooking days, and many kids' birthday parties. In these instances, it was the immigrant participants who presented me to their families and loved ones, and I shared my research purpose with them. Eventually I got to know some of the families very well.

My observations were documented in several formats. When possible, I jotted down notes during the observed situation. This was easy, for instance, during the women's support group and religious gatherings, since other people also had notebooks and pens. In most cases, however, I recounted my observations in a voice recorder either by taking bathroom breaks during an event or in my car promptly after. Taking notes during a three-year-old's birthday party, for example, would be disruptive to the party and possibly interfere with my ability to build trust with participants. Like the interviews, my observations that were recorded were also transcribed.

I analyzed interview transcripts and field notes as the project progressed. This allowed me to revise the ways I asked questions to ensure that participants felt more comfortable and to find instances where my questions were confusing and as a result produced unclear answers. The analytical strategy was also inductive, which allowed for the data to guide findings. This is how the main argument/thesis for the book came about. I did not begin this project looking at the differences between Indigenous and mestizo immigrants. Rather, it was their experiences that pushed me to reconsider how colonial legacies are maintained and (re)produced in transnational spaces. I utilized line-by-line coding to get a well-rounded estimation of the data. Initially I coded too intricately, making my initial analysis overly complicated. However, my coding became better with practice, and eventually subthemes were clustered into major themes, which are presented in the various chapters of this book.

I did not pay any immigrants to participate in this study—a common practice in sociology and the social sciences that I fully support. However, other forms of support developed organically. As immigrants shared intimate aspects of their lives with me, whether it was through interviews or in the spaces where I was invited, trust was developed, so they began to share some of their ongoing troubles and the needs they encountered. I provides support as much as I could. In some instances, this involved connecting immigrants with allies in the community, including nonprofits and service organizations. Other times, it involved helping to fill out forms for schools, health care, and immigration processes; interpreting conversations in person or over the phone; and driving folks to work, medical appointments, and immigration-related appointments. In other cases it was more complicated, particularly when it involved interactions with state agents including with the courts, policing and immigration enforcement, and the welfare system. And sometimes, more often than I wished, there were just no resources in the community to meet immigrants' needs. So, we—the immigrant families and I—had to create our own resources, involving creative forms of mutual aid. All these forms of support were provided at no cost and with no expectation of participation in the study. Some of the immigrants I met while conducting the study and gave rides to or helped fill out paperwork, for instance, never became interview participants. However, for those who did, these interactions allowed for a deeper connection that allowed me to gain a profound understanding of their social world and the ongoing hostility that the Trump administration was brewing.

Families felt comfortable enough to call me at all times of the day including in the middle of the night, which happened a few times. During this period I was in my midtwenties. I was a graduate student, I had no children, and I had a loving and supportive partner. I had a car and a generous fellowship, which allowed me the time to be able to do these tasks. As much as I felt the responsibility to provide support and as much as I tried, however, I simply could not fulfill all the needs or solve the ongoing crisis that immigrant families encountered in the heartland. Thus, I sometimes felt like I was letting immigrant families down, especially when, for example, the little girl introduced at the beginning of this appendix shared her high hopes of me bringing help to immigrants in her community. So, how can we conduct research that is not extracting and that provides the support that study participants need in moments of crisis during and after research is concluded, honoring their lives and worldviews, while at the same time contributing to important academic conversations? I turn to other scholars for guidance.

COMPASSIONATE AND CARING RESEARCH PRACTICES

Scholars have written extensively about practices that researchers can incorporate to address the tensions in research dynamics, particularly when working with harmed populations.[1] Much of these academic discussions surround the impossibility of "subjectivity" and "objectivity" in research—particularly in qualitative methods—and how this may or may not lead to rigorous research findings. For me as a Mexicana young student doing work with mostly Mexican and Central American immigrants during a very hostile political climate, these tensions seemed to get in the way of actually *doing* the research. As Leisy Abrego has argued, it is sometimes impossible and not useful to create distance and "objectivity" between research and personal life.[2] Abrego introduces accompaniment as a research method: "understanding of the state of the academic field(s) of interest and a deep familiarity with the processes, practices, and emotions of the people and communities in question."[3] Instead of trying to distance ourselves as researchers from participants, accompaniment as a research method highlights the wealth that the close relationships and the embracing of emotions associated with such relationships can generate to develop new and creative research and rigorous findings and ultimately how these practices can bring important contributions and change to immigrants' well-being.

Emphasizing care and well-being is beneficial for both immigrant participants and researchers. For instance, scholars León, Abrego, and Negrón-Gonzales also highlight the complexities of time when doing research with undocumented immigrants.[4] This includes time for academics trying to conduct projects that lead to steps in their careers (i.e., finishing a dissertation, getting a job, getting tenure, etc.) but also time for immigrants in their immigration processes and time focusing on the fast-changing immigration policies. The authors argue for the importance of time in a deliberate and caring manner within research practices that could facilitate collaboration and cooperation between researchers and undocumented immigrants. Throughout my research project, time was of extreme importance: sometimes this included time to provide support during moments of need, such as nonscheduled phone interpretation support, a four-hour car ride, filling out complicated forms, and accompanying immigrants to a difficult appointment. Sometimes time involved hours trying to find resources for immigrants or their loved ones, spending several hours calling the immigration enforcement bureaucracy trying to find a detained loved one, accompanying immigrants through various bureaucratic processes, and waiting in all kinds of waiting rooms—health clinics, attorney offices, schools, and immigration offices. Acknowledging the importance of time and unplanned time in research practices can develop more caring and empathetic outcomes that ultimately centers on immigrants' well-being and allows for deeper connections between researchers and participants, allowing for more in-depth data and robust findings.

Importantly, deciphering the role of violence in the context of research and within our research practices can create more a complete picture of what we are trying to learn—or provide evidence for in regard to needed change—while acknowledging who are the true knowledge creators.[5] I completed my fieldwork during very turbulent times in the immigration landscape of the United States. Immigrants were scared, with well-founded reasons. The anti-immigrant rhetoric was at an all-time high, and policy changes criminalizing undocumented immigrants came quickly. Understanding the mechanisms of fear within immigration policies, the creation of fear as a control mechanism of the state, and therefore a form of violence allowed me to adjust my research program to better comprehend immigrant experiences and form deeper connections. I had to understand the ways in which my presence could sometimes reproduce fear and find creative ways to navigate such sociopolitical context. For instance, knocking at the front door of an immigrant's home could create a lot of anxiety and fear. With the increased presence of ICE in immigrant communities, "Know Your Rights" campaigns told immigrants that if immigration enforcement came knocking at their door, they should not open the door. Early on in my research days I was ignorant of this dynamic, especially because my research began in 2016 prior to these specific recommendations shared in "Know Your Rights" campaigns. However, very quickly after the 2017 elections, I realized that when I knocked at immigrants' doors while visiting caused unintended harm, as a summary from my field notes indicates:

> I knocked at the front door of a two level, run-down house, and no one answered. There were cars in the driveway, though, so I walked around the back. I found a back door, and I knocked again; this time, after seeing me through the window, Luz, an Indigenous Maya Guatemalan woman, opened the door and told me "Ay pensé que eras la migra (I thought you were ICE)."

Of course, I never intended to increase immigrants' fears during my interactions. Thereafter, instead of knocking the door, I most often texted or called participants ahead of time to let them know I was outside. Only with their permission given ahead of time—at the time when we scheduled the interview—would I knock when I was at the door. Most often, I waited patiently outside until they saw me or heard their phones.

Some of the experiences that immigrants shared with me detailed heavy traumatic events. When I started this project, I did not realize the impact this would have on my well-being. Secondary trauma refers to the effect of indirect exposure to traumatic experiences of others.[6] Symptoms associated with secondary trauma include physical manifestations such as headaches, changes in body weight, irritability, or nightmares; cognitive manifestations such as disruption in perceptions of safety, trust, intimacy, flashbacks, and changes of memory and views of self and of the world; emotional reactions such as guilt, shame, helplessness, self-blaming, and grief anxiety; and behavioral changes.[7] I experienced many of these symptoms during my research project and even after I completed my graduate degree. And it was not until very recently— when I read the appendix of a book written by a friend, Stephanie Canizales, that I realized that I was also experiencing "empathy-based stress."[8] This relates to the stress associated with the empathetic reactions that I had after being exposed to secondary trauma.[9] However, I did not have the language to talk about these experiences with my academic mentors (who would have supported me without question). How I managed secondary trauma and empathy-based stress emerged organically. At the time, I was very active into exercising, which luckily helps reduce stress and supports emotional well-being.[10] I also had a small group of friends who were doing critical work that also had exposure to secondary trauma. We met weekly for writing and talked about our work, we called ourselves *Sister Scholars*. And some days I just cried in my car after an interview, binge-watched Netflix in bed for an entire day, or ate too many chips and cookies. Acknowledging these possible stressors on researchers could help us be better prepared beforehand while also confronting the multiple emotions that come with doing work with harmed populations. Centering emotions surrounding violence and trauma within the core of research can ultimately lead to better research practices, more robust data, and impactful findings. As researchers, we must incorporate trauma-informed practices within our methodologies to care for the study participants and study collaborators but also care for ourselves while remaining compassionate, empathetic, and in solidarity.[11]

A MEXICANA IMMIGRANT FIRST-GEN SCHOLAR

I am both an insider and an outsider when it comes to my ties to the Latina/o/x immigrant community in the heartland. As an immigrant from Mexico, I could easily connect with many of the immigrants I met on the trials and errors of making a home in a new country. Although I arrived at the United States at age twelve, Spanish has remained my first language to this day, and thus having conversations and interviews in Spanish came easily. I was also young when I was doing this project, and my status as a graduate student softened immigrants' concerns about my research. Most often, the immigrants I met wanted to *help me* finish my degree. Families were welcoming, and after our time together sometimes they gave me nicknames such as Andreita and Andy. My demeanor was purposefully friendly and respectful. I always used formal Spanish (*usted*, meaning "you") unless invited to use informal Spanish (*tú*). I did not grow up in Kansas and had no family there either. I was there only temporarily for the period of my graduate program. I spent a lot of time in the immigrant community as a volunteer English-language teacher and volunteering at health clinics, visiting Hispanic-serving organizations, participating in cultural events, and shopping at the local Mexican stores as part of my everyday life. Yet I had no intention of staying in Kansas after finishing my graduate program, thus making me also an outsider to the local immigrant community.

My immigration story is both transnational and multigenerational and motivates my scholarship as well as this book project. I was born in Mexico City. My father and his family migrated to Mexico from Galicia, Spain, during Francisco Franco's dictatorship. My mom was born in Mexico to a Costa Rican mother and a Mexican father. My Costa Rican great-grandma's parents were from Nicaragua and El Salvador. Becoming an immigration scholar was meant to happen, I guess, with migration running deep in my family lineage. My migration-related experiences have also shaped how I approached this book and how I approach my scholarship more broadly. When I was little, my Costa Rican *abuelita* (grandma), Julieta, was the center of my universe. She raised me, since my mom was a divorced single mom, working long hours to make ends meet, and my dad was not very involved. When I was around four years old and living in Mexico, my *abuelita* was voluntarily returned to Costa Rica—that is, deported—because she had been living undocumented, with *papeles chuecos* (crooked papers), in Mexico. Although I cannot recall all the details, I remember feeling sad and scared. Crying in my *abuelita*'s room, I wondered if I was also going to have to move to Costa Rica—a place I had never been to—or if I would ever see her again. The complex thing about childhood trauma is that when it is combined with secondary trauma as an adult, sometimes the veil that had covered forgotten events as a protection mechanism (such as my *abuelita*'s "voluntary" deportation) gets ripped away, leaving you with unhealed memories to process unexpectedly.

When I arrived in the United States to suburban Michigan as a sixth grader, I was one of two non-English speakers in the six elementary schools of the district, a landscape that has since changed drastically; by 2020 there was even a bilingual Spanish-immersion elementary school in that same district. I remember vividly my first days in school: the brown carpet, the green lockers, the minilibrary in the classroom, and a TV in the corner where we watched the crashes of 9/11. I remember trying to play with the other kids during recess but being left behind because they could not understand me. And I remember the first day I touched snow and the feeling of the icy-cold air on my face. Migrating as part of the 1.5 generation also meant that while I never felt fully "American," I was also not Mexican enough. I was a *pocha* (term used in Mexico to describe US-born Mexicans) when visiting my *primos* (cousins) and family in Mexico and an outsider to my Anglo peers in the United States. Thus, I did not fit into either country, a challenge that many immigrants of the 1.5- and second-generation experience.[12]

My experiences as a Mexicana immigrant in the United States and coming from a family of transnational and multigenerational migrations do shape my researcher lens, the types of questions I ask, the methods I rely on, and the groups I am able to connect with. Particularly surrounding immigration issues and immigrant understandings, I can create deep and intimate connections with immigrants that lead to collaborations of knowledge production rooted in compassion, empathy, and care. But my positionality also has drawbacks. Some of my colleagues may deem my scholarship—and this book—not "rigorous enough." And of course, due to my positionality there might be some populations that I too may have difficulties building rapport with.[13] Nonetheless, I strongly believe that this book brings nuanced and important contributions to sociology and the social sciences. And I truly believe that we can use sociological research as a tool for transformative change. In Cecilia Menjívar's words, "Identifying urgent issues that need our research attention is key to doing this work more effectively to contribute to social change."[14] Given the turbulent sociopolitical context that immigrants in the United States have faced, this book will hopefully help shape discussions for purposeful and transformative change even in challenging times. As a Mexicana, an immigrant, and a first-gen scholar in the United States, I am hopeful that this book will help other minoritized and nontraditional scholars in their academic paths, inspire new questions and solutions to old and new problems, and bring about the realities and hopes of Indigenous and mestizo immigrants to broader conversations with prospects to alter their realities now and in the future.

Notes

FOREWORD

1. Guttentag 2025.

2. Klein 2010.

3. Social science evidence demonstrates that immigrants have no association with increases in crime rates in the United States. See Ousey and Kubrin 2018.

4. Ousey and Kubrin 2018.

5. Santana and Aleman 2025.

6. Osgood 2025.

7. On June 27, 2025, in a historic decision, the Supreme Court ruled in *Trump v. CASA* to end universal injunctions, making it impossible for federal courts to block executive orders or related decisions made by the executive branch (*Trump v. CASA* 606 U.S. 2025).

8. Federal Register 2025.

9. Alvord et al. 2018.

10. Pearson 2025.

11. Duehren 2025.

12. Frank 2025.

13. Bustillo 2025.

14. Federal Register 2025.

15. US Department of Justice 2025.

16. Lopez 2025.

17. Taylor and Dastin 2025.

18. Nungesser 2024.

19. Rosenberg 2025; and Trevizo and Rosenberg 2025.

20. Oladipo 2025.

21. Ortuaty 2025.

22. Al-Badawi 2025.

23. Massey et al. 2002.

24. Beauregard 2025.

25. Johnson 2025.

26. Federal Register 2025. As of June 27, 2025, the Supreme Court in *Trump v. CASA*, a challenge to Executive Order 14160 aiming to end birthright citizenship for individuals born in the United States to parents with certain immigration statuses, did not decide on the constitutionality of this executive order and instead blocked universal injunctions. The court gave leeway for this order to come into effect thirty days from its decision date, allowing for various organizations to prepare class action lawsuits and causing confusion and enhancing fear across the country (*Trump v. CASA* 2025).

27. Lee 2007.

28. Martínez-Beltrán 2025.

29. Chischti and Putzel-Kavanaugh 2025.

30. Faheid and Park 2025.

31. Menjívar and Abrego 2012.

32. Brabeck and Xu 2010.

33. Rosenberg 2017.

34. Enriquez 2020.

35. Sugarman 2025.

36. Friedman and Venkataramani 2021.

37. Alvord et al. 2018.

38. Menjívar 2021.

39. Arriaga 2017.

40. Baumer and Xie 2023.

41. Donato and Rodríguez 2014.

42. Gómez Cervantes 2021.

43. Menjívar and Lakhani 2016; and García 2018.

44. Novak et al. 2017.

45. Saadi, Patler, and Langer 2025.

46. Payan and Rodriguez-Sánchez 2025.

47. De Genova 2004.

48. Kapoor 2022.

49. Rattner 2025.

50. Hsu 2025.

51. PBS News 2024; Bennett et al. 2024; and López et al. 2016.

52. Bonilla-Silva 2004, 933.

INTRODUCTION

1. Throughout the book, I translate most of the interview quotes to English to assist non-Spanish-speaking readers. However, in instances where the translation would dilute meaning or intent, I present the original quotes in Spanish followed with the English translation in parenthesis.

2. *Güero* is a term used in Mexico to refer to people with blond hair, lighter skin tone, and light eye color. This is also a term that many Mexican and Latin American immigrants use to refer to US-born Anglo white people.

3. I use the terms "Latino," "Latina," and "Hispanic" interchangeably throughout the book. While terms to de-gender Latinidad such as "Latinx," "Latine," and "Latin+" have also emerged, none of the immigrants I met identified with these terms—at least during the time of our conversations and the period of the study. For this reason, I rely on the terminology commonly used by the immigrants I met during this study throughout the book.

4. Urrieta 2013; Blackwell, Boj Lopez, and Urrieta 2017; and Boj Lopez 2017.

5. Fox and Rivera-Salgado 2004.

6. Critical Latinx Indigeneities scholarship has placed significant attention on the educational and work experiences of Indigenous immigrants in the United States, mainly in traditional destinations such as California (Blackwell

et al. 2017; Urrieta and Calderón 2019), and highlights the racialization mechanisms that lead to different experiences for Indigenous versus non-Indigenous groups.

7. Gómez Cervantes 2021.

8. Jiménez 2009.

9. Golash-Boza and Valdez 2018; Portes and Rumbaut 2001; and Schmalzbauer 2014.

10. Brown, Jones, and Becker 2018; Golash-Boza and Valdez 2018; and Jones 2019. Examining Latinos' experiences in a new destination in North Carolina, Jones (2019) noted that immigrants initially found a welcoming context of reception, with accessible housing and jobs and welcoming institutions and almost no local-level immigration enforcement. Yet as federal immigration policies tightened during the 2000s, the local context shifted, complicating Latino immigrants' experiences of integration.

11. Flippen and Farrell-Bryan 2021.

12. Oppenheimer 1985.

13. Jiménez 2009.

14. US Census 2020.

15. Quijano 2019.

16. Wolfe 2006.

17. I acknowledge that presenting the historical colonial context of all Latin American nations as one hegemonic experience is problematic and impossible in just a few pages. As previous scholars have noted, however, there is value in highlighting commonalities across nations to understand migration processes and experiences. See Blackwell et al. 2017; and Speed 2019.

18. Castellanos 2017; Gott 2007; and Speed 2019.

19. Fanon 1963.

20. Quijano 2000, 2019.

21. Lugones 2008; and Oyěwùmí 1997.

22. Rivera Cusicanqui 1997.

23. Curiel 2007, 98.

24. Walsh 2010.

25. Irving Reynoso, 2013.

26. Velázquez Gutiérrez and Iturralde Nieto 2016.

27. Taracena Arriola 2019.

28. The logic of elimination, according to Wolfe (2006, 388), is "encouraged miscegenation, the breaking-down of native title into alienable individual free-holds, native citizenship, child abduction, religious conversion, resocialization in total institutions such as missions or boarding schools, and a whole range of cognate biocultural assimilation . . . along with homicide of the frontier."

29. Wolfe 2006.

30. Haney-Lopez 1996.

31. Glenn 2015; and Wolfe 2006.

32. Hixson 2013.

33. Glymph 2008.

34. Rumbaut 2009.

35. Gómez 2007.

36. Menchaca 1993.

37. Rodríguez 2000.

38. The US Census defines the "Hispanic or Latino" category as "include[ing] individuals of Mexican, Puerto Rican, Salvadoran, Cuban, Dominican, Guatemalan, and other Central or South American or Spanish culture or origin" (Marks 2024).

39. Mora 2014.

40. Mora 2014.

41. Boj Lopez 2017, 12.

42. Cardoso 2014; and Gonzales 1984.

43. Menjívar 2021; Molina 2014; and Hernández 2017.

44. Transactional Records Access Clearinghouse 2022.

45. Van Hook, Gelatt, and Ruiz Soto 2023.

46. Armenta 2017; Flores and Schachter 2018; Gómez Cervantes 2021; and Menjívar 2021.

47. Lee 2002.

48. Enchautegui and Menjívar 2015.

49. Bonjour and Chauvin 2018.

50. Dowling and Inda 2013; Martínez 2022; Provine et al. 2016; and Stumpf 2006.

51. Once farmworkers were able to shift their immigration status, however, they quickly moved to better-paying and more stable occupations, leaving the agriculture industry in need of workers and thus maintaining a demand for

(undocumented) workers even after amnesty was granted (Massey, Durand, and Malone 2002).

52. Massey et al. 2002.

53. De Genova 2002.

54. De Genova 2004.

55. Massey, Durand, and Pren 2016.

56. De León 2015; and Martínez 2022.

57. Romero 2006.

58. Initially, the only charges associated with aggravated felony for immigrants were murder, federal drug trafficking, and arms dealing. By 2018, however, Congress expanded the definition of aggravated felony to cover over thirty types of offenses, including theft, filing a wrong tax return, failing to appear in court, and illegal reentry (Menjívar, Gómez Cervantes, and Alvord 2018). These behaviors are not usually considered felonies for citizens. Conviction of an aggravated felony within the immigration system is retroactive even if the charge was not originally considered as such (American Immigration Council 2021). This means that even if an immigrant was convicted and served a punishment assigned by the criminal legal system and Congress added a new behavior to the list of aggravated felonies thirty years later, the immigrant would then be subject to deportation retroactively (see also Tosh 2019).

59. Abrego et al. 2017.

60. Ryo 2019.

61. American Immigration Council 2019.

62. Kubrin 2014.

63. Coleman and Kocher 2019, 1189.

64. Transactional Records Access Clearinghouse 2022.

65. Ngai 2004.

66. Abrego and Villalpando 2021.

67. Adler 2006; Gómez Cervantes 2021.

68. Flores and Schachter 2018; and Santa Ana 2002.

69. Golash-Boza and Hondagneu-Sotelo 2013.

70. Menjívar and Gómez Cervantes 2024.

71. Llewellyn 2020.

72. Gómez Cervantes, Alvord, and Menjívar 2018.

73. Alvord, Menjívar, and Gómez Cervantes 2018; Romero 2018.

74. Deferred Action for Childhood Arrival is a two-year semipermanent status that grants relief from deportation and provides immigrants with a work permit.

75. Pierce 2019.

76. Guttentag 2025.

77. Gonzales and Burciaga 2018.

78. Viruell-Fuentes, Morenoff, and Williams 2013.

79. Menjívar 2000.

80. Cranford 2005; Hagan 1994; Del Real 2019; and Rosales 2020.

81. Curran and Rivero-Fuentes 2003; Hondagneu-Sotelo 1994; Kibria 1993; Mahler and Pessar 2006; and Menjívar 2000.

82. Hagan 1998.

83. Hagan 1998.

84. Schmalzbauer 2014.

85. Menjívar 2000, 35.

86. Rosales 2020.

87. Canizales 2024.

88. Del Real 2019.

89. Blackwell 2010; and Herrera 2016.

90. Urrieta and Calderón 2019; and Ramos and Karin 2019.

91. Although I can pronounce the phrases the families taught me, I had a difficult time finding the Western equivalents for the phrases. In Chuj "how are you" sounds like *wa-cha kojol* (see Az'un Papul Xuvan 2017), and in Tlapaneco "see you later" is *mbáyaa rá* (see Gobierno de México 2016).

92. Families who lived in rural Kansas were contacted through another research project led by Professor Cecilia Menjívar. To learn more about immigration and immigrant experiences in rural destinations, see our coauthored works Gómez Cervantes et al. 2018; and Menjívar and Gómez Cervantes 2024.

CHAPTER 1. "VENIMOS POR NECESIDAD":
MIGRATING NORTH

1. Messina and Silva 2021.

2. I use the term "non-Indigenous" in this chapter when documenting the inequities that Indigenous groups face in Latin America. In some countries

such as Mexico, mestizos are not "counted" as such, and African-origin groups only began being documented in recent years, so there is little data that helps contextualize the "only mestizo" experience. Rather, existing data divides groups as Indigenous and non-Indigenous. In Guatemala, statistics surrounding non-Indigenous population ranges from 50 to 62 percent (López de León and Yela Sayle 2018). The inequality measures are available in relation to Indigenous and non-Indigenous groups more broadly.

3. Sánchez García et al. 2023.

4. Consejo Nacional de Evaluación de la Política de Desarrollo Social 2019.

5. Instituto Nacional de Estadística y Geografía 2022; and Mazari and Ruiz 2019.

6. Oxfam Mexico 2017.

7. Cumes 2012.

8. Gauster and Romero 2019.

9. Inter-American Commission on Human Rights 2015.

10. Gauster and Romero 2019; and Ola 2020.

11. Inter-American Commission on Human Rights 2015.

12. Gomes 2013; Lagarde 2006; and Menjívar 2011.

13. *Femincidios* is a term coined by Mexican scholar-activist Marcela Lagarde (2006), pointing at the interconnection of gender violence that results in multiple levels of oppression and harm and ultimately death among women, with undue impunity from the state. There have been debates on the term *feminicidio* that emerged from the Mexican context and "femicide" from US scholars. However, regardless of theoretical labels, women in Latin American continue to face high levels of gender-based violence and torturous conditions throughout their lifetimes, which often ends in death.

14. Menjívar and Diossa-Jiménez 2023; and Menjívar and Walsh 2017.

15. Inter-American Commission on Human Rights 2015.

16. *Vine a luchar* was a common phrase used by immigrants when talking about their experiences of migration. The literal translation is "to fight." However, it also means to struggle, to overcome, or to work hard to get ahead.

17. Ventura Patiño 2008. The Mexican Constitution, enacted after the Mexican Revolution that began in 1910, created the *ejido* system, which was dismantled with the neoliberal turn of the 1980s and finalized with the North American Free Trade Agreement.

18. McCarty 2008.

19. Speed, Castillo, and Stephen 2006.

20. Martínez Coria et al. 2015.

21. Instituto Nacional de Estadística Guatemala 2018.

22. Rincón 2010.

23. Sanford 2008.

24. Bastos and León 2015; Gauster and Isakson 2007; and Rincón 2010.

25. Gransovsky-Larsen 2017.

26. Gauster and Isakson 2007.

27. United Nations 2009.

28. Centro de Estudios para el Desarrollo Rural Sustentable y la Soberanía Alimentaria 2015.

29. Galtung 1969.

30. Centro de Estudios para el Desarrollo Rural Sustentable y la Soberanía Alimentaria 2015; Naciones Unidas 2016; and Organización Panamericana de la Salud/Organización Mundial de la salud en Guatemala 2016.

31. Angotti 2013.

32. Angotti 2017.

33. Banco Central de Reserva de El Salvador 2016; and Secretaría Nacional de Planificación y Desarrollo 2013.

34. Bassi, Busso, and Munoz 2013.

35. Enchautegui and Menjívar 2015.

36. We will delve into family sponsorship as a path for shifting immigration status in Chapter 5. For now, I focus on immigrants' access to visas regarding their method of entry to the United States, not their use of visas to shift their immigration status once they are settled in their Kansas communities. This is an important difference, because as we will learn in Chapter 5, the form of entry marks immigrants' pathways to remain undocumented or gain some protective status later on.

37. Loza (2016) finds that temporary work visas were given primarily to men who "looked Indigenous," given stereotypical associations between indigeneity and farmworker labor during the Bracero program. However, these same stereotypes racialize who is considered a tourist versus a labor migrant. Thus, racialization processes interlock with class and gender through visa eligibility requirements, automatically classifying those who do not qualify

(including Indigenous immigrants in this study) as undesirable and systematically excluded from legal migration. Furthermore, I highlight the importance of place, unlike farmworker immigrant networks, primarily in California. Indigenous immigrants in this study did not report access to temporary work visas, and none of the participants worked as farmworkers in land and food cultivation (some participants worked in meat processing). The visas that Loza's work points to, however, focus on labor in land cultivation. Most Indigenous informants disclosed that they did not know where to find information on the process for a temporary or a work visa or how to apply. See also Asad and Hwang 2019.

38. Médecins Sans Frontières 2024; and Vogt 2013.

39. Abrego 2014; and Menjívar 2011.

40. Cortés 2018.

41. For accounts of Central American migrant journeys via rail, see Vogt (2018) and Speed (2019). The cargo trains are known as *la bestia* (the beast) due their dangers.

42. In Mexico, drug cartels, gangs, police, and immigration officials often work together to target immigrants (Speed 2019).

43. International Organization of Migration 2019.

44. Mexico has seen a sweeping increase in violence since the 1980s (Bergman 2012). A combination of growing drug cartels, gangs, corruption, and state militarization has led to some Mexican regions having higher levels of violence than countries experiencing civil conflicts (Nájar 2019a; Redacción 2018). Immigrants traveling through Mexico suffer the collateral damage of this violence and become targets of violence themselves, given their status as unauthorized immigrants. See also Agren (2020) and Fuentes-Reyes and Ortiz-Ramírez (2012).

45. Speed 2019; and United Nations High Commissioner for Refugees 2015.

46. Nájar 2019b.

47. Lakhani 2019.

48. Speed 2019.

49. Schapendonk 2018.

50. Massey, Durand, and Pren 2016.

51. Fernandez 2017; and Slack et al. 2016.

52. De León 2015; and Reineke and Martinez 2024.

53. Inskeep 2014; and Joffe-Block 2014.

54. Bejarano, Morales, and Saddiki 2012.

55. Menjívar 2000.

56. Gómez Cervantes 2021; and Romero 2006, 2008.

57. *Güero* is a term that Latino immigrants use to refer to Anglo white US citizens and also refers to people with blond hair, light-color eyes, or light-color skin.

58. A summarized version of Vicente's account can be found in Gómez Cervantes (2021).

59. Chacón and Coutin 2018; and Gómez Cervantes 2021.

60. Cruz 2021.

61. Romo 2018.

62. Lytle Hernandez 2017.

63. Menjívar and Gómez Cervantes 2024; and Speed 2019.

64. Menjívar and Gómez Cervantes 2024; and Speed 2019.

65. Menjívar and Gómez Cervantes 2024.

66. For more details on the asylum process as a continuum of state control, see Menjívar and Gómez Cervantes 2024.

CHAPTER 2. "UN AMBIENTE HOSTIL":
KANSAS DURING TRUMP'S FIRST PRESIDENCY

1. Peterson 2016.

2. *Dos Mundos* 2016.

3. Peterson 2017.

4. Cancino 2017.

5. Institute for Policy and Social Research 2023.

6. Migration Policy Institute 2023.

7. American Immigration Council 2015; and Migration Policy Institute 2019.

8. Jones 2019; and Marrow 2020.

9. Following Trump's election, on February 22, 2017, Srinivas Kuchibhotla was killed by a white supremacist while sitting in a local bar in Olathe, Kansas. Adam Purinton harassed Srinivas and his friends, asking if they were "illegal," and after yelling, "Get out my country" he shot and killed Srinivas (Barajas 2018). In Garden City, Kansas, three men were arrested in November 2016 for

plotting to plant a bomb in an apartment complex where Somali immigrants lived (Fortin 2019).

10. Sorensen 2008.

11. According to the Pew Research Center (2016), 66 percent of registered voters who supported Trump in the 2016 election viewed immigration as a "very big problem." Only 17 percent of Hillary Clinton supporters felt the same way. Seventy-nine percent of Trump supporters strongly agreed with Trump's proposal to build a wall, and 59 percent associated unauthorized immigrants with serious crimes. The majority of Trump supporters viewed law enforcement as a priority for addressing immigration issues.

12. Anonymous 2017.

13. Berenson 2016.

14. De Genova 2004.

15. Alvord, Menjívar, and Gómez Cervantes 2018.

16. This phenomenon was not exclusive to immigrants in the heartland. Simmons and colleagues (2021), for example, examined the impact of Trump's 2017 reinstitution of ICE's Secure Communities programs, which promoted collaborations between local policing agencies and immigration enforcement, leaving immigrants and Latinos who fit ideals of illegality at risk of apprehensions. Focusing on Chicago, Houston, Los Angeles, and Phoenix, they found that immigration enforcement led to immigrants' social isolation and disengagement with social institutions and public spaces, similar to immigrants in the heartland.

17. Tabares 2017 (my translation).

18. American Immigration Lawyers Association 2021.

19. Moorefield 2022, quoting Professor Jonathan Abramowitz.

20. Rosenberg 2017, summary of Mary Moller's presentation at the 2017 Neuroscience Education Institute Congress.

21. García 2018 has documented how the fear of deportation reproduces chronic stress.

22. Bonilla Silva (2015, 11) describes color-blind racism as a racial structure that is "based on the superficial extension of the principles of liberalism to racial matters that results in 'raceless' explanations for all sort of race-related affairs."

23. Bonilla-Silva 2015.

24. Flores-González and Salgado 2022.

25. Haltiwanger 2020.

26. Finley and Esposito 2020.

27. BBC News 2016.

28. Davis 2018.

29. Edwards and Rushin 2018.

30. Bialik 2018. Although nativist ideologies fueled Trump's campaign, his presidency did not achieve the highest rates of immigrant detention or deportation. The Obama administration apprehended and deported the largest number of immigrants in modern US history. Between 2012 and 2014, over four hundred thousand immigrants were deported each year, lending Barack Obama the title of "Deporter in Chief" among immigrant rights organizations. See the data at Transactional Records Access Clearinghouse 2022.

31. Gómez Cervantes, Menjívar, and Staples 2017.

32. Guttentag 2021.

33. Benner and Dickerson 2018.

34. American Civil Liberties Union 2018. While this order was blocked by a federal judge, it nevertheless impacted women who were fleeing their countries due to brutalities of gender violence, leaving them at deadly risk if deported.

35. Southern Poverty Law Center 2016.

36. Torche and Sirois 2019.

37. Several investigative journalistic sources as well as research centers have identified Kris Kobach's close ties to nativist, anti-immigrant organizations. See Khimm 2012; and Southern Poverty Law Center 2016.

38. American Immigration Council 2020.

39. Transactional Records Access Clearinghouse 2023.

40. Transactional Records Access Clearinghouse 2023.

41. Transactional Records Access Clearinghouse 2018.

42. Siddiqui 2018.

43. Gómez Cervantes and Menjívar 2020.

44. The term "chilling effects" is largely used in public health scholarship to document the indirect consequences of immigration policies on immigrant families, mostly in relation to access to health care as well as access to welfare benefits among mixed-status families.

45. Gonzales 2024.

46. Rodriguez Vega 2023.

47. Ee and Gándara 2019. Title I of the Elementary and Secondary Education Act provides resources to schools that have high numbers of students from low-income families.

48. Bellows 2019.

49. Canizales and Vallejo 2021.

50. Friedman and Venkataramani 2021.

51. Twersky 2022.

52. Lambert, Discepolo, and Elani 2022.

53. Ifft and Jodlowski 2022.

54. East and Velásquez 2024.

55. Ngai 2004.

56. Oppenheimer 1985.

57. Massey, Durand, and Malone 2002.

58. Jiménez 2009.

59. Hernandez 2024.

60. Edelman 2021.

61. Torres 2018, 381.

62. Aldama 2003, 1.

63. Korac 2020.34.

CHAPTER 3. "AGUANTANDO SIN PAPELES": LIFE WITHOUT PAPERS

1. Menjívar and Abrego 2012.

2. Abrego and Menjívar 2011, 11.

3. Gleeson and Gonzales 2012.

4. De Genova 2002.

5. The first version of the employment verification program was established in 1996 under the Illegal Immigration Reform and Immigrant Responsibility Act, with three pilot programs: Basic Pilot, the Citizen Attestation Pilot, and the Machine-Readable Document Pilot. Earlier programs verified employees' work eligibility by communicating between the Social Security Administration office and the Immigration and Naturalization Services office (which is now part of the Department of Homeland Security). In 2004, the Basic Program

began to use the internet to share its data between agencies, and from there it was renamed E-Verify in 2007. By 2011 the program incorporated data from the Department of Motor Vehicles to check for employees driver's licenses, which was further refined by 2018 (E-Verify 2024).

6. E-Verify 2024.

7. US Department of Homeland Security 2018.

8. Chauvin and Garcés-Mascareñas 2014; and De Genova 2002.

9. 140 S. Ct. 791 (2020).

10. Hagan 1994; Menjívar 2000; and Schmalzbauer 2014.

11. During the period of this study, Kansas utilized the federal minimum wage, $7.25, as its standard.

12. Lee 2014.

13. De Genova 2007.

14. Novak et al. 2017.

15. Lopez et al. 2018.

16. Workplace violence is a form of legal violence. See also Menjívar and Abrego 2012.

17. Blackwell 2010; Morales Waugh 2010; and Villegas 2019.

18. Villegas 2019.

19. Graunke 2002; Kristen, Banuelos, and Urban 2015; Menjívar and Abrego 2012; and Villegas 2019.

20. Hall and Stringfield 2014.

21. Thacher 2008.

22. The government uses SSNs to track employment, earned income, and use of public benefits. SSNs are also used for criminal background checks. Individual Taxpayer Identification Numbers do not provide immigration status, protection from deportation, work authorization, or access to public benefits.

23. Jordan 2019.

24. Hall and Greenman 2013.

25. Gómez Cervantes and Menjívar 2020; and Schmalzbauer 2014.

26. Barron et al. 2009; and Gómez Cervantes and Menjívar 2020.

27. Gómez Cervantes and Menjívar 2020.

28. For a summarized version of Flor's experience with *raiteros*, see Gómez Cervantes and Menjívar 2020.

29. Gómez Cervantes 2021.

30. In a study of immigration enforcement and policing in New Jersey, Adler (2006) found that Indigenous Latin American immigrants were targeted by police and immigration enforcement agents at higher rates than other mestizo Latin American and Italian immigrants. This certainly rang true among the immigrants I met in Kansas.

31. De Genova 2002.

32. Abrego and Menjívar 2011; and Menjívar and Abrego 2012.

33. Barron et al. 2009.

34. For similar experiences of immigrant women in rural Montana, see Schmalzbauer 2014.

CHAPTER 4. "NO VINE A APRENDER INGLÉS":
LANGUAGE IN THE COMMUNITY AND AT HOME

1. Rosa and Flores 2017.

2. Rickford 2016.

3. Bourdieu 1991, 45.

4. Silver 2005, 50.

5. Yosso 2016.

6. Chiswick and Miller 2007.

7. Yosso 2016.

8. Yosso 2016, 123.

9. As observed in Chapter 1, many Indigenous and rural regions in Mexico lack nearby public schools, and there is no public school transportation.

10. Instituto Nacional de Estadística y Geografía 2020.

11. Latapí Sarre 2009; and Schmelkes 2013.

12. Schmelkes 2013.

13. Although the United Nations Declaration of Indigenous Peoples, Article 14, affirms the right to an education, Indigenous knowledge (including languages) has been either devalued or co-opted by Western practices for centuries (Cusicanqui 2012; Quijano 1999). Thus, access to bilingual and multilingual education in Indigenous languages is often limited and lacks Indigenous knowledge and worldviews (Latapí Sarre 2009; Schmelkes 2013).

14. Rosa and Flores 2017.

15. Bourdieu 1991.

16. Pew Research Center 2016.

17. Capps and Ruiz Soto 2016.

18. Hagan 1994; and Portes and Rumbaut 2001.

19. Higher education institutions such as community colleges and universities also offer English-language programs; however, none of the immigrants I met had experiences in these spaces.

20. In her work with Indigenous immigrant youths in California, Canizales (2021) found that Indigenous youths viewed English-language classes as a means to increase their educational opportunities.

21. Reierson and Celedón-Pattichis 2014.

22. Gómez Cervantes and Menjívar 2020.

23. Dovchin 2019; Rosa and Flores 2017; and Gómez Cervantes 2023.

24. Fishmann 1966.

25. Alba 2004; Alba et al. 2002; Portes and Rumbaut 2001; Rumbaut, Massey, and Bean 2006; and Waters 1990.

26. Golash-Boza 2005; Portes and Lingxin 1998; and Tran 2010.

27. Bauer, Epstein, and Gang 2005.

28. Velasco 2014.

29. Boj Lopez 2017; and Morales 2016.

30. Canizales and O'Connor 2021; Estrada 2013; and Ruiz and Barajas 2012.

31. Bourdieu 1977.

32. Morales, Saravia, and Pérez-Iribe 2019; Velasco 2014; and Yoshioka 2010.

33. Barajas 2014.

34. Samson and Gigoux 2016.

35. Boj Lopez 2017.

36. Tseng and Fuligni 2000.

37. King and Lanza 2019.

38. Yosso 2016.

39. Méndez, Flores-Haro, and Zucker 2020.

CHAPTER 5. "TAL VEZ UN DÍA ME PUEDO ARREGLAR": HOPES AND WORRIES

1. Abrego 2011; and Sarat 1990.

2. DACA was enacted as executive action under President Barack Obama in June 2012 to provide work authorization and temporary deportation relief to undocumented youths who came to the United States as minors. The program has strict eligibility requirements, including timing, age of entry, time living in the United States, and educational attainment, and an expensive processing fee of $495. The program was rescinded by Trump in 2017; however, federal litigation pushed for the program to be maintained although limiting it to renewals only. During the Biden administration, an attempt was made to move the program into law with a rule change, but this was stopped by the US District Court for the Southern District of Texas (Immigration Legal Resource Center 2024). The future of DACA remained wary as the second Trump administration began in 2025.

3. In 2015 the US Supreme Court's decision in *Obergefell v. Hodges* (576 U.S. 644) legalized same-sex marriage in all states.

4. Qian, Lichter, and Tumin 2018.

5. In her book *Of Love and Papers*, Laura Enriquez (2020) conducted an in-depth analysis of undocumented and semilegal immigrant youths' romantic relationships. The opportunity to shift status through marriage is especially limited given the up to ten-year entry ban that most undocumented immigrants would face.

6. Menjívar 2006; and Menjívar, Agadjanian, and Oh 2022.

7. In 2014 following decades of undocumented immigrants' collective organizing and a period of the highest deportation rates in US history, the Obama administration introduced the Deferred Action for Parents of Americans and Lawful Permanent Residents (DAPA) program through an executive order (National Immigration Law Center 2015). The goal of DAPA was to provide temporary protection from deportation to (eligible) parents of US citizens. Shortly after, however, a district court in Texas issued an order to block DAPA. This case went to the US Supreme Court in 2016, and under a split 4–4 decision, the block was maintained. In 2017, Trump rescinded the program completely (Kopan 2017).

8. Immigrant Legal Resource Center 2023.

9. The U visa program was initially created in 2000 through the Victims of Trafficking and Violence Protection Act to provide safety for immigrants who

experience criminal violence within US territory as long as they are willing to aid US authorities in the prosecution or investigation of the case. Criminal activity for U visa eligibility is designated by Congress as "abduction, abusive sexual contact, blackmail, domestic violence, extortion, false imprisonment, felonious assault, female genital mutilation, fraud in foreign labor contracting, hostage, incest, involuntary servitude, kidnapping, manslaughter, murder, obstruction of justice, peonage, perjury, prostitution, rape, sexual assault, sexual exploitation, slave trade, stalking, torture, trafficking, witness tampering, and unlawful criminal restraint" (US Department of Homeland Security 2019). The U visa lasts four years, is renewable, and can serve as a path to legal permanent residency and eventually naturalization. These visas are capped at ten thousand each year; however, the number of petitions continues to grow, and as a result there is a long waiting list accumulating each year. In 2018, there were 134,714 pending applications (US Department of Homeland Security 2019).

10. The American Bar Association advises newly arrived immigrants to be careful with "notaries" and "immigration representation." These highly advertised firms are all over the country, but they do not provide legal representation and instead steal migrants' money through false and often fraudulent information (American Bar Association 2019). This may have been what happened to Felipe with the attorney who never called him back after the initial consultation.

11. Mathema 2017.

12. Dreby 2015.

13. Abrego 2016; and Menjívar and Abrego 2012.

14. Enriquez 2015.

15. Enriquez 2020.

16. In 1984 the Reagan administration established the Lifeline program, a subsidy that would help low-income eligible households pay for a telephone land line. To qualify, households must earn less than 135% of the poverty line. Since then, the program has moved to provide subsidies for cell phone and internet services. At the time of the project, the program paid $9.25 toward the household's cell or internet bill.

17. The Public Charge Rule went into effect in 2020 and was paused by the Biden administration in 2021 and eventually thrown out by the courts.

However, income restrictions and financial proof had been a prerequirement for any legal permanent residency application well before the 2019 changes were established. Additionally, under other policies immigrants do not qualify for most federally funded subsidized programs, including welfare and Medicaid, unless individual states decide to allow this (Gómez Cervantes and Menjívar 2020).

18. For an in-depth analysis of unaccompanied minors growing up without their parents, see Canizales 2024.

19. Brabeck and Xu 2010; and Dreby 2015.

CHAPTER 6. "VOY A SALIR ADELANTE": STRATEGIES TO GET AHEAD

1. Canizales 2023.

2. National Center for Education Statistics 2023; and Quintana 2020.

3. Batalova 2024.

4. American Immigration Council 2023; and Murillo 2021.

5. Cha, Enriquez, and Ro 2019; and Murillo 2021.

6. Higher ED Immigration Portal 2024.

7. Barillas-Chón 2010; and Sanchez 2018.

8. According to structural education theorists, school policies, teachers, and punishment mechanisms all play significant roles in students' educational outcomes (Annamma et al. 2019; Mireles-Rios, Rios, and Reyes 2020; Rios 2011). In this view, students do not simply drop out of school on their own; rather, processes within schools *push* students out of the educational system (Rios 2011). "Pull out" theories, on the other hand, take into consideration factors outside of school—such as financial and parenting pressures—that dissuade students from continuing with formal schooling (Mireles-Rios et al. 2020).

9. Stephanie Canizales's book *Sin Padres ni Papeles* (2024) examined the experiences of Mayan unaccompanied minors living in Los Angeles without their parents. Her in-depth account sheds light on how Indigenous youths built social ties to make Los Angeles their home, including in their work and educational experiences.

10. This was many years prior to the COVID-19 pandemic, when online learning became more accessible and widely used in the United States.

11. Abrego 2014.

12. Barillas-Chón 2010; and Sanchez 2018.

13. Canizales 2024.

14. Abrego 2011; and Gonzales 2015.

15. Yosso 2016, 122.

16. Alba and Nee 1997.

17. Chiswick, Lee, and Miller 2005.

18. Portes, Fernandez-Kelly, and Haller 2005; and Portes and Zhou 1993.

19. Carneiro, Fortuna, and Varejão 2012; Flippen 2016; and Marrow 2011.

20. Waldinger and Lichter 2003.

21. De Genova 2002; and Gleeson and Gonzales 2012.

22. Hagan, Hernandez-Leon, and Demonsat 2015.

23. Connley 2020.

24. Blackwell 2010.

25. Previous studies have found similar ethnoracial hierarchies among Latin American immigrant workers in farming (Blackwell 2010; Holmes 2013) and day labor (Herrera 2016). These ethnoracial hierarchies relegate Indigenous workers to the most vulnerable and poorly paid working situations (Holmes 2013).

26. Damaske 2013.

27. Abrego 2006; and Murillo 2021.

28. Herrera 2016.

CONCLUSION

1. Mora 2014.

2. Blackwell et al. 2017; and Urrieta and Calderón 2019.

3. Speed 2019; and Radhakrishnan and Solari 2023.

4. Jones 2019.

5. Vega 2015; and Schmalzbauer 2014.

6. Jones 2019; and Ribas 2015.

7. Jiménez 2009.

8. Wolfe 2006.

9. Bailey et al. 2016; Dixon 2019; Ortiz Hernández et al. 2018; and Telles and Paschel 2014.

10. Gauster and Romero 2019; and Rivera Cusicanqui 2010.

11. Adler 2006; and Gómez Cervantes 2021. See also Chacón and Coutin 2018.

12. Harris 1993.

13. Gómez Cervantes 2021.

14. Blackwell 2010; and Speed 2019.

15. Gómez Cervantes 2021.

16. Chiswick and Miller 2007.

17. Bourdieu 1977, 1991.

18. Yosso 2016.

19. Menjívar 2000.

20. Del Real 2019.

21. Abrego 2016.

22. Coutin 2005; De Genova 2004; and Stumpf 2006.

23. 8 U.S.C. § 1325(a); and Eagly 2020.

24. 8 U.S.C. § 1326. Magistrates oversee illegal entry cases, while federal prosecutors under the Department of Justice preside in illegal reentry cases (Eagly 2020).

25. For example, Operation Streamline diverts immigration hearings from civil immigration courts into criminal courts, subjecting migrants to incarceration in federal prisons and local jails before deportation (Corrandini et al. 2018). These hearings are often conducted en masse, with multiple immigrants processed at the same time (Lydgate 2010). Operation Streamline was first instituted in 2005 in Texas and was utilized throughout the southwest border regions thereafter in order to deter migration. Studies show that such operations fail in deterring migration. Instead, they break cyclical migration patterns and make it more difficult for migrants to return to their home countries (Slack et al. 2015).

26. Kanstroom 2018.

27. Eagly 2020, 1976.

28. Almost 48 percent of deportees from 2003 to 2020 had no convictions (Transactional Records Access Clearinghouse 2022).

29. Alvord, Menjívar, and Gómez Cervantes 2018.

30. Eagly 2020, 1975.

31. Alvord et al. 2018; and Eagly 2020.

32. National Immigrant Justice Center 2020.

33. Morin 2021.

34. Abrego et al. 2017; Durand and Massey 2019; Massey 2020; and Slack et al. 2015.

35. Eagly 2020; and Mijente 2018.

36. Eagly 2020.

37. Kanstroom 2018.

38. Pistone and Hoeffner 2005.

39. Beginning in 2020, the Trump administration implemented Title 42, denying entrance to asylum seekers during the pandemic, which was maintained by the Biden administration (Rose and Neuman 2021).

40. Other offenses include money laundering, prostitution, drug offenses, firearm possession, suspicion of engaging in terrorist activities, and suspicion of being a drug trafficker (Torrey 2015).

41. Torrey 2015.

42. American Civil Liberties Union 2021.

43. Transactional Records Access Clearinghouse 2022.

44. Armenta 2017; Gómez Cervantes 2021; and Menjívar 2021.

45. Alvord et al. 2018.

46. Chacón and Coutin 2018.

47. Anderson 2020.

48. Ryo and Peacock 2020.

49. Armenta 2017; and Arriaga 2017.

50. See also Bailliard 2013; Gómez Cervantes and Menjívar 2020; and Simmons, Menjívar, and Valdez 2021.

51. Adler 2006; and Gómez Cervantes 2021.

52. Menjívar and Gómez Cervantes 2024; and Speed 2019.

53. Menjívar and Walsh 2016; and Adamson, Menjívar, and Walsh 2020.

54. Llewellyn 2020; and Menjívar and Gómez Cervantes 2024.

55. Enchautegui and Menjívar 2015; and Kibria 2019.

56. López 2015.

57. Montecinos 2020.

58. Immigrant Legal Resource Center 2020.

59. Gómez Cervantes and Menjívar 2020; and Hagan et al. 2003.

60. Gómez Cervantes 2021.

61. Mathews, Lins, and Vega 2012; and McMichael 2010.

62. Institute for Economics and Peace 2019.

63. Menjívar and Walsh 2016, 2017.

64. Menjívar and Diossa-Jiménez 2023.

65. Casamérica 2022.

66. Oxfam 2020.

67. Samson and Gigoux 2017.

68. Fox and Rivera-Salgado 2004.

69. Ruiz Soto 2024.

70. Corvino et al. 2022.

71. Acevedo and Mora-Tagle 2021.

APPENDIX: LESSONS LEARNED
FROM A MEXICANA SCHOLAR

1. Abrego 2024; Aranda 2023; Harding 1987; León, Abrego, and Negrón-Gonzales 2024; Luna and Pirtle 2021; Menjívar 2023; Mollard, Hatton-Bowers, and Tippens 2020; Smith 2021; Smith 1987; and Sumida Huaman and Martin 2023.

2. Abrego 2024.

3. Abrego 2024, 42.

4. León et al., 2024.

5. Smith 2021.

6. Berger 2021; and van der Merwe and Hunt 2019.

7. For details, see Berger 2021.

8. Canizales 2024.

9. Rauvola, Vega, and Lavigne 2019.

10. National Institute on Aging 2024.

11. For similar discussions, see Canizales 2024; Enriquez 2020; van der Merwe and Hunt 2019; and Small and Calarco 2022.

12. Anzaldúa 1987.

13. Social scientists have debated the benefits and drawbacks of the rigor and validity of data when researchers are an "outsider" versus an "insider" of a particular group under study for decades. Yet scholars also have shown ways

to conduct research rooted in practices of respect, ethical care, and solidarity regardless of the researchers' positionality in relation to the population under study that brings about significant contributions to academia and our social worlds (Small and Calarco 2022; Smith 2021).

14. Menjívar 2023, 10.

Bibliography

Abrego, Leisy J. 2006. "'I Can't Go to College Because I Don't Have Papers': Incorporation Patterns of Latino Undocumented Youth." *Latino Studies* 4: 212–31.

Abrego, Leisy J. 2011. "Legal Consciousness of Undocumented Latinos: Fear and Stigma as Barriers to Claims-Making for First- and 1.5-Generation Immigrants." *Law & Society Review* 45(2): 337–70.

Abrego, Leisy J. 2014. *Sacrificing Families: Navigating Laws, Labor, and Love across Borders.* Stanford University Press.

Abrego, Leisy J. 2016. "Illegality as a Source of Solidarity and Tension in Latino Families." *Journal of Latino/Latin American Studies* 8(1): 5–21.

Abrego, Leisy J. 2024. "Research as Accompaniment: Reflections on Objectivity, Ethics and Emotions." In *Out of Place, Power, Person, and Difference in Socio-Legal Research*, ed. L. Chua and M. F. Massoud. Cambridge University Press.

Abrego, Leisy J., Mathew Coleman, Daniel E. Martínez, Cecilia Menjívar, and Jeremy Slack. 2017. "Making Immigrants into

Criminals: Legal Processes of Criminalization in the Post-IIRIRA Era." *Journal on Migration and Human Security* 5(3): 694–715.

Abrego, Leisy J., and Cecilia Menjívar. 2011. "Immigrant Latina Mothers as Targets of Legal Violence." *International Journal of Sociology of the Family* 37(1): 9–26.

Abrego, Leisy J., and Alejandro Villalpando. 2021. "Racialization of Central Americans in the United States." In *Precarity and Belonging: Labor, Migration, and Noncitizenship*, ed. C. Ramirez, S. Falcon, J. Poblete, and F. A. Schaeffer. Rutgers University Press.

Acevedo, Nicole, and Rogelio Mora-Tagle. 20213. "Topeka, Kansas, Bets on Economic Incentives to Attract New Latino Residents." NBC News. https://www.nbcnews.com/news/latino/topeka-kansas-urges-latinos-move-financial-incentives-rcna120876.

Adamson, Erin, Cecilia Menjívar, and Shannon Drysdale Walsh. 2020. "The Impact of Adjacent Laws on Implementing Violence against Women Laws: Legal Violence in the Lives of Costa Rican Women." *Law & Social Inquiry* 45(2): 432–59.

Adler, Rachel H. 2006. "'But They Claimed to Be Police, Not La Migra!': The Interaction of Residency Status, Class, and Ethnicity in a (Post–PATRIOT Act) New Jersey Neighborhood." *American Behavioral Scientist* 50(1): 48–69.

Agren, David. 2020. "More Than Two-Thirds of Migrants Fleeing Central American Region Had Family Taken or Killed." *The Guardian*, February 11.

Al-Badawi, Mohammed. 2025. "US Cancels Visas as Trump Seeks to Revive Muslim Travel Ban." *New Arab*, March 9.

Alba, Richard. 2004. "Language Assimilation Today: Bilingualism Persists More Than in the Past, but English Still Dominates." Lewis Mumford Center for Comparative Urban and Regional Research at the University of Albany Working paper No. 11: 1–32.

Alba, Richard, John Logan, Amy Lutz, and Brian Stults. 2002. "Only English by the Third Generation? Loss and Preservation of the Mother Tongue among the Grandchildren of Contemporary Immigrants." *Demography* 39(3): 467–84.

Alba, Richard, and Victor Nee. 1997. "Rethinking Assimilation Theory for a New Era of Immigration." *International Migration Review* 31(4): 826–74.

Aldama, Arturo J. 2003. "Violence, Bodies, and the Color of Fear: An Introduction." In *Violence and the Body: Race, Gender, and the State*, ed. A. J. Adalma. Indiana University Press.

Alvord, Daniel R., Cecilia Menjívar, and Andrea Gómez Cervantes. 2018. "The Legal Violence in the 2017 Executive Orders: The Expansion of Immigrant Criminalization in Kansas." *Social Currents* 5(5): 411–20.

American Bar Association. 2019. *El Peligro de Fraude de Notario.* Washington, DC.

American Civil Liberties Union. 2018. "Federal Judge Blocks Trump's Policy Gutting Asylum for People Fleeing Domestic and Gang Violence." Washington, DC.

American Civil Liberties Union. 2021. "Analysis of Immigration Detention Policies." Washington, DC. https://www.aclu.org/other/analysis-immigration -detention-policies.

American Immigration Council. 2015. *Immigrants in Kansas.* Washington, DC.

American Immigration Council. 2019. *A Primer on Expedited Removal.* Washington, DC.

American Immigration Council. 2020. *Immigrants in Kansas.* Washington, DC.

American Immigration Council. 2021. *Aggravated Felonies: An Overview.* Washington, DC.

American Immigration Council. 2023. *Undocumented Students in Higher Education.* Washington, DC.

American Immigration Lawyers Association. 2021. "Announcements of ICE Enforcement Actions." https://www.aila.org/infonet/ice-announcements-of -enforcement-actions.

Anderson, April J. 2020. "Racial Profiling: Constitutional and Statutory Considerations for Congress." Congressional Research Service. https://sgp.fas .org/crs/misc/LSB10524.pdf.

Angotti, Tom. 2013. "Urban Latin America: Violence, Enclaves, and Struggles for Land." *Latin American Perspectives* 40(2): 5–20.

Angotti, Tom. 2017. *Urban Latin America: Inequalities and Neoliberal Reforms.* Rowman & Littlefield.

Animal Político. 2020. "Unos cuantos acumulan billones, mientras mujeres que hacen trabajo de cuidados son explotadas: Oxfam." Blog, January 20, 2020. https://www.animalpolitico.com/2020/01/desigualdad-mujeres-trabajo -cuidados-oxfam-informe/.

Annamma, Subini Ancy, Yolanda Anyon, Nicole M. Joseph, Jordan Farrar, Eldridge Greer, Barbara Downing, and John Simmons. 2019. "Black Girls and

School Discipline: The Complexities of Being Overrepresented and Under-studied." *Urban Education* 54(2): 211–42.

Anonymous. 2017. "Kansas Election Results 2016." *New York Times*, August 1.

Anzaldúa, Gloria. 1987. *Borderlands: The New Mestiza.* Aunt Lute Books.

Aranda, Elizabeth. 2023. "Im/Migrant Well-Being Part I: The Impact of Immigration Laws and Enforcement Measures." *American Behavioral Scientist* 0(0).

Armenta, Amada. 2017. *Protect, Serve, and Deport: The Rise of Policing as Immigration Enforcement.* University of California Press.

Arriaga, Felicia. 2017. "Relationships between the Public and Crimmigration Entities in North Carolina: A 287(g) Program Focus." *Sociology of Race and Ethnicity* 3(3): 417–31.

Asad, Asad L., and Jackelyn Hwang. 2019. "Indigenous Places and the Making of Undocumented Status in Mexico-US Migration." *International Migration Review* 53(4): 1032–77.

Az'un Papul Xuvan, dir. 2017. *Let's Learn to Greet People in Chuj: One of Many Maya Languages.* YouTube. https://www.youtube.com/watch?v=ok190gXcCqQ

Bailey, Stanley R., Fabrício M. Fialho, and Andrew M. Penner. 2016. "Interrogating Race: Color, Racial Categories, and Class across the Americas." *American Behavioral Scientist* 60(4): 538–55.

Bailliard, Antoine. 2013. "Laying Low: Fear and Injustice for Latino Migrants to Small Town, USA." *Journal of Occupational Science* 20(4): 342–56.

Banco Central de Reserva de El Salvador. 2016. *Análisis de Impactos de Aumento al Salario Mínimo En 2017 En El Salvador.* San Salvador, El Salvador.

Barajas, Joshua. 2018. "Kansas Man Sentenced to Life in Prison for 2017 Shooting That Targeted Indian Men." PBS News, August 7. https://www.pbs.org/newshour/nation/kansas-man-sentenced-to-life-in-prison-for-2017-shooting-that-targeted-indian-men.

Barajas, Manuel. 2014. "Colonial Dislocations and Incorporation of Indigenous Migrants from Mexico to the United States." *American Behavioral Scientist* 58(1): 53–63.

Barillas-Chón, David W. 2010. "Oaxaqueño/a Students' (Un)Welcoming High School Experiences." *Journal of Latinos and Education* 9(4): 303–20.

Barron, P., A. Bory, S. Chauvin, N. A. Fall, N. Jounin, and L. Tourette. 2009. "Travailleurs sans Papiers: La Précarité Interdite." *Les Mondes Du Travail* 7: 63–74.

Bassi, Marina, Matias Busso, and Juan Sebastian Munoz. 2013. "Is the Class Half Empty or Half Full? School Enrollment, Graduation, and Dropout Rates in Latin America." *IDB Working Paper Series* IBD-WP-462: 1–36.

Bastos, Santiago, and Quimy León. 2015. "Guatemala: Construyendo El Desarrollo Propio En Un Neoliberalismo de Postguerra." *Revista Pueblos y Fronteras* 10(19): 52–79.

Batalova, Jeanne. 2024. *College-Educated Immigrants in the United States.* Migration Policy Institute.

Bauer, T., G. S. Epstein, and I. N. Gang. 2005. "Enclaves, Language, and the Location Choice of Migrants." *Journal of Population Economics* 18(4): 649–62.

Baumer, Eric P., and Min Xie. 2023. "Federal-Local Partnerships on Immigration Law Enforcement: Are the Policies Effective in Reducing Violent Victimization?" *Criminology & Public Policy* 22(3): 417–55.

BBC News. 2016. "What Trump Has Said about Mexicans." August 31.

BBC News Mundo. 2018. "Los cinco estados de México que Estados Unidos considera tan violentos como Siria y Afganistán."

Beauregard, Luis Pablo. 2025. "United States Suspends Green Card Processing for Some Refugees and Asylees." *El País*, March 26.

Bejarano, Cynthia, Maria Cristina Morales, and Said Saddiki. 2012. "Understanding Conquest through a Border Lens: A Comparative Analysis of the Mexico-U.S. and Morocco-Spain Regions." In *Beyond Walls and Cages: Prisons, Borders, and Global Crisis*, ed. A. Burridge, M. Mtchelson, and J. M. Loyd. University of Georgia Press.

Bellows, Laura. 2019. "Immigration Enforcement and Student Achievement in the Wake of Secure Communities." *AERA* 5(4): 1–20.

Bellows, Laura. 2021. "The Effect of Immigration Enforcement on School Engagement: Evidence from 287(g) Programs in North Carolina." *AERA* 7(1): 1–20.

Benner, Katie, and Caitlin Dickerson. 2018. "Sessions Says Domestic and Gang Violence Are Not Grounds for Asylum." *New York Times.*

Bennett, Geoff, Shrai Popat, and Saher Khan, dirs. 2024. *Exploring Why More Latinos Voted for Trump and What It Means for Future Elections.* PBS News.

Berenson, Tessa. 2016. "Middle School Students Chant 'Build That Wall' after Trump Victory." *Time Magazine.*

Berger, Roni. 2021. "Studying Trauma: Indirect Effects on Researchers and Self and Strategies for Addressing Them." *European Journal of Trauma & Dissociation* 5(1): 100149.

Bergman, Marcelo. 2012. "La violencia en México: algunas aproximaciones académicas." *Desacatos: Revista de Ciencias Sociales* 40: 65–76.

Bialik, Kristen. 2018. *ICE Arrests Went Up in 2017, with Biggest Increases in Florida, Northern Texas, Oklahoma*. Pew Research Center.

Blackwell, Maylei. 2010. "Líderes Campesinas Nepantla Strategies and Grassroots Organizing at the Intersection of Gender and Globalization." *Aztlán: A Journal of Chicano Studies* 35(1): 13–47.

Blackwell, Maylei, Floridalma Boj Lopez, and Luis Urrieta. 2017. "Special Issue: Critical Latinx Indigeneities." *Latino Studies* 15(2): 126–37.

Boj Lopez, Floridalma. 2017. "Mobile Archives of Indigeneity: Building La Comunidad Ixim through Organizing in the Maya Diaspora." *Latino Studies* 15(2): 201–18.

Bonilla-Silva, Eduardo. 2004. "From Bi-Racial to Tri-Racial: Towards a New System of Racial Stratification in the USA." *Ethnic and Racial Studies* 27(6): 931–50.

Bonilla-Silva, Eduardo. 2015. "The Structure of Racism in Color-Blind, 'Post-Racial' America." *American Behavioral Scientist* 59(11): 1358–76.

Bonjour, Saskia, and Sébastien Chauvin. 2018. "Social Class, Migration Policy and Migrant Strategies: An Introduction." *International Migration* 56(4): 5–18.

Bourdieu, Pierre. 1977. "The Economics of Linguistic Exchanges." *Social Science Information* 16(6): 645–68.

Bourdieu, Pierre. 1991. *Language and Symbolic Power*. Cambridge, MA: Harvard University Press.

Brabeck, Kalina, and Qingwen Xu. 2010. "The Impact of Detention and Deportation on Latino Immigrant Children and Families: A Quantitative Exploration." *Hispanic Journal of Behavioral Sciences* 32(3): 341–61.

Brenner, Katie, and Caitlin Dickerson. 2018. "Sessions Says Domestic and Gang Violence Are Not Grounds for Asylum." *New York Times*, June 11.

Brown, Hana E., Jennifer A. Jones, and Andrea Becker. 2018. "The Racialization of Latino Immigrants in New Destinations: Criminality, Ascription, and Countermobilization." *RSF: The Russell Sage Foundation Journal of the Social Sciences* 4(5): 118–40.

Bustillo, Ximena. 2025. "In Child Care Centers and on Farms, Businesses Are Bracing for More Immigration Raids." *National Public Radio,* February 28. https://www.npr.org/2025/02/28/g-s1-50958/business-workplace-raids-immigration-ice-deportation.

Cancino, Jorge. 2017. "El miedo invade a la comunidad inmigrante por los informes de redadas en al menos seis estados." Univision Noticias, February 11.

Canizales, Stephanie L. 2021. "Educational Meaning Making and Language Learning: Understanding the Educational Incorporation of Unaccompanied, Undocumented Latinx Youth Workers in the United States." *Sociology of Education* 94(3): 175–90.

Canizales, Stephanie L. 2023. "Work Primacy and the Social Incorporation of Unaccompanied, Undocumented Latinx Youth in the United States." *Social Forces* 101(3): 1372–95.

Canizales, Stephanie L. 2024. *Sin Padres, Ni Papeles: Unaccompanied Migrant Youth Coming of Age in the United States.* University of California Press.

Canizales, Stephanie, and Jody Agius Vallego. 2021. "Latinos & Racism in the Trump Era." *Daedalus* 150(2): 150–64. https://www.jstor.org/stable/48691409.

Canizales, Stephanie L., and Brendan H. O'Connor. 2021. "From Preparation to Adaptation: Language and the Imagined Futures of Maya-Speaking Guatemalan Youths in Los Angeles." In *Refugee Education across the Lifespan: Mapping Experiences of Language Learning and Use,* ed. Doris Warriner. Springer.

Capps, Randy, and Ariel G. Ruiz Soto. 2016. "Immigration to the Heartland: A Profile of Immigrants in the Kansas City Region." Migration Policy Institute.

Cardoso, Cláudia Pons. 2014. "Amefricanizando o Feminismo: O Pensamento de Lelia Gonzalez." *Estudos Feministas* 22(3): 965–86.

Carneiro, Anabela, Natércia Fortuna, and José Varejão. 2012. "Immigrants at New Destinations: How They Fare and Why." *Journal of Population Economics* 25(3): 1165–85.

Casamérica. 2022. "La situación actual de las mujeres en América Latina." Madrid, España. https://www.casamerica.es/sociedad/la-situacion-actual-de-las-mujeres-en-america-latina.

Castellanos, M. Bianet. 2017. "Introduction: Settler Colonialism in Latin America." *American Quarterly* 69(4): 777–81.

Centro de Estudios para el Desarrollo Rural Sustentable y la Soberanía Alimentaria. 2015. *La población indígena en el México rural: Situación actual y perspectivas.* Ciudad de México.

Cha, Biblia S., Laura E. Enriquez, and Annie Ro. 2019. "Beyond Access: Psychosocial Barriers to Undocumented Students' Use of Mental Health Services." *Social Science & Medicine* 233: 193–200.

Chacón, Jennifer, and Susan Coutin. 2018. "Racialization through Enforcement." In *Race, Criminal Justice and Migration Control: Enforcing the Boundaries of Belonging,* ed. Mary Bosworth, Alpa Parmar, and Yolanda Vázquez. Oxford University Press.

Chauvin, Sébastien, and Blanca Garcés-Mascareñas. 2014. "Becoming Less Illegal: Deservingness Frames and Undocumented Migrant Incorporation." *Sociology Compass* 8(4): 422–32.

Chistchti, Muzaffar, and Colleen Putzel-Kavanaugh. 2025. "Tapping Ancient Wartime and Security Laws, Trump Administration Dramatically Expands Immigration Powers." Migration Policy Institute.

Chiswick, Barry R., Yew Liang Lee, and Paul W. Miller. 2005. "A Longitudinal Analysis of Immigrant Occupational Mobility: A Test of the Immigrant Assimilation Hypothesis." *International Migration Review* 39(2): 332–53.

Chiswick, Barry R., and Paul W. Miller. 2007. *The Economics of Language: International Analyses.* Routledge.

Coleman, Mat, and Austin Kocher. 2019. "Rethinking the 'Gold Standard' of Racial Profiling: §287(g), Secure Communities and Racially Discrepant Police Power." *American Behavioral Scientist* 63(9): 1185–220.

Connley, Courtney. 2020. "Latinas Earn $0.55 for Every Dollar Paid to White Men, a Pay Gap That Has Barely Moved in 30 Years." CNBC, October 29.

Consejo Nacional de Evaluación de la Política de Desarrollo Social. 2019. *La pobreza en la población indígena de México, 2008–2018.* Mexico City, Mexico.

Corrandini, Michael, Jonathan Allen Kringen, Karen Berberich, and Meredith Emigh. 2018. "Operation Streamline: No Evidence That Criminal Prosecution Deters Migration." Vera Institute of Justice. https://www.immigration research.org/system/files/Operation_Streamline.pdf.

Cortés, Almudena. 2018. "Violencia de género y frontera: Migrantes centroamericanas en México hacia los EEUU." *European Review of Latin American and*

Caribbean Studies/Revista Europea de Estudios Latinoamericanos y Del Caribe 105: 39–60.

Corvino, Chiara, Sara Martinez-Damia, Mattia Belluzzi, Daniela Marzana, and Chiara D'angelo. 2022. "'Even Though We Have Different Colors, We Are All Equal Here': Immigrants Building a Sense of Community and Wellbeing through Sport Participation." *Journal of Community Psychology* 51(1): 201–18.

Coutin, Susan Bibler. 2005. "Contesting Criminality: Illegal Immigration and the Spatialization of Legality." *Theoretical Criminology* 9(1): 5–33.

Cranford, Cynthia J. 2005. "Networks of Exploitation: Immigrant Labor and the Restrcturing of the Los Angeles Janitorial Industry." *Social Problems* 52(3): 379–97.

Cruz, Melissa. 2021. *ICE May Have Deported as Many as 70 US Citizens in the Last Five Years.* American Immigration Council.

Cumes, Aura Estela. 2012. "Mujeres indígenas patriarcado y colonialismo: Un desafío a la segregación comprensiva de las formas de dominio." *Anuario de Hojas de Warmi* 17: 1–16.

Curiel, Ochy. 2007. "Crítica poscolonial desde las prácticas políticas del feminismo antirracista." *Nómadas* 26: 92–102.

Curran, Sara R., and Estela Rivero-Fuentes. 2003. "Engendering Migrant Networks: The Case of Mexican Migration." *Demography* 40(2): 289–307.

Cusicanqui, S. R. 2012. "Ch'ixinakax Utxiwa: A Reflection on the Practices and Discourses of Decolonization." *South Atlantic Quarterly* 111(1): 95–109.

Damaske, Sarah. 2013. "Work, Family, and Accounts of Mothers' Lives Using Discourse to Navigate Intensive Mothering Ideals." *Sociology Compass* 7(6): 436–44.

Davis, Julie Hirschfeld. 2018. "Trump Calls Some Unauthorized Immigrants 'Animals' in Rant." *New York Times*, May 16.

Deeb, Lara, and Jessica Winegar. 2024. "Resistance to Repression and Back Again: The Movement for Palestinian Liberation in US Academia." *Middle East Critique* 33(3): 313–34.

De Genova, Nicholas. 2002. "Migrant 'Illegality' and Deportability in Everyday Life." *Annual Review of Anthropology* 31(1): 419–47.

De Genova, Nicholas. 2004. "The Legal Production of Mexican/Migrant 'Illegality.'" *Latino Studies* 2(2): 160–85.

De Genova, Nicholas. 2007. "The Production of Culprits: From Deportability to Detainability in the Aftermath of 'Homeland Security.'" *Citizenship Studies* 11(5): 421–48.

De León, Jason. 2015. *The Land of Open Graves: Living and Dying on the Migrant Trail.* University of California Press.

Del Real, Deisy. 2019. "Toxic Ties: The Reproduction of Legal Violence within Mixed-Status Intimate Partners, Relatives, and Friends." *International Migration Review* 53(2): 548–70.

Dixon, Angela R. 2019. "Colorism and Classism Confounded: Perceptions of Discrimination in Latin America." *Social Science Research* 79 (March): 32–55.

Dohery, Caroll. 2016. *5 Facts about Trump Supporters' Views of Immigration.* Pew Research Center.

Donato, Katherine. M., and Leslie Ann Rodríguez. 2014. "Police Arrests in a Time of Uncertainty: The Impact of 287(g) on Arrests in a New Immigrant Gateway." *American Behavioral Scientist* 58(13): 1696–722.

Dos Mundos. 2016. Political Cartoon: Mister President. Volume 36, Issue 45. Kansas City, KS.

Dovchin, Sender. 2019. "Language Crossing and Linguistic Racism: Mongolian Immigrant Women in Australia." *Journal of Multicultural Discourses* 14(4): 334–51.

Dowling, Julie, and Jonatahn Xavier Inda. 2013. *Governing Immigration through Crime.* Stanford University Press.

Dreby, Joanna. 2015. "U.S. Immigration Policy and Family Separation: The Consequences for Children's Well-Being." *Social Science and Medicine* 132: 245–51.

Duehren, Andrew. 2025. "Homeland Security Officials Push I.R.S. for 700,000 Immigrants' Addresses." *New York Times*, February 28.

Durand, Jorge, and Douglas S. Massey. 2019. "Debacles on the Border: Five Decades of Fact-Free Immigration Policy." *ANNALS of the American Academy of Political and Social Science* 684(1): 6–20.

Eagly, Ingrid V. 2020. "The Movement to Decriminalize Border Crossing." *Boston College Law Review* 61(6): 1967–2030.

East, Chloe N., and Andrea Velásquez. 2024. "Unintended Consequences of Immigration Enforcement: Household Services and High-Educated Mothers' Work." *Journal of Human Resources* 59(5): 1458–502.

Edelman, Marc. 2021. "Hollowed Out Heartland, USA: How Capital Sacrificed Communities and Paved the Way for Authoritarian Populism." *Journal of Rural Studies* 82: 505–17.

Edwards, Griffin Sims, and Stephen Rushin. 2018. "The Effect of President Trump's Election on Hate Crimes." SSRN. http://dx.doi.org/10.2139/ssrn.3102652.

Ee, Jongyeon, and Patricia Gándara. 2020. "The Impact of Immigration Enforcement on the Nation's Schools." *American Educational Research Journal* 57(2): 840–71.

Enchautegui, María E., and Cecilia Menjívar. 2015. "Paradoxes of Family Immigration Policy: Separation, Reorganization, and Reunification of Families under Current Immigration Laws." *Law & Policy* 37(1–2): 32–60.

Enriquez, Laura E. 2015. "Multigenerational Punishment: Shared Experiences of Undocumented Immigration Status within Mixed-Status Families." *Journal of Marriage and Family* 77(4): 939–53.

Enriquez, Laura E. 2020. *Of Love and Papers: How Immigration Policy Affects Romance and Family.* University of California Press.

Estrada, Alicia Ivonne. 2013. "Ka Tzij: The Maya Diasporic Voices from Contacto Ancestral." *Latino Studies* 11(2): 208–27.

E-Verify. 2024. *History and Milestones | E-Verify.* US Government, Washington, DC.

Faheid, Dalia, and Hanna Park. 2025. "Jocelynn Rojo Carranza Suicide: Texas District Releases Findings from Bullying Investigation of 11-Year-Old." CNN, February 27.

Fanon, Franz. 1963. *The Wretched of the Earth.* Grove.

Federal Register. 2025. *2025 Donald J. Trump Executive Orders.* Washington, DC.

Fernandez, Manny. 2017. "A Path to America Marked by More and More Bodies." *New York Times*, May 4.

Finley, Laura, and Luigi Esposito. 2020. "The Immigrant as Bogeyman: Examining Donald Trump and the Right's Anti-Immigrant, Anti-PC Rhetoric." *Humanity & Society* 44(2): 178–97.

Fishmann, Joshua. 1966. *Language Loyalty in the United States: The Maintenance and Perpetuation of Non-English Mother Tongues by American Ethnic and Religious Groups.* Mouton & Company.

Flippen, Chenoa A. 2016. "Shadow Labor: Work and Wages among Immigrant Hispanic Women in Durham, North Carolina." *ANNALS of the American Academy of Political and Social Science* 666(1): 110–30.

Flippen, Chenoa A., and Dylan Farrell-Bryan. 2021. "New Destinations and the Changing Geography of Immigrant Incorporation." *Annual Review of Sociology* 47(1): 479–500.

Flores, René D., and Ariela Schachter. 2018. "Who Are the 'Illegals'? The Social Construction of Illegality in the United States." *American Sociological Review* 83(5): 839–68.

Flores-González, Nilda, and Casandra D. Salgado. 2022. "Shifting Racial Schemas: From Post-Racial to New 'Old-Fashioned' Racism." *Sociological Inquiry* 92(2): 341–63.

Fortin, Jacey. 2019. "3 Men Sentenced in Plot to Bomb Somali Immigrants in Kansas." *New York Times*, January 27.

Fox, Jonathan, and Gaspar Rivera-Salgado, eds. 2004. *Indigenous Mexican Migrants in the United States*. Center for US-Mexican Studies.

Frank, Thomas. 2025. "FEMA Blocks $10B in Disaster Aid over Immigration Concerns." *Politico*, March 28.

Friedman, Abigail S., and Atheendar S. Venkataramani. 2021. "Chilling Effects: US Immigration Enforcement and Health Care Seeking among Hispanic Adults; Study Examines the Effects of US Immigration Enforcement and Health Care Seeking among Hispanic Adults." *Health Affairs* 40(7): 1056–65.

Fuentes-Reyes, Gabriela, and Luis Raúl Ortiz-Ramírez. 2012. "El migrante centroamericano de paso por México: Una revisión a su condición social desde la perspectiva de los derechos humanos." *Convergencia: Revista de Ciencias Sociales* 19(58): 157–82.

Fussell, Elizabeth. 2011. "The Deportation Threat Dynamic and Victimization of Latino Migrants: Wage Theft and Robbery." *Sociological Quarterly* 52(4): 593–615.

Galtung, Johan. 1969. "Violence, Peace, and Peace Research." *Journal of Peace Research* 6(3): 167–91.

Garcia, Matthew. 2007. "Labor, Migration, and Social Justice in the Age of the Grape Boycott." *Gastronómica* 7(3): 68–74.

García, San Juanita. 2018. "Living a Deportation Threat: Anticipatory Stressors Confronted by Undocumented Mexican Immigrant Women." *Race and Social Problems* 10(3): 221–34.

Gauster, Susana, and S. Ryan Isakson. 2007. "Eliminating Market Distortions, Perpetuating Rural Inequality: An Evaluation of Market-Assisted Land Reform in Guatemala." *Third World Quarterly* 28(8): 1519–36.

Gauster, Susanne, and Wilson Romero. 2019. "Entre el suelo y el cielo: Radiografía multidimensional de la desigualdad en Guatemala." Oxfam. https://oi-files-d8-prod.s3.eu-west-2.amazonaws.com/s3fs-public/file_attachments/entre_el_suelo_y_el_cielo_0.pdf.

Gleeson, Shannon, and Roberto G. Gonzales. 2012. "When Do Papers Matter? An Institutional Analysis of Undocumented Life in the United States." *International Migration* 50(4): 1–19.

Glenn, Evelyn Nakano. 2015. "Settler Colonialism as Structure: A Framework for Comparative Studies of U.S. Race and Gender Formation." *Sociology of Race and Ethnicity* 1(1): 52–72.

Glymph, Thavolia. 2008. *Out of the House of Bondage: The Transformation of the Plantation Household*. Cambridge University Press.

Gobierno de México. 2016. *Prontuario En Tlapaneco/ Español*. Ciudad de México, México.

Golash-Boza, Tanya. 2005. "Assessing the Advantages of Bilingualism for the Children of Immigrants." *International Migration Review* 39(3): 721–53.

Golash-Boza, Tanya, and Pierrette Hondagneu-Sotelo. 2013. "Latino Immigrant Men and the Deportation Crisis: A Gendered Racial Removal Program." *Latino Studies* 11(3): 271–92.

Golash-Boza, Tanya, and Zulema Valdez. 2018. "Nested Contexts of Reception: Undocumented Students at the University of California, Central." *Sociological Perspectives* 61(4): 535–52.

Gomberg-Muñoz, Ruth. 2015. "The Punishment/El Castigo: Undocumented Latinos and US Immigration Processing." *Journal of Ethnic and Migration Studies* 41(14): 2235–52.

Gomes, Izabel Solyszko. 2013. "Femicidio y feminicidio: Avances para nombrar la expresión letal de la violencia de género contra las mujeres." *GénEroos* 13(2): 23–42.

Gómez, Laura E. 2007. *Manifest Destinies: The Making of the Mexican American Race.* New York University Press.

Gómez Cervantes, Andrea. 2021. "'Looking Mexican': Indigenous and Non-Indigenous Latina/o Immigrants and the Racialization of Illegality in the Midwest." *Social Problems* 68(1): 100–17.

Gómez Cervantes, Andrea. 2023. "Language, Race, and Illegality: Indigenous Migrants Navigating the Immigration Regime in a New Destination." *Journal of Ethnic and Migration Studies* 49(7): 1610–29.

Gómez Cervantes, Andrea, Daniel R. Alvord, and Cecilia Menjívar. 2018. "'Bad Hombres': The Effects of Criminalizing Latino Immigrants through Law and Media in the Rural Midwest." *Migration Letters* 15(2): 167–81.

Gómez Cervantes, Andrea, and Cecilia Menjívar. 2020. "Legal Violence, Health, and Access to Care: Latina Immigrants in Rural and Urban Kansas." *Journal of Health and Social Behavior* 61(3): 307–23.

Gómez Cervantes, Andrea, Cecilia Menjívar, and William G. Staples. 2017. "'Humane' Immigration Enforcement and Latina Immigrants in the Detention Complex." *Feminist Criminology* 12(3): 269–92.

Gonzales, Lélia. 1984. "Racismo e Sexismo Na Cultura Brasileria." *Revista Ciências Sociais Hoje,* 223–44.

Gonzales, Roberto G. 2015. *Lives in Limbo: Undocumented and Coming of Age in America.* University of California Press.

Gonzales, Roberto G. 2024. "Policy and Place: Immigration, Schooling, and the Local Context." *AERA Open* 10(1): 1–7.

Gonzales, Roberto G., and Edelina M. Burciaga. 2018. "Segmented Pathways of Illegality: Reconciling the Coexistence of Master and Auxiliary Statuses in the Experiences of 1.5-Generation Undocumented Young Adults." *Ethnicities* 18(2): 178–91.

Gott, Richard. 2007. "Latin America as a White Settler Society." *Bulletin of Latin American Research* 26(2): 269–89.

Gransovsky-Larsen, Simon. 2017. "The Guatemalan Campesino Movement and the Post Conflict Neoliberal State." *Latin American Perspectives* 44(5): 53–73.

Graunke, Kristi L. 2002. "Just Like One of the Family: Domestic Violence Paradigms and Combating on-the-Job Violence against Household Workers in the United States." *Michigan Journal of Gender & Law* 9(1): 131–206.

Gretzinger, Erin, Maggie Hicks, Christina Dutton, and Jasper Smith. 2024. "Tracking Higher Ed's Dismantling of DEI." *Chronicle of Higher Education*, December 13.

Guttentag, Lucas. 2025. "Immigration Policy Tracking Project." https://immpolicy tracking.org/.

Hagan, Jacqueline Maria. 1994. *Deciding to Be Illegal: A Maya Community in Houston*. Temple University Press.

Hagan, Jacqueline Maria. 1998. "Social Networks, Gender, and Immigrant Incorporation: Resources and Constraints." *American Sociological Review* 63(1): 55–67.

Hagan, Jacqueline, Ruben Hernandez-Leon, and Jean-Luc Demonsat. 2015. *Skills of the Unskilled: Work and Mobility among Mexican Migrants*. University of California Press.

Hagan, Jacqueline, Nestor Rodriguez, Randy Capps, and Nika Kabiri. 2003. "The Effects of Recent Welfare and Immigration Reforms on Immigrants' Access to Health Care." *International Migration Review* 37 (2): 444–63.

Hall, Mathew, and Emily Greenman. 2013. "Housing and Neighborhood Quality among Undocumented Mexican and Central American Immigrants." *Social Science Research* 42(6): 1712–25.

Hall, Mathew, and Jonathan Stringfield. 2014. "Undocumented Migration and the Residential Segregation of Mexicans in New Destinations." *Social Science Research* 47: 61–78.

Haltiwanger, John. 2020. "Trump Has Repeatedly Been Endorsed by White Supremacist Groups and Other Far-Right Extremists, and They've Looked to Him as a Source of Encouragement." Business Insider, September 30. https://www.businessinsider.com/trumps-history-of-support-from-white-supremacist-far-right-groups-2020-9.

Haney-Lopez, Ian Haney. 1996. *White by Law: The Legal Construction of Race*. New York University Press.

Harding, Sandra G. 1987. *Feminism and Methodology: Social Science Issues*. Indiana University Press.

Harris, Cheryl I. 1993. "Whiteness as Property." *Harvard Law Review* 106 (8): 1707–91.

Hernandez, Joseph. 2024. "When Was the Last Time Kansas or Missouri Voted for a Democrat for President?" *Kansas City Star*, November 6.

Hernández, Kelly Lytl. 2017. *City of Inmates: Conquest, Rebellion, and the Rise of Human Caging in Los Angeles, 1771–1965*. University of California Press.

Herrera, Juan. 2016. "Racialized Illegality: The regulation of informal labor and space." *Latino Studies* 14(3): 320.

Higher ED Immigration Portal. 2024. "State Data." https://www.highered immigrationportal.org/state/kansas/.

Hixson, Walter. 2013. *American Settler Colonialism: A History*. Palgrave Macmillan.

Holmes, Seth. 2013. *Fresh Fruit: Migrant Farmworkers in the United States*. University of California Press.

Hondagneu-Sotelo, Pierrette. 1994. *Gendered Transitions: Mexican Experiences of Immigration*. University of California Press.

Hsu, Andrea. 2025. "Trump Signs Order Ending Union Bargaining Rights for Wide Swaths of Federal Employees." National Public Radio, March 28.

Ifft, Jennifer, and Margaret Jodlowski. 2022. "Is ICE Freezing US Agriculture? Farm-Level Adjustment to Increased Local Immigration Enforcement." *Labour Economics* 78: 102203.

Immigrant Legal Resource Center. 2020. "National Map of 287(g) Agreements." https://www.ilrc.org/national-map-287g-agreements.

Immigrant Legal Resource Center. 2023. "How US Citizens Can Petition Their Parents for Permanent Residence." https://www.ilrc.org/sites/default/files /2023-03/How%20USC%20can%20petition%20their%20parents%20for %20LPR_March%202023.pdf.

Immigration Legal Resource Center. 2024. *What Is the DACA Rule and How Does It Impact Me?* https://www.ilrc.org/sites/default/files/2024-06/Updated_2022% 20DACA%20Rule_June%202024.pdf.

Inskeep, Steve. 2014. "The Rarely Told Stories of Sexual Assault against Female Migrants." National Public Radio, March 23.

Institute for Policy and Social Research. 2023. "Population in Kansas and U.S., by Race and Hispanic Origin, 2010 and 2020." https://ksdata.ku.edu/ksdata /ksah/population/2pop7.pdf.

Institute for Economics and Peace. 2019. "Global Peace Index 2019: Measuring Peace in a Complex World." https://www.visionofhumanity.org/wp-content /uploads/2020/10/GPI-2019web.pdf.

Instituto Nacional de Estadística Guatemala. 2018. "Resultados república de Guatemala censo 2018." Guatemala.

Instituto Nacional de Estadística y Geografía. 2020. "Población: Hablantes de lengua indígena." Ciudad de México, México. https://cuentame.inegi.org.mx/poblacion/lindigena.aspx.

Instituto Nacional de Estadística y Geografía. 2022. "Estadísticas a propósito del día internacional de los pueblos indígenas." Ciudad de México, México. https://www.inegi.org.mx/app/saladeprensa/noticia/7519.

Inter-American Commission on Human Rights. 2015. *Pueblos indígenas: Diversidad, desigualdad y exclusión. Situación de Derechos Humanos en Guatemala.* Guatemala.

International Organization of Migration. 2019. "Missing Migrants Project." Geneva, Switzerland. https://missingmigrants.iom.int/.

Irving Reynoso, Jaime. 2013. "Manuel Gamio y las bases de la política indigenista en México." *Andamios* 10(22): 333–55.

Jiménez, Tomas. 2009. *Replenished Ethnicity: Mexican Americans, Immigration, and Identity.* University of California Press.

Joffe-Block, Jude. 2014. "Facing Risk of Rape, Migrant Women Prepare with Birth Control." *Fronteras*, March 12.

Johnson, Gene. 2025. "Things to Know about the Ruling Blocking President Trump's Refugee Ban." Associated Press, February 26.

Jones, Jennifer. 2019. *The Browning of the New South.* University of Chicago Press.

Jones, Lee, and Jeanett Castellanos, eds. 2023. *The Majority in the Minority: Expanding the Representation of Latina/o Faculty, Administrators and Students in Higher Education.* Taylor & Francis.

Jordan, Chuck. 2019. "Another Barrier for Immigrants: Their Credit History." *The Hill*, September 6.

Kansas v. García. 2020. 140 S. Ct. 791.

Kanstroom, Daniel. 2018. "Expedited Removal and Due Process: A Testing Crucible of Basic Principle in the Time of Trump." *Washington and Lee Law Review* 75: 1323–60.

Kapoor, Sampada. 2022. "The U.S. Labor Union Spike." American Bar Association.

Khimm, Suzy. 2012. "Kris Kobach, Nativist Son." *Mother Jones.*

Kibria, Nazli. 1993. *Family Tightrope: The Changing Lives of Vietnamese Americans.* Princeton University Press.

Kibria, Nazli. 2019. "#FamiliesBelongTogether: Facts and Fictions of Race and Family in U.S. Immigration Policy." *Sociological Forum* 34(4): 809–17.

King, Kendall, and Elizabeth Lanza. 2019. "Ideology, Agency, and Imagination in Multilingual Families: An Introduction." *International Journal of Bilingualism* 23(3): 717–23.

Klein, Naomi. 2010. *The Shock Doctrine: The Rise of Disaster Capitalism.* Henry Holt.

Kopan, Tal. 2017. "Trump Administration Reverses DAPA in 'House Cleaning.'" *CNN*, June 16.

Korac, Maja. 2020. "Gendered and Racialised Border Security: Displaced People and the Politics of Fear." *International Journal for Crime, Justice and Social Democracy* 9(3): 75–86.

Kristen, Elizabeth, Blanca Banuelos, and Daniela Urban. 2015. "Workplace Violence and Harassment of Low-Wage Workers." *Berkeley Journal of Employment and Labor Law* 36(1): 169–214.

Kubrin, Charis E. 2014. "Secure or Insecure Communities: Seven Reasons to Abandon the Secure Communities Program Immigration Enforcement, Policing, and Crime: Essay." *Criminology and Public Policy* 13(2): 323–38.

Lagarde, Marcela. 2006. "Del Femicidio al Feminicidio." *Desde El jardín de Freud* 6: 216–25.

Lakhani, Nina. 2019. "Indigenous Mexicans Tortured in Migrant Crackdown Win Public Apology." *The Guardian*, November 7.

Lambert, Frederick, Keri E. Discepolo, and Hawazin W. Elani. 2022. "Chilling Effects on Immigrants' Health Insurance Coverage after the 2016 Presidential Election." *Journal of Immigrant and Minority Health* 24: 819–26.

Lartey, Jamiles. 2017. "'Day without Immigrants' Protests Close Restaurants across the US." *The Guardian*, February 17.

Latapí Sarre, Pablo. 2009. "El Derecho a La Educación: Su Alcance, Exigibilidad y Relevancia Para La Política Educativa." *Revista Mexicana de Investigación Educativa* 14(40): 255–87.

Lee, Erika. 2002. "The Chinese Exclusion Example: Race, Immigration, and American Gatekeeping, 1882–1924." *Journal of American Ethnic History* 21(3): 36–62.

Lee, Fred I. 2007. "The Japanese Internment and the Racial State of Exception." *Theory & Event* 10(1). https://dx.doi.org/10.1353/tae.2007.0043.

Lee, Stephen. 2014. "Policing Wage Theft in the Day Labor Market Part V: Employment Law." *Immigration and Nationality Law Review* 35: 627–50.

León, Lucia, Leisy J. Abrego, and Genevieve Negrón-Gonzales. 2024. "Cultivating Ethical and Politically Rooted Research Practices with Undocumented Migrants." *Social Inclusion* 12: 8555.

Llewellyn, Cheryl. 2020. "(In)Credible Violence: An Analysis of Post-Alvarado Domestic Violence Asylum Cases in the United States." *Journal of Women, Politics & Policy* 41 (2): 170–93.

Lopez, Jane Lilly. 2015. "Impossible Families: Mixed-Citizenship Status Couples and the Law." *Law and Policy* 37(1–2): 93–118.

Lopez, Mark Hugo, Ana Gonzalez-Barrera, Jens Manuel Krogstad, and Gustavo López. 2016. "2. The Latino Vote in the 2016 Presidential Election." Pew Research Center. https://www.pewresearch.org/race-and-ethnicity/2016/10/11/the-latino-vote-in-the-2016-presidential-election/.

Lopez, Todd. 2025. "Hegseth Gives Order to Enhance Military Mission at Southern Border." U.S. Department of Defense.

Lopez, William D., Nicole L. Novak, Melanie Harner, Ramiro Martinez, and Julia S. Seng. 2018. "The Traumatogenic Potential of Law Enforcement Home Raids: An Exploratory Report." *Traumatology* 24(3): 193–99.

López de León, Silvia, and José Alberto Yela Sayle. 2018. *Compendio estadístico de pueblos 2018*. Instituto Nacional de Estadística.

Loza, Mireya. 2016. *Defiant Braceros: How Migrant Workers Fought for Racial, Sexual, and Political Freedom*. University of North Carolina Press.

Lugones, María. 2008. "Colonialidad y Género." *Tabula Rasa* 9: 73–101.

Luna, Zakiya, and Whitney Pirtle. 2021. *Black Feminist Sociology: Perspectives and Praxis*. Routledge.

Lydgate, Joanna Jacobbi. 2010. "Assembly-Line Justice: A Review of Operation Streamline." *California Law Review* 98(2): 481–544.

Lytle Hernandez, Kelly. 2017. *City of Inmates: Conquest, Rebellion, and the Rise of Human Caging in Los Angeles, 1771–1965*. University of North Carolina Press.

Mahler, Sarah J., and Patricia R. Pessar. 2006. "Gender Matters: Ethnographers Bring Gender from the Periphery toward the Core of Migration Studies." *International Migration Review* 40(1): 27–63.

Marks, Rachel. 2024. *What Updates to OMB's Race/Ethnicity Standards Mean for the Census Bureau*. US Census Bureau.

Marrow, Helen B. 2011. *New Destination Dreaming: Immigration, Race, and Legal Status in the Rural South*. Stanford University Press.

Marrow, Helen B. 2020. "Hope Turned Sour: Second-Generation Incorporation and Mobility in US New Immigrant Destinations." In *The End of Compassion*, ed. Alejandro Portes and Patricia Fernandez-Kelly. Routledge.

Martínez Coria, Ramón, Jesús Armando Haro Encinas, Ramón Martínez Coria, and Jesús Armando Haro Encinas. 2015. "Derechos territoriales y pueblos indígenas en México: Una lucha por la soberanía y la nación." *Revista pueblos y fronteras digital* 10(19): 228–56.

Martínez, Daniel E. 2022. "The Racialized Dimensions of Contemporary Immigration and Border Enforcement Policies and Practices." *Public Administration Review* 82(3): 598–603.

Martínez-Beltrán, Sergio. 2025. "Trump Asks Supreme Court to Allow Deportations under Alien Enemies Act." National Public Radio, March 28.

Massey, Douglas S. 2020. "Immigration Policy Mismatches and Counterproductive Outcomes: Unauthorized Migration to the U.S. in Two Eras." *Comparative Migration Studies* 8(1): 21.

Massey, Douglas S., Jorge Durand, and Nolan J. Malone. 2002. *Beyond Smoke and Mirrors: Mexican Immigration in an Era of Economic Integration*. Russell Sage Foundation.

Massey, Douglas S., Jorge Durand, and Karen A. Pren. 2016. "Why Border Enforcement Backfired." *American Sociological Journal* 121(5): 1557–1600.

Mathema, Silva. 2017. "Keeping Families Together." Center for American Progress. https://www.americanprogress.org/issues/immigration/reports/2017/03/16/428335/keeping-families-together/.

Mathews, Gordon, Gustavo Lins Ribeiro, and Carlos Alba Vega. 2012. *Globalization from Below: The World's Other Economy*. Routledge.

Mazari, Ivania, and César Ruiz. 2019. *Desigualdad en México: El que quiere no siempre puede*. Instituto Mexicano para la Competitividad.

McCarty, Dawn. 2008. "The Impact of the North American Free Trade Agreement (NAFTA) on Rural Children and Families in Mexico: Transnational Policy and Practice Implications." *Journal of Public Child Welfare* 1(4): 105–23.

McMichael, Philip. 2010. *Contesting Development: Critical Struggles for Social Change*. Routledge.

McEwen, Bruce S. 2017. "Neurobiological and Systemic Effects of Chronic Stress." *Chronic Stress* 1. doi:10.1177/2470547017692328.

Médecins Sans Frontières. 2024. "Violence, Desperation and Abandonment on the Migration Route: The Medical-Humanitarian Impact of an Unprecedented Crisis in Mexico and Central America." https://www.msf.org/violence -desperation-and-abandonment-migration-route.

Menchaca, Martha. 1993. "Chicano Indianism: A Historical Account of Racial Repression in the United States." *American Ethnologist* 20(3): 583–603.

Méndez, Michael, Genevieve Flores-Haro, and Lucas Zucker. 2020. "The (in) Visible Victims of Disaster: Understanding the Vulnerability of Undocumented Latino/a and Indigenous Immigrants." *Geoforum; Journal of Physical, Human, and Regional Geosciences* 116 (November): 50–62.

Menjívar, Cecilia. 2000. *Fragmented Ties: Salvadoran Immigrant Networks in America*. University of California Press.

Menjívar, Cecilia. 2006. "Liminal Legality: Salvadoran and Guatemalan Immigrants' Lives in the United States." *American Journal of Sociology* 111(4): 999–1037.

Menjívar, Cecilia. 2011. *Enduring Violence: Ladina Women's Lives in Guatemala*. University of California Press.

Menjívar, Cecilia. 2021. "The Racialization of 'Illegality.'" *Daedalus* 150(2): 91–105.

Menjívar, Cecilia. 2023. "Publicly Engaged Sociological Research for Immigrant Well-Being." *American Behavioral Scientist*. doi.org/10.1177/0002764223 1217626.

Menjívar, Cecilia, and Leisy J. Abrego. 2012. "Legal Violence: Immigration Law and the Lives of Central American Immigrants." *American Journal of Sociology* 117(5): 1380–421.

Menjívar, Cecilia, Victor Agadjanian, and Byeongdon Oh. 2022. "The Contradictions of Liminal Legality: Economic Attainment and Civic Engagement of Central American Immigrants on Temporary Protected Status." *Social Problems* 69(3): 678–98.

Menjívar, Cecilia, and Leydy Diossa-Jiménez. 2023. "Blocking the Law from Within: Familyism Ideologies as Obstacles to Legal Protections for Women in El Salvador, Guatemala, Honduras, and Nicaragua." *Latin American Research Review* 58(3): 501–18.

Menjívar, Cecilia, and Shannon Drysdale Walsh. 2016. "Subverting Justice: Socio-Legal Determinants of Impunity for Violence against Women in Guatemala." *Laws* 5(31). https://doi.org/10.3390/laws5030031.

Menjívar, Cecilia, and Shannon Drysdale Walsh. 2017. "The Architecture of Feminicide: The State, Inequalities, and Everyday Gender Violence in Honduras." *Latin American Research Review* 52(2): 221–40.

Menjívar, Cecilia, and Andrea Gómez Cervantes. 2024. "Maya Guatemalans Seeking Asylum: Race and Gender in a Continuum of State Control." *Sociology of Race and Ethnicity* 11(1): 69–84.

Menjívar, Cecilia, Andrea Gómez Cervantes, and Daniel Alvord. 2018. "The Expansion of 'Crimmigration,' Mass Detention, and Deportation." *Sociology Compass* 12(4):e12573.

Menjívar, Cecilia, and Sarah M. Lakhani. 2016. "Transformative Effects of Immigration Law: Immigrants' Personal and Social Metamorphoses through Regularization." *American Journal of Sociology* 121(6): 1818–55.

Messina, Julian, and Joana Silva. 2021. "Twenty Years of Wage Inequality in Latin America." *World Bank Economic Review* 35(1): 117–47.

Migration Policy Institute. 2019. "Profile of the Unauthorized Population: Kansas." https://www.migrationpolicy.org/data/unauthorized-immigrant-population /state/KS.

Migration Policy Institute. 2023. "State Demographics Data: Kansas." Washington, DC. https://www.migrationpolicy.org/data/state-profiles/state/demographics /KS/US.

Mijente. 2018. "Free Our Future: An Immigration Policy Platform for beyond the Trump Era." https://mijente.net/wp-content/uploads/2018/06/Mijente -Immigration-Policy-Platform_0628.pdf.

Mireles-Rios, Rebeca, Victor M. Rios, and Augustina Reyes. 2020. "Pushed Out for Missing School: The Role of Social Disparities and School Truancy in Dropping Out." *Education Sciences* 10(4): 108–23.

Molina, Natalia. 2014. *How Race Is Made in America: Immigration, Citizenship, and the Historical Power of Racial Scripts.* University of California Press.

Mollard, Elizabeth, Holly Hatton-Bowers, and Julie Tippens. 2020. "Finding Strength in Vulnerability: Ethical Approaches When Conducting Research with Vulnerable Populations." *Journal of Midwifery & Women's Health* 65(6): 802–7.

Montecinos, Claudia. 2020. "Millions of Undocumented Immigrants Are Essential to America's Recovery, New Report Shows." 2020. Center for American Progress. https://www.americanprogress.org/press/release/2020/12/02

/493404/release-millions-undocumented-immigrants-essential-americas -recovery-new-report-shows/.

Moorefield, Nicole. 2022. *This Is Your Brain (and Body) on Fear*. University of North Carolina.

Mora, G. Cristina. 2014. *Making Hispanics: How Activists, Bureaucrats, and Media Constructed a New American*. University of Chicago Press.

Morales, P. Zitlali, Lydia A. Saravia, and María Fernanda Pérez-Iribe. 2019. "Multilingual Mexican-Origin Students' Perspectives on Their Indigenous Heritage Language." *Association of Mexican American Educators Journal* 13(2): 91–121.

Morales, P. Zitlali. 2016. "Transnational Practices and Language Maintenance: Spanish and Zapoteco in California." *Children's Geographies* 14(4): 375–89.

Morales Waugh, Irma. 2010. "Examining the Sexual Harassment Experiences of Mexican Immigrant Farmworking Women." *Violence Against Women* 16(3): 237–61.

Morin, Rebecca. 2021. "DHS: More than 3,900 Children Separated under Trump 'Zero Tolerance' Policy." *USA. Today*, June 8. https://www.usatoday.com /story/news/politics/2021/06/08/dhs-task-force-children-separated-trump -zero-tolerance-policy/7594577002/.

Murillo, Marco A. 2021. "Undocumented and College-Bound: A Case Study of the Supports and Barriers High School Students Encounter in Accessing Higher Education." *Urban Education* 56(6): 930–58.

Muzychenko, I. N., L. Zhang, I. A. Apollonova, A. P. Nikolaev, and A. V. Pisareva. 2018. "Development of a Method for Assessing the Effects of Chronic Stress on the Human Body." *Journal of Physics* 7.

Naciones Unidas. 2016. *La matriz de la desigualdad social en América Latina*. Comisión Economica para América Latina y el Caribe. Santiago, Chile.

Nájar, Alberto. 2019a. "4 claves que explican por qué México registró un nuevo récord en el número de homicidios." *BBC News*, July 22.

Nájar, Alberto. 2019b. "Cómo la crisis migratoria despierta al Trump que muchos mexicanos llevan dentro." *BBC News*.

National Center for Education Statistics. 2023. *Educational Attainment of Young Adults*. US Department of Education, Institute of Education Sciences.

National Immigrant Justice Center. 2020. "A Legacy of Injustice: The U.S. Criminalization of Migration." https://immigrantjustice.org/research/report -a-legacy-of-injustice-the-u-s-criminalization-of-migration/.

National Immigration Law Center. 2015. *DAPA and Expanded DACA Programs.* Washington, DC.

National Institute on Aging. 2024. *Mental Health Benefits of Exercise and Physical Activity.* Washington, DC.

Ngai, Mae N. 2004. *Impossible Subjects: Illegal Aliens and the Making of Modern America.* Princeton University Press.

Nicholls, Walter J. 2013. *The DREAMers: How the Undocumented Youth Movement Transformed the Immigrant Rights Debate.* Stanford University Press.

Nicholls, Walter J. 2019. *The Immigrant Rights Movement: The Battle over National Citizenship.* Stanford University Press.

Nolan, Rachel. 2019. "A Translation Crisis at the Border." *New Yorker*, December 30.

Novak, Nicole L., Arline T. Geronimus, and Aresha M. Martinez-Cardoso. 2017. "Change in Birth Outcomes among Infants Born to Latina Mothers after a Major Immigration Raid." *International Journal of Epidemiology* 46(3): 839–49.

Nungesser, Frithjof. 2024. "Defying Guantánamo: Resistance to Indefinite Detention and Torture in a Prison Camp." *International Journal of Comparative Sociology* 66(3): 388–419.

Ola, Ana Lucia. 2020. "Cifras que llaman a la reflexión sobre la reinvidicación de la mujer en Guatemala." Prensa Libre, March 7. https://www.prensalibre .com/guatemala/comunitario/cifras-que-llaman-a-la-reflexion-sobre-la -reinvidicacion-de-la-mujer-en-guatemala/.

Oladipo, Gloria. 2025. "'A Warning for Students of Color': ICE Agents Are Targeting Certain Protesters, Say Experts." *The Guardian*, March 26.

Oppenheimer, Robert. 1985. "Acculturation or Assimilation: Mexican Immigrants in Kansas, 1900 to World War II." *Western Historical Quarterly* 16(4): 429–48.

Organización Panamericana de la Salud/Organización Mundial de la salud en Guatemala. 2016. *Perfil de salud de los pueblos indígenas.* Guatemala.

Ortiz Hernández, Luis, César Iván Ayala Guzmán, Diana Pérez-Salgado, Luis Ortiz Hernández, César Iván Ayala Guzmán, and Diana Pérez-Salgado. 2018. "Posición socioeconómica, discriminación y color de piel en México." *Perfiles latinoamericanos* 26 (51): 215–39.

Ortutay, Barbara. 2025. "US Immigration Officials Look to Expand Social Media Data Collection." Associated Press, March 30.

Osgood, Brian. 2025. "How the 'War on Terror' Paved the Way for Student Deportations in the US." Al Jazeera, March 28.

Ousey, Graham C., and Charis E. Kubrin. 2018. "Immigration and Crime: Assessing a Contentious Issue." *Annual Review of Criminology* 1: 63–84.

Oxfam Mexico. 2017. "Todo nuestro trabajo vale: Mujeres y hombres en equidad." https://www.oxfammexico.org/historias/todo-nuestro-trabajo-vale -mujeres-y-hombres-en-equidad.

Oyěwùmí, Oyèrónkẹ́. 1997. *The Invention of Women: Making an African Sense of Western Gender Discourses*. University of Minnesota Press.

Palumbo-Liu, David. 2024. "How Gaza Is Changing US Campuses." Al Jazeera, April 13. https://www.aljazeera.com/opinions/2024/4/13/how-gaza-is-changing -us-campuses.

Payan, Tony, and José Iván Rodríguez-Sánchez. 2025. "Social and Economic Effects of Expanded Deportation Measures." Baker Institute for Public Policy.

PBS News. 2024. "Interactive: How Key Groups of Americans Voted in 2024." https://www.pbs.org/newshour/politics/interactive-how-key-groups-of -americans-voted-in-2024-according-to-ap-votecast.

Pearson, Lynn Damiano. 2025. "Factsheet: Trump's Rescission of Protected Areas Policies Undermines Safety for All." National Immigration Law Center. https://www.nilc.org/wp-content/uploads/2025/01/Protected-Areas-Policies -Undermines-Safety-for-All-.pdf.

Peterson, Nicholas. 2016. "Sesiones de Información Publica Sobre Trump e Inmigración." *Dos Mundos*.

Peterson, Nicholas. 2017. "ICE Genera Miedo, Infórmate." *Dos Mundos Bilingual Newspaper*, February 17, Vol. 37(07).

Pew Research Center. 2016. "Demographic and Economic Profiles of Hispanics by State and County, 2014." https://www.pewresearch.org/hispanic/states/.

Pew Research Center. 2022. "Hispanic Population Growth and Dispersion across U.S. Counties, 1980–2020." https://www.pewresearch.org/race-and -ethnicity/feature/hispanic-population-by-county/.

Pierce, Sarah. 2019. *Immigration-Related Policy Changes in the First Two Years of the Trump Administration*. Migration Policy Institute.

Pistone, Michele R., and John J. Hoeffner. 2005. "Rules Are Made to Be Broken: How the Process of Expedited Removal Fails Asylum Seekers." *Georgetown Immigration Law Journal* 20: 167–211.

Portes, Alejandro, Patricia Fernandez-Kelly, and William Haller. 2005. "Segmented Assimilation on the Ground: The New Second Generation in Early Adulthood." *Ethnic and Racial Studies* 28(6): 1000–40.

Portes, Alejandro, and Hao Lingxin. 1998. "E Pluribus Unum: Bilingualism and Loss of Language in the Second Generation." *Sociology of Education* 71(4): 269–94.

Portes, Alejandro, and Rubén Rumbaut. 2001. *Legacies: The Story of the Immigrant Second Generation*. University of California Press.

Portes, Alejandro, and Min Zhou. 1993. "The New Second Generation: Segmented Assimilation and Its Variants." *ANNALS of the American Academy of Political and Social Science* 530: 74–96.

Provine, Doris Marie, Monica W. Varsanyi, Paul G. Lewis, and Scott H. Decker. 2016. *Policing Immigrants: Local Law Enforcement on the Front Lines*. University of Chicago Press.

Qian, Zhenchao, Daniel T. Lichter, and Dmitry Tumin. 2018. "Divergent Pathways to Assimilation? Local Marriage Markets and Intermarriage among U.S. Hispanics." *Journal of Marriage and Family* 80(1): 271–88.

Quijano, Aníbal. 1999. "Colonialidad del poder, cultura y conocimiento en América Latina." *Dispositio* 24 (51, Crítica cultural en Latinoamérica: Paradigmas globales y enunciaciones locales): 137–48.

Quijano, Aníbal. 2000. "Coloniality of Power and Eurocentrism in Latin America." *International Sociology* 15(2): 215–32.

Quijano, Aníbal. 2019. "Colonialidad del poder, eurocentrismo y América Latina." *Espacio Abierto* 28(1): 255–301.

Quintana, Chris. 2020. "More Latino Students Than Ever Are Trying to Get Their Degree, but It's Fraught and Costly." *USA Today*, January 6.

Radhakrishnan, Smitha, and Cinzia D. Solari. 2023. *The Gender Order of Neoliberalism*. John Wiley & Sons.

Ramos, Pedraza, and Alejandro Karin. 2019. "El indigenismo en México como racismo de estado: Mestizaje asimilacionista y esterilización forzada." *Itinerarios. Revista de estudios lingüísticos, literarios, históricos y antropológicos* (Itinerarios no. 29/2019): 215–36.

Rattner, Steven. 2025. "How Bad Is This Bill? The Answer in 10 Charts." *New York Times,* July 3.

Rauvola, Rachel S., Dulce M. Vega, and Kristi N. Lavigne. 2019. "Compassion Fatigue, Secondary Traumatic Stress, and Vicarious Traumatization: A Qualitative Review and Research Agenda." *Occupational Health Science* 3(3): 297–336.

Reierson, Shannon, and Sylvia Celedón-Pattichis. 2014. "Transforming Experience through English Use and Service-Oriented Cultural Capital: Indigenous Honduran Immigrants to the U.S. Southwest." *Latin American Perspectives* 41(3): 208–19.

Reineke, Robin C., and Daniel E. Martinez. 2024. "Excessive Use of Force and Migrant Death and Disappearance in Southern Arizona." *Journal on Migration and Human Security* 12(3): 243–56.

Ribas, Vanesa. 2015. *On the Line: Slaughterhouse Lives and the Making of the New South.* University of California Press.

Rickford, John R. 2016. *Raciolinguistics: How Language Shapes Our Ideas about Race.* Oxford University Press.

Rincón, Luis Felipe. 2010. "¡Hombres de maíz! Una mirada a la actualidad organizativa campesina en Guatemala." *REvista NERA* 13(17): 49–65.

Rios, Victor M. 2011. *Punished: Policing the Lives of Black and Latino Boys.* New York University Press.

Rivera Cusicanqui, Silvia. 1997. "La noción de 'derecho' o las paradojas de la modernidad postcolonial: Indígenas y mujeres en Bolivia." *Temas Sociales* (19): 27–52.

Rivera Cusicanqui, Silvia. 2010. *Ch'ixinakax utxiwa. Una reflexión sobre prácticas y discursos descolonizadores.* Buenos Aires, Argentina: Tinta limón.

Robbins, Liz, and Annie Correal. 2017. "On a 'Day Without Immigrants,' Workers Show Their Presence by Staying Home." *New York Times,* February 16.

Rodríguez, Clara E. 2000. *Changing Race: Latinos, the Census and the History of Ethnicity.* New York University Press.

Rodriguez Vega, Silvia. 2023. *Drawing Deportation: Art and Resistance among Immigrant Children.* New York University Press.

Romero, Mary. 2006. "Racial Profiling and Immigration Law Enforcement: Rounding Up of Usual Suspects in the Latino Community." *Critical Sociology* 32(2–3): 447–73.

Romero, Mary. 2008. "Crossing the Immigration and Race Border: A Critical Race Theory Approach to Immigration Studies." *Contemporary Justice Review* 11(1): 23–37.

Romero, Mary. 2011. "Keeping Citizenship Rights White: Arizona's Racial Profiling Practices in Immigration Law Enforcement." *Law Journal for Social Justice* 1(1): 97–113.

Romero, Mary. 2018. "Trump's Immigration Attacks, In Brief." *Contexts* 17(1): 34–41.

Romo, Vanessa. 2018. "U.S. Border Agents Seen on Video Trying to Deport a Man Who 'Looks Mexican.'" *National Public Radio*, April 12.

Rosa, Jonathan, and Nelson Flores. 2017. "Unsettling Race and Language: Toward a Raciolinguistic Perspective." *Language in Society* 46(5): 621–47.

Rosales, Rocio. 2014. "Stagnant Immigrant Social Networks and Cycles of Exploitation." *Ethnic and Racial Studies* 37(14): 2564–79.

Rosales, Rocío. 2020. *Fruteros: Street Vending, Illegality, and Ethnic Community in Los Angeles.* University of California Press.

Rose, Joel, and Scott Neuman. 2021. "The Biden Administration Is Fighting in Court to Keep a Trump-Era Immigration Policy." *National Public Radio*, September 20. https://www.npr.org/2021/09/20/1038918197/the-biden-administration-is-fighting-in-court-to-keep-a-trump-era-immigration-po.

Rosenberg, Jaime. 2017. "The Effects of Chronic Fear on a Person's Health." AMJC. https://www.ajmc.com/view/the-effects-of-chronic-fear-on-a-persons-health.

Rosenberg, Carol. 2025. "Another Dozen Migrants Are Transferred to Guantánamo Bay." *New York Times*, June 12.

Ruiz, Nadeen T., and Manuel Barajas. 2012. "Multiple Perspectives on the Schooling of Mexican Indigenous Students in the U.S.: Issues for Future Research." *Bilingual Research Journal* 35(2): 125–44.

Ruiz Soto, Ariel G. 2024. "Explainer: Immigrants and Crime in the United States." Migration Policy Institute.

Rumbaut, Rubén. 2009. "Pigments of Our Imagination: On the Racialization and Racial Identities of 'Hispanics' and 'Latinos.'" In *How the United States Racializes Latinos: White Hegemony and Its Consequences,* ed. J. A. Cobas, J. Duany, and J. R. Feagin. Boulder, CO: Paradigm Publishers.

Rumbaut, Ruben G., Douglas S. Massey, and Frank D. Bean. 2006. "Linguistic Life Expectancies: Immigrant Language Retention in Southern California." *Population and Development Review* 32(3): 447–60.

Ryo, Emily. 2019. "Understanding Immigration Detention: Causes, Conditions, and Consequences." *Annual Review of Law and Social Science* 15(1): 97–115.

Ryo, Emily, and Ian Peacock. 2020. "Jailing Immigrant Detainees: A National Study of County Participation in Immigration Detention, 1983–2013." *Law & Society Review* 54(1): 66–101.

Saadi, Altaf, Caitlin Patler, and Paola Langer. 2025. "Duration in Immigration Detention and Health Harms." *JAMA Network Open* 8(1): 1–10.

Samson, Colin, and Carlos Gigoux. 2016. *Indigenous Peoples and Colonialism: Global Perspectives*. Polity.

Sanchez, Daina. 2018. "Racial and Structural Discrimination toward the Children of Indigenous Mexican Immigrants." *Race and Social Problems* 10(4): 306–19.

Sánchez García, Carolina, Juan Mario Pérez Martínez, Rocío Becerra Montané, and José del Val. 2023. *El mundo indígena 2023: México*. Copenhagen: International Work Group for Indigenous Affairs.

Sanford, Victoria. 2008. "From Genocide to Feminicide: Impunity and Human Rights in Twenty-First Century Guatemala." *Journal of Human Rights* 7(2): 104–22.

Santa Ana, Otto. 2002. *Brown Tide Rising: Metaphors of Latinos in Contemporary American Public Discourse*. University of Texas Press.

Santana, Rebecca, and Marcos Aleman. 2025. "Trump Administration Deports 17 More 'Violent Criminals' to El Salvador." Associated Press, March 31.

Sarat, Austin. 1990. "The Law Is All Over: Power, Resistance and the Legal Consciousness of the Welfare Poor." *Yale Journal of Law & the Humanities* 2: 343.

Schapendonk, Joris. 2018. "Navigating the Migration Industry: Migrants Moving through an African-European Web of Facilitation/Control." *Journal of Ethnic and Migration Studies* 44(4): 663–79.

Schmalzbauer, Leah. 2014. *The Last Best Place? Gender, Family, and Migration in the New West*. Stanford University Press.

Schmelkes, Sylvia. 2013. "Educación y pueblos indígenas: Problemas de medición." Instituto Nacional de Estadística y Geografía. http://www.inegi.org.mx/rde/rde_08/Doctos/RDE_08_Art1.pdf.

Secretaría Nacional de Planificación y Desarrollo. 2013. *Atlas de las desigual-dades socio-económicas del Ecuador.* Quito, Ecuador.

Siddiqui, Sabrina. 2018. "'On a Mission to Destroy Families': Ice Targets Migrants in Once Safe Spaces." *The Guardian,* July 14.

Silver, Rita Elaine. 2005. "The Discourse of Linguistic Capital: Language and Economic Policy Planning in Singapore." *Language Policy* 4(1): 47–66.

Simmons, William Paul, Cecilia Menjívar, and Elizabeth Salerno Valdez. 2021. "The Gendered Effects of Local Immigration Enforcement: Latinas' Social Isolation in Chicago, Houston, Los Angeles, and Phoenix." *International Migration Review* 55(1): 108–34.

Slack, Jeremy, Daniel E. Martínez, Alison Elizabeth Lee, and Scott Whiteford. 2016. "The Geography of Border Militarization: Violence, Death and Health in Mexico and the United States." *Journal of Latin American Geography* 15(1): 7–32.

Slack, Jeremy, Daniel E. Martínez, Scott Whiteford, and Emily Peiffer. 2015. "In Harm's Way: Family Separation, Immigration Enforcement Programs and Security on the US-Mexico Border." *Journal on Migration and Human Security* 3(2): 109–28.

Small, Mario Luis, and Jessica McCrory Calarco. 2022. *Qualitative Literacy: A Guide to Evaluating Ethnographic and Interview Research.* University of California Press.

Smith, Dorothy E. 2012. *The Everyday World as Problematic: A Feminist Sociology.* Northeastern University Press.

Smith, Linda Tuhiwai. 2021. *Decolonizing Methodologies: Research and Indigenous Peoples.* Bloomsbury Academic.

Soledad O'Brien Productions and Retro Report, dir. 2024. *Campus D.E.I. Programs Under Fire after Supreme Court Ruling on Race.*

Sorensen, Majken Jul. 2008. "Humor as a Serious Strategy of Nonviolent Resistance to Oppression." *Peace & Change* 33(2): 167–90.

Southern Poverty Law Center. 2016. "Kris Kobach: Lawyer for America's Nativist Movement." November 18. https://www.splcenter.org/resources/reports/kris-kobach-lawyer-americas-nativist-movement/.

Speed, Shannon. 2019. *Incarcerated Stories: Indigenous Women Migrants and Violence in the Settler-Capitalist State.* University of North Carolina Press.

Speed, Shannon, R. Aída Hernández Castillo, and Lynn M. Stephen. 2006. *Dissident Women: Gender and Cultural Politics in Chiapas.* University of Texas Press.

Stumpf, Juliet. 2006. "The Crimmigration Crisis: Immigrants, Crime, and Sovereign Power." *American University Law Review* 56(2): 367–420.

Sugarman, Julie. 2025. "Schools and Immigrant Students Navigate an Era of Rising Immigration Enforcement." Migration Policy Institute, April. https://www.migrationpolicy.org/news/schools-immigrant-students-enforcement.

Sumida Huaman, Elizabeth, and Nathan D. Martin, eds. 2023. *Indigenous Research Design Transnational Perspectives in Practice.* Canadian Scholars.

Tabares, Maria Luisa. 2017. "Si soy indocumentado, ¿debo tener un plan de custodia para mis hijos menores? Univision Noticias, February 7.

Taracena Arriola, Arturo. 2019. *Guatemala: Del Mestizaje a La Ladinizacion, 1524–1964.* Centro de Investigaciones Regionales de Mesoamerica (CIRMA).

Taylor, Marisa, and Jeffrey Dastin. 2025. "Exclusive: Trump Administration Is Pointing Spy Satellites at US Border." Reuters, March 27.

Telles, Edward, and Tianna Paschel. 2014. "Who Is Black, White, or Mixed Race? How Skin Color, Status, and Nation Shape Racial Classification in Latin America." *American Journal of Sociology* 120(3): 864–907.

Terriquez, Veronica, and Ruth Milkman. 2021. "Immigrant and Refugee Youth Organizing in Solidarity with the Movement for Black Lives." *Gender & Society* 35(4): 577–87.

Thacher, David. 2008. "The Rise of Criminal Background Screening in Rental Housing." *Law & Social Inquiry* 33(1): 5–30.

Torche, Florencia, and Catherine Sirois. 2019. "Restrictive Immigration Law and Birth Outcomes of Immigrant Women." *American Journal of Epidemiology* 188(1): 24–33.

Torres, M. Gabriela. 2018. "Chapter 22. State Violence." In *The Cambridge Handbook of Social Problems*, Vol. 2, ed. A. J. Treviño. Cambridge University Press.

Torrey, Philip L. 2015. "Rethinking Immigration's Mandatory Detention Regime: Politics, Profit, and the Meaning of Custody." *University of Michigan Journal of Law Reform* 48(4): 879–914.

Tosh, Sarah. 2019. "Drugs, Crime, and Aggravated Felony Deportations: Moral Panic Theory and the Legal Construction of the 'Criminal Alien.'" *Critical Criminology* 27(2): 329–45.

Tran, Van. 2010. "English Gain vs. Spanish Loss? Language Assimilation among Second-Generation Latinos in Young Adulthood." *Social Forces* 89(1): 257–84.

Transactional Records Access Clearinghouse. 2018. *Immigration and Customs Enforcement Arrests*. Syracuse, NY.

Transactional Records Access Clearinghouse. 2022. *Latest Data: Immigration and Customs Enforcement Removals*. Syracuse, NY.

Transactional Records Access Clearinghouse. 2023. *Immigration and Customs Enforcement Detainers*. Syracuse, NY.

Trevizo, Mica, and Perla Rosenberg. 2025. "U.S. Claims Immigrants Held at Guantanamo Are 'Worst of the Worst.' Their Families Say They're Being Unfairly Targeted." ProPublica, February 13.

Trump v. CASA. 2025. 606 U.S.

Tseng, Vivian, and Andrew J. Fuligni. 2000. "Parent-Adolescent Language Use and Relationships among Immigrant Families with East Asian, Filipino, and Latin American Backgrounds." *Journal of Marriage and Family* 62(2): 465–76.

United Nations. 2009. *Guatemala: Análisis de la situación del país 2008*.

United Nations High Commissioner for Refugees. 2015. *Women on the Run*. Washington, DC.

US Census Bureau. 2020. *U.S. Census Bureau QuickFacts: Kansas*. Washington, DC.

US Department of Homeland Security. 2018. *Participating Employers*. Washington, DC.

US Department of Homeland Security. 2019. *Number of Form I-918, Petition for U Nonimmigrant Status, by Fiscal Year, Quarter, and Case Status 2009- 2019*. Washington, DC.

US Department of Justice. 2025. "Memorandum Operation Take Back America." March 6. https://www.justice.gov/dag/media/1393746/dl?inline.

Urrieta, Luis. 2013. "Familia and Comunidad-Based Saberes: Learning in an Indigenous Heritage Community." *Anthropology & Education Quarterly* 44(3): 320–35.

Urrieta, Luis, Jr., and Dolores Calderón. 2019. "Critical Latinx Indigeneities: Unpacking Indigeneity from Within and Outside of Latinized Entanglements." *Association of Mexican American Educators Journal* 13(2): 145–74.

van der Merwe, Amelia, and Xanthe Hunt. 2019. "Secondary Trauma among Trauma Researchers: Lessons from the Field." *Psychological Trauma: Theory, Research, Practice, and Policy* 11(1): 10–18.

Van Hook, Jennifer, Julia Gelatt, and Airel G. Ruiz Soto. 2023. *A Turning Point for the Unauthorized Immigrant Population in the United States*. Migration Policy Institute.

Vaquera, Elizabeth, Elizabeth Aranda, and Roberto G. Gonzales. 2014. "Patterns of Incorporation of Latinos in Old and New Destinations: From Invisible to Hypervisible." *American Behavioral Scientist* 58(14): 1823–33.

Vega, Sujey. 2015. *Latino Heartland: Of Borders and Belonging in the Midwest Latino Heartland*. New York University Press.

Velasco, Patricia. 2014. "The Language and Educational Ideologies of Mixteco-Mexican Mothers." *Journal of Latinos and Education* 13(2): 85–106.

Velázquez Gutiérrez, María Elisa, and Gabriela Iturralde Nieto. 2016. *Afrodescendientes en México: Una historia de silencio y discriminación*. 2nd ed. Consejo Nacional para Prevenir la Discriminación.

Ventura Patiño, María de Carmen. 2008. "Nueva Reforma Agraria Neoliberal y Multiculturalismo: Territorios Indígenas, Un Derecho Vuelto a Negar." *Revista Pueblos y Fronteras* 3(5): 1–35. https://doi.org/10.22201/cimsur.18704115e.2008.5.211.

Villegas, Paloma E. 2019. "'I Made Myself Small like a Cat and Ran Away': Workplace Sexual Harassment, Precarious Immigration Status and Legal Violence." *Journal of Gender Studies* 28(6): 674–86.

Viruell-Fuentes, Edna A., Jeffrey D. Morenoff, and David R. Williams. 2013. "Contextualizing Nativity Status, Latino Social Ties, and Ethnic Enclaves: An Examination of the 'Immigrant Social Ties Hypothesis.'" *Ethnicity and Health* 18(6): 586–609.

Vogt, Wendy A. 2013. "Crossing Mexico: Structural Violence and the Commodification of Undocumented Central American Migrants." *American Ethnologist* 40(4): 764–80.

Vogt, Wendy A. 2018. *Lives in Transit: Violence and Intimacy on the Migrant Journey*. University of California Press.

Waldinger, Roger, and Michael I. Lichter. 2003. *How the Other Half Works: Immigration and the Social Organization of Labor*. University of California Press.

Walsh, Catherine. 2010. "'Raza', Mestizaje y Poder: Horizontes Coloniales Pasados y Presentes." *Crítica y Emancipación: Revista Latinoamericana de Ciencias Sociales* 2(3): 95–127.

Waters, Mary C. 1990. *Ethnic Options: Choosing Identities in America*. University of California Press.

Watson, Tara, and Jonathon Zars. 2024. *What to Expect on Immigration Policy from a Trump White House*. Brookings.

Wolfe, Patrick. 2006. "Settler Colonialism and the Elimination of the Native." *Journal of Genocide Research* 8(4): 387–409.

Yoshioka, Hirotoshi. 2010. "Indigenous Language Usage and Maintenance Patterns among Indigenous People in the Era of Neoliberal Multiculturalism in Mexico and Guatemala." *Latin American Research Review* 45(3): 5–34.

Yosso, Tara J. 2016. "Whose Culture Has Capital? A Critical Race Theory Discussion of Community Cultural Wealth." In *Critical Race Theory in Education: All God's Children Got a Song*, ed. Addrienne Dixson, Celia K. Rousseau Anderson, and Jamel K. Donnor. Abingdon, UK: Taylor & Francis.

Index

Fourth Amendment, 200–201
Francisca, interviewee, 40
frontera, la. See US-Mexico border
future (for immigrants in heartland), 208–11

gender: discrimination, 181; driving mobility, 101–4; entanglement with illegality, 16; as factor in shaping power dynamics, 18; and federal-level policies, 201–2; gender violence crossing borders, 42, 46–47; gendered expectations, 119, 131, 175; hierarchies, 191; and hypercriminalization of immigrants, xix; illegality and, 15–16; mobility at work, 180–85; navigating illegality, 17–19; playing role in working lives of immigrants, 187; power relations, 180; "pushed and pulled out" of school, 163–69; role alignment, 9, 15–16; and state and local policies, 205; violence, 16, 43, 72, 161, 196, 201–2, 206–7, 232n13; workplace violence, 94–96. *See also* intensive motherhood ideal; pregnancy; violence; women
Geo Group, 71
Gerado, interviewee: and occupational mobility, 178–79; stolen wages and workplace violence, 88–89; workplace raids and apprehensions, 36, 91–92, 149
getting ahead, strategies for: educational journeys, 162–74; overview, 161–62, 185–87; work trajectories, 174–85
"good immigrant" perspective, xix, xv–xvi
Great Depression, 77

Guantánamo Bay, xv
Guatemala, 189; agricultural landscape of, 30; colonial racial hierarchy of, 8; crossing Mexico, 39–44; fighting for land rights in, 31–32; Guatemalan Peace Accords, 32; Guatemalan Revolution, 32; Indigenous experiences in, 29–33; Indigenous groups in, 28; Maya Guatemalans, 32, 39–42, 65–66, 85–86, 88, 93, 95, 102, 104, 112, 121, 124–25; mestizo experiences, 33–36; motivation to move from, 32–33; women in, 28–29. *See also* Mexico
güero, 2, 49, 92, 227n2, 235n57

harmed populations, doing research with, 214–18
health care: allowing access to, 204; chilling effects and access to, 76; facilities, xviii; professionals, 20, 108; settings, 113, 134; systems, 116, 130
heartland, illegality in: colonial legacies in home countries of immigrants, 6–9, 26–54; conclusions, 188–211; illegality as legal and social construct, 12–17; immigration status, 136–60; importance of place, 4–6; introduction, 1–25; Kansas sociopolitical climate, 55–80; language in community and at home, 108–35; Latinidad, 10–12; life without papers, 81–107; navigating illegality, 17–19; strategies for getting ahead, 161–88; studies, 19–24; studying immigrant life in heartland, 4–6. *See also* immigrants; Kansas, USA
Hernández, Lytle, 51

heterosexual nuclear family, enforcing, 7

Hispanic, term, 227n3

"Hispanics," political group, 11

Honduras, 12, 23, 39, 137–38, 161

hopes and dreams, listening to, 202–3

hostilities, creating: cementing links between undocumented status and criminality, 70; "chilling effects" of immigration policies, 74–76; direct ties to heartland, 72–73; executive order usage, 70–71; formal and informal policy changes, 71–72; historical context, 69–70; immigrant detainers, 73–74, 74fig.; restricting asylum options, 72

housing, life without papers and, 97–100

Hugo, interviewee, 199; and mixed-status youths, 154–55; and sibling relationships, 155–58

Humanitarian Parole, xvi

hypercriminalization, xix, xv

ICE. See Immigration and Customs Enforcement

IIRIRA. See Illegal Immigration Reform and Immigrant Responsibility Act

illegal entry and reentry: accelerating individual cases of, 197; convictions, 198; and federal-level policies, 198; penalties for, 198

Illegal Immigration Reform and Immigrant Responsibility Act (IIRIRA), 14–15, 202–3, 238n5

illegality: border experiences influenced by racialization of, 49–51; and colonial systems of power, 15; establishing boundaries of, 82; fitting ideals of,

236n16; gender and, 15–16; internalization of, 159; as legal and social construct, 12; mechanisms of, 82; navigating, 17–19; perceptions of, 200; presumptions of, 193; racialization of, 12–15, 49, 69, 75, 101, 103–4, 106, 127, 192–96, 200–201, stereotypes of, 50, 105. See also heartland, illegality in

"illegal reentry," offense, 14

immigrants: and beginnings of studies, 19–23; colonial legacies in home countries of, 26–54; conclusions, 188–211; connecting with, 222–24; immigration status, 136–60; and importance of place, 4–6; and Kansa sociopolitical climate, 55–80; language in community and at home, 108–35; life without papers, 81–107; manufacturing panic against, xiii–xvii; meeting with, 215–18; navigating illegality, 17–19; racialization and illegality, 192–96; resources used by, 1–4; shock politics and, xii–xiii; strategies for getting ahead, 161–88. See also Indigenous immigrants; mestizo immigrants

Immigration and Customs Enforcement (ICE), xv, xvii, 60, 145; apprehensions, 73, 93–94; avoiding encounters with, 60; detainers, 74f, 104, 158; headlines, 55–56; and "Know Your Rights" campaigns, 220–21; potential of interacting with, 215; and undocumented parents, 150–52

Immigration and Nationality Act of 1965, 12–13, 201

Immigration and Naturalization Service, 83

Immigration Reform and Control Act (IRCA), 13, 77, 83

immigration status: farmers and, 229n51; mixed-status families, 146–58; overview, 159–60; overview of, 136–37; shifting, 137–42; "stuck" in undocumented situation, 142–46. *See also* immigrants

indigenismo, 7–8, 43, 191, 193, 215. See also *mestizaje,* reliance on

Indigenous immigrants, 11, 15, 19–23; conclusions, 188–211; crossing borders, 36–53; crossing Mexico, 39–44; driving, 100–105; English linguistic capital of, 117–22; gendered mobility at work, 180–85; housing for, 97–100; Kansas as *un lugar tranquilo,* 56–61; language barriers and tensions, 122–27; language in community and at home, 108–35; life without papers, 81–107; linguistic wealth of, 111–14; mixed-status families, 146–58; multilingual homes of, 128–30; navigating school barriers, 169–74; and occupational mobility, 175–80; racialization and illegality, 192–96; resources used by, 1–4; seeking asylum, 51–53; sharing fears and worries, 61–69; shifting immigration status, 137–42; sibling relationships, 155–58; Spanish linguistic wealth, 114–17; stolen wages and workplace violence, 87–91; "stuck" in undocumented situation, 142–46; undocumented parents, 146–52; US-Mexico border, 44–51; visas of, 37–39; workplace raids and apprehensions in, 91–94

intensive motherhood ideal: bilingual homes and, 131–33; and English linguistic capital, 119; resistance and gendered mobility at work, 183–87. *See also* women

Internal Revenue Service, xiv, 21

interpretation services, 53, 122, 124, 134, 204–5

interviews: compassionate and caring research practices, 218–21; conducting, 19–23; doing research with harmed populations, 214–18; transcript analysis, 217. *See also various interviewees*

invasion. *See* panic, manufacturing

IRCA. *See* Immigration Reform and Control Act

Isabel, interviewee, 97–98, 119, 130–31

Jaime, interviewee, 57–58, 133; and driving, 103; English linguistic capital, 118–19; and housing, 98–99; language barriers and tensions, 122; language in community and at home, 108–9; multilingual homes, 130; and occupational mobility, 175–76, 179; Spanish linguistic wealth, 115–16

Jazmin, interviewee, 126; experiences of, 29–32; seeking asylum, 52–53; and unauthorized travel, 41; workplace raids and apprehensions, 93–94, 200

Jenny, interviewee, 1–4; English linguistic capital, 120; unauthorized travel, 47–50

Jiménez, Thomas, 5–6

jobs, finding, 83–87. *See also* undocumented workers

Jones, Jennifer, 228n10

migration: flows of, 191, 196–97; as human right, 197–98; journeys, 4, 6, 23; mestizo migration, 9, 27; navigating illegality, 18–19; patterns of, 5, 246n25; and policy criminalization, 198–99; processes, 27, 37, 158, 228n17; Ronald Reagan on, 13. *See also* immigrants

mixed-status families, 18, 68, 76; mixed-status youths, 152–55; sibling relationships, 155–58; undocumented parents, 146–52

Mixteco Mexicans, 45, 57, 98, 112, 115, 147, 164, 179, 267

motivations (of immigrants), exploring: crossing borders, 36–53; life before migration, 27–37; overview, 26–27, 53–54

multigenerational families, colonial languages and, 129

multigenerational immigrant communities, 209–10

multigenerational punishment, 147. *See also* undocumented parents

multilingual homes, Indigenous families and, 128–30

NAFTA. *See* North American Free Trade Agreement

National Origins Act of 1924, 12

National Public Radio, 50

National Quota Law of 1929, 12

Native Americans, 8–10

neighbors, protecting, xxi

networks and resources, access to, 47–49

"new" immigrant destinations, 4–6. *See also* Kansas, USA

Nina, interviewee: and driving, 104; gendered workplace violence, 95–96; language barriers and tensions, 124–25; and multilingual homes, 129–30

non-Indigenous, term, 231n2

nonlinear workplace mobility, 178–80

North American Free Trade Agreement (NAFTA), 29–30, 31, 232n17

North Carolina, examining Latinos' experiences in, 228n10

occupational mobility, 175–80

Ofelia, interviewee, 42; Indigenous linguistic wealth, 112

Olga, interviewee: navigating school barriers, 171–72; sibling relationships, 155–58

Operation Streamline, 246n25

Operation Take Back America, xiv

Paco, interviewee, 45, 144, 167–69

Paloma, interviewee, 34, 132; and gendered mobility at work, 181, 183–84

panic, manufacturing, xiii–xvii

papers, life without: driving, 100–105; housing, 97–100; overview, 81–83, 105–7; workers, 83–96. *See also* undocumented workers; workplace

Pastor José, 89–91

Patricio, interviewee, 103, 126

Pew Research Center, 236n11

place, importance of, 4–6

policies, reforming: federal level, 197–203; local policies, 203–5; overview, 196–97; state policies, 203–5

pollero, 42

post-traumatic stress disorder, 93

pregnancy: and Spanish linguistic
wealth, 115–17; violence and, 94–96.
See also intensive motherhood ideal;
women

Pregnancy Discrimination Act, 96

preocupaciones. See worries

"Prevention through Deterrence," 13–14

"protected areas," xiv

Protected Status, xvi

protests, organizing, 20, 210–11, 216

Public Charge Rule, 113, 148, 244n17

Puerto Ricans, 10, 77

"pushed and pulled out" of school,
163–69; theories, 244n8. *See also* school

Quijano, Aníbal, 7

race, idea of, 7

race, intersections with. *See* immigrants

racialization, 5, 7, 9; illegality and, 12–15,
49, 69, 75, 101, 103–4, 106, 127, 192–96,
200–201; and immigration detention
system, 51; Latinidad and, 192–96;
processes of, 233n37; of undocumented
immigrants, 43–44

racial profiling, ending, 201–3

raids, 68; consequences of, xix–xx; in
workplace, 91–94

raiteros (drivers). *See* driving

rallies, organizing, 210–11

reactions (to Trump 2.0 administration),
xvii–xxi

Regan, Ronald, 13, 243n16

Reierson, Shannon, 120

Reinalda, interviewee, 35; and authorized
travel, 38; Kansas as *un lugar tranquilo,*
58–59; and mixed-status youths, 152–53

Renata, interviewee: driving, 102;
English linguistic capital, 120; and
fear of being deported, 65–66; Kansas
as *un lugar tranquilo,* 60–61

research practices, emphasizing care and
well-being in, 218–21

Rita, interviewee, 68, 98; authorized
travel, 38–39; driving, 102–3; life
without papers, 83–84; mestizo
experiences before migration, 33–34;
navigating school barriers, 170

Rodolfo, interviewee, 139

romantic ties, forming, 139–41

Roosevelt, Franklin, 78

Rosales, Rocio, 18

rural-to-urban migration, 33–34

salir adelante. See getting ahead,
strategies for

sanctuary cities, xiv

Saturnina, interviewee, 130, 133; housing
and, 98–99; language barriers and
tensions, 122; occupational mobility,
179; Spanish linguistic wealth, 115–17

Schmalzbauer, Leah, 18

school: cumulative barriers, 167–69;
economic motivations, 164–65;
gendered mothering roles, 164–67;
navigating barriers of, 169–74;
"pushed and pulled out" of, 163–69

Secure Communities, 62, 71, 73, 75–76,
236n16. *See also* Immigration and
Customs Enforcement (ICE)

seguro. See Social Security Number

Sessions, Jeff, 198

settler colonialism, 7–9

shock politics, xi–xiii

undocumented life, worries about. *See* fear (*miedo*)

undocumented parents: detention and deportation, 149–51; exclusion faced by, 146–47; managing apprehensions and deportations, 151–52; opportunities for children of, 147–48; and subsidized aid, 148

undocumented population, expansion of, xvi

undocumented workers: apprehensions, 91–94; English linguistic capital, 121–22; E-Verify, 83–87; finding jobs, 83–87; passage of the Immigration Reform and Control Act of 1986, 83; raids, 91–94; stolen wages, 87–91; workplace violence, 87–91

United States. *See* educational journeys; heartland, illegality in; Kansas, USA

Universal Declaration of Human Rights, 197

Univision, 56, 66

Univision Noticias, 67

un lugar tranquilo, Kansas as, 56–61, 76, 78, 190. *See also* Kansas, USA

US Border Patrol, 13, 49–50

US Census, defining "Hispanic or Latino" category in, 229n38

US-Mexico border, crossing: access to networks and resources, 47–49; border surveillance, 45–46; gendered violence, 46–47; getting lost in deserts, 45–46; profiting from undocumented crossing, 44–45; racialization of illegality influencing border experiences, 49–51; seeking asylum, 51–53

US Supreme Court, 84–85

U visa program, 242n9

Valentina, interviewee, 67, 141–42

Venezuela, 23

Vicente, interviewee, 84; driving, 100–101; English linguistic capital, 118–19; and occupational mobility, 176–77; unauthorized travel, 49–51; undocumented parents, 146–47

Victims of Trafficking and Violence Protection Act, 242n9

Victoria, interviewee, 87, 145; authorized travel, 37–38; and gendered mobility at work, 181–83; Indigenous linguistic wealth, 111–12; language barriers and tensions, 124–25; workplace raids and apprehensions, 94–96

Villegas, Paloma, 96

violence: and accountability, 205–8; acts of, 27; domestic violence, 179, 242n9; forms of, 6–9, 34, 44, 47, 53, 206; gender violence, 16, 72, 161, 189, 201, 232n13, 237n34, 238n63; gendered workplace violence, 94–96; legacies of, 21; legal, 81–82, 88, 93–94, 96, 100, 105–7, 190, 192, 200; racial violence, 70; reproduction of, 33, 96; state, 9, 27, 79–80, 190; testimonies of, 202; victims of, 71–72; in workplace, 87–91; workplace raids, 91–94. *See also* undocumented workers; women

visas, immigrants obtaining, 37–39

vulnerable populations, doing research with, 214–18

wages, theft of, 87–91. *See also* undocumented workers

wealth, linguistic: definition, 109–10; Indigenous linguistic wealth, 111–14; overview, 132–35; Spanish linguistic wealth, 114–17

well-being, emphasizing, 218–21

WIC. *See* Women, Infant, and Children

Wolfe, Patrick, 229–28

women: and accountability, 205–8; accounts of community English-language classes, 119; border crossings, 46–47; colonizing, 7; and driving, 100–105; finding work, 87; gendered mobility at work, 180–85; gendered workplace violence, 94–96; gender playing role in working lives of, 187; illegality and, 15–16; and K–12 system experiences, 164–67; navigating illegality, 17–19; and occupation mobility, 177–78; pre-migration life in Guatemala, 28–29; pre-migration life in Mexico, 28. See also gender; intensive motherhood ideal; pregancy

Women, Infant, and Children (WIC), 147–48

work, trajectories of: occupational mobility, 175–80; overview, 174–75; resistance, 180–85. *See also* undocumented workers; workplace

workers, paperless life of. *See* papers, life without; undocumented workers

working class, growing up in, 36

workplace, 18, 60, 68, 84, 86, 88, 90, 107, 114, 175, 209; gendered workplace violence, 94–96; informal workplace interactions, 120; language barriers in, 122; mobility in, 178; raids in, 91–94, 150; violence in, 87–91, 174. *See also* gender; undocumented workers; women; violence

World Bank, 32

worries (*preocupaciones*), 55–56; chronic fear, 69; conversations regarding, 62–64; creation of hostile environment, 64–65; and election of Trump, 61–62; family separation, 65–66; "fight-or-flight" response, 68–69; threat of deportation, 65–68

Ximena, interviewee, 141–42, 153–54, 169–70

Yosso, Tara J., 110, 132, 173

youths, mixed-status, 152–55

Founded in 1893,
UNIVERSITY OF CALIFORNIA PRESS
publishes bold, progressive books and journals
on topics in the arts, humanities, social sciences,
and natural sciences—with a focus on social
justice issues—that inspire thought and action
among readers worldwide.

The UC PRESS FOUNDATION
raises funds to uphold the press's vital role
as an independent, nonprofit publisher, and
receives philanthropic support from a wide
range of individuals and institutions—and from
committed readers like you. To learn more, visit
ucpress.edu/supportus.

www.ingramcontent.com/pod-product-compliance
Lightning Source LLC
Chambersburg PA
CBHW020823270326
41928CB00006B/426